Beyond Proprietorship

Beyond Proprietorship

Murphree's Laws on Community-Based Natural Resource Management in Southern Africa

Edited by
B.B. Mukamuri, J.M. Manjengwa & S. Anstey

Weaver Press
HARARE

International Development Research Centre
OTTAWA · CAIRO · DAKAR · MONTEVIDEO · NAIROBI
NEW DELHI · SINGAPORE

Weaver Press
PO Box A1922
Avondale, Harare
Zimbabwe
www.weaverpresszimbabwe.com

ISBN 0-77922-072-1

Chapter 7 ('More Than Socially Embedded: The
Distinctive Character of "Communal Tenure" Regimes
in South Africa and its Implications for Land Policy')
was first publishedin the *Journal of Agrarian Change*,
Vol. 7, No. 3, July 2007, pp. 281–315, and is
reproduced with permission.

The publishers would like to express their gratitude to
the International Development Research Centre
(IDRC), Ottawa, whose financial assistance
made this publication possible.

Cover design by Heath Manyepa
Cover photograph by Frédéric Baudron, CIRAD, Harare
Typesetting by forzalibro designs
Printed and bound in Mauritius by Précigraph Ltd.

Contents

6
Rural Institutions
Challenges and Prospects for the active participation in Natural Resources Governance in Zimbabwe
Billy Mukamuri

7
More than Socially Embedded
The Distinctive Character of 'Communal Tenure' Regimes in South Africa & its Implications for Policy
Ben Cousins
89

8
Conflicts & Commercialization Pressures over Forest Resources in the Post-Fast Track Land Reform Context in Zimbabwe
A case of Seke Communal Lands
Shylock Muyengwa
123

9
Gender Issues Surrounding Water Development & Management in Chishawasha Settlement Area
Chipo Plaxedes Mubaya
136

10
Participatory Development of Community-based Management Plans for Livestock Feed Resources in Semi-arid Areas of Zimbabwe
Experiences from Lower Guruve District
B.G. Mombeshora, F. Chinembiri & T. Lynam
151

1

Introduction

Billy Mukamuri, Jeanette Manjengwa & Simon Anstey

This book seeks to capture the spirit of Professor Marshall Murphree's work and convictions from the past, present and in shaping future research initiatives. The book is based on a collection of papers that were prepared for and presented at a conference hosted in honour of Murphree's work, held at Leopard Rock Hotel, Vumba, Zimbabwe, in May 2007. Professor Marshall Murphree contributed immensely to academia, to the conservation of wildlife resources, to community development and to race relations for more than four decades. His professional career as an academic and social developer was anchored at the Centre for Applied Social Sciences (CASS), formerly called the Centre for Race Relations, which he opened in the 1960s.

The book covers a wide range of issues that are in the purview of Professor Murphree's scholarship, and conveys a central concern with the notion of equality and fairness to all humankind. There is a deliberate focus on the poor and marginalised people living in Southern Africa's most impoverished and remote regions, characterised by low rainfall, limited agricultural potential, and poor infrastructure and social services. However, these remote regions have latent opportunities for economic development and conservation of natural resources, particularly wildlife. This opportunity for wildlife-based development was noted by Murphree and his colleagues while they worked with the Department of National Parks and Wildlife Management.

Following the attainment of Zimbabwe's independence in 1980, race became sidelined in economic debates; access, management and benefit sharing of the country's natural resources took centre stage. Murphree and his colleagues spearheaded the wildlife proprietorship initiatives. The group's effort led to the creation of the world acclaimed Communal Areas Management Programme for Indigenous Resources (Campfire) programme in the mid-1980s. The programme, though encompassing other natural resources, was centred on wildlife in Communal Areas adjacent to National Parks and other protected areas. It was, and is still, based on the principles set by Murphree and his colleagues, notably Rowan Martin, who crafted the initial Campfire document. These principles centre on proprietorship of wildlife by communal people living with wildlife and their right to benefit from funds generated through wildlife-based activities including trophy hunting, culling and eco-tourism. Wildlife management was devolved from the state to local communities in partnership with or through their respective Rural District Councils (RDCs). Murphree and colleagues, together with students largely from CASS, provided academic and professional advice to Campfire.

The first decade of Campfire implementation was characterised by success, evidenced by financial dividends that were channelled to the communities through their respective RDCs. Funds derived from Campfire activities were used to build or upgrade schools, clinics, community centres, as well as remit dividends to households. However, reviews of the programme have indicated reversals in these benefits, particularly following the implementation of economic reforms which led to reduced government subsidies to RDCs. There is recognition that RDCs tend to derive more benefit from the wildlife remittances than do local communities, and that RDCs have retained most of the power related to decision making. Despite these problems, recent research indicates that the design of Campfire has not been found wanting. What needs to be promoted is how to make local authorities more responsive to the needs and aspirations of local communities. Achieving this requires more transparency and accountability, as well as communities being able to set up institutions that can deal with all these issues.

Contributors to the book have interacted with Professor Murphree in various capacities: people who have worked with him over the last 20 or more years, his former students and friends, academics currently based at CASS who have benefited immensely from his scholarship and leadership, as well as postgraduate students who continue to be inspired by him. The chapters are predicated on past and present community-based natural resource management initiatives in Southern Africa. The strand running through them borrows from a series of Murphree's principles governing the relationship between bureaucracy and local communities: devolution, decentralisation and rights over decision making and property, and the inclusion of marginalised communities who bear the consequences of living with wildlife.

Community-based natural resource management principles

Rowan Martin's chapter summarises the core values and principles espoused by Murphree. Though the laws, or perhaps more correctly 'principles', are not sorted by order of importance, readers are able to get to the core of Murphree's thinking, notably that community conservation is a long process, and a product of negotiation, requiring involvement of multiple disciplines. Local people, particularly the marginalised, need to be central. Other principles present conditions for sustainability, which include a developmental rather than conservational focus, benefits being perceived as more than the costs of management; and planning for a broader cultural, political and economic base (multiple stakeholders). Above all, regulatory mechanisms need to be in place.

Roselyn Duffy's chapter contributes to the understanding of CBNRM within the international framework. Although many commentators view CBNRM as an internally driven agenda, her chapter clearly shows that the process is very much imbedded in donor-driven politics and agendas.

Governance, institutional issues & land tenure

Simon Anstey (a PhD student of Professor Murphree) and Liz Rihoy focus on community-based natural resource management and evolution of governance in Mozambique and Zimbabwe. Their chapter draws on Murphree's academic contributions on the important role community-based natural resource management plays in highlighting the inter-relatedness of natural resources governance and democracy at the local level. What is clear from this contribution is the inalienable linkage between natural resources governance and people's rights and liberties. Rights relate to issues of land tenure and the ability of rural people to make meaningful and rational decisions over their resources. Another interesting feature is the role of the 'context' in shaping community-based natural resource management outcomes in different parts of southern Africa. National and local history plays a critical role in this, as is further corroborated by Ben Cousins' contribution on land tenure issues and community-based natural resource management in South Africa.

The challenges currently facing Campfire and other programmes in southern Africa should be viewed as a helical or incremental academic and practical learning curve. Central to this debate is the anticipated ascendancy of rural households from poverty, illiteracy and disenfranchisement to becoming proprietors of high value resources competing for political space. Case-studies from Mozambique, Zimbabwe and South Africa illustrate communities at different stages along this trajectory. Ultimately it is clear that institutional evolution is a political and academic process.

Billy Mukamuri's contribution suggests strategies for empowering local communities so that they minimise the effects of inherent hegemonic tendencies by state structures. The issue of local people's rights is seen as a process linked to the granting of legally recognised rights to ownership of natural resources by local people. This is widely viewed as a strategy to make local people active participants in both management and the decision making process concerning their lives and natural resources. Campfire and other initiatives should be viewed as political processes rather than purely as milch-cows.

Chaka Chirozva explores theoretical and practical aspects of decentralisation as an organising framework in a resettled area in Zimbabwe; he reviews both politics and practice, especially regarding access to natural resources by old and new settlers in the study area. Chaka Chirozva and Simon Anstey have independently demonstrated that devolution efforts in natural resource management can act to empower the marginalised in local governance against elite capture, for example, by the state or 'traditional' authority.

Gender

A gendered approach to community-based natural resource management issues is increasingly becoming central to research in southern Africa. Interest in gender and access to natural resources has been generated by the realisation that natural resources play an important role in poverty alleviation and income generation, particularly for female-headed households living in Communal Areas. Chipo Mubaya's chapter is an interesting contribution on how rural women in a small-scale community access water resources that are owned communally. She also examines institutional arrangements in the context of water access and management.

Land tenure

Land tenure issues in southern Africa are largely characterised by the existence of multiple land tenure regimes. Since independence, legislation has sought to centralise state control of the land while maintaining land access rights along state, private and communal models. These anomalies reverberate through most of the discussions on ownership and benefit sharing in the use of natural resources.

Ben Cousins' chapter analyses debates over tenure reform policy in South Africa following the enactment of the Communal Land Rights Act of 2004. The notion of dynamism is highlighted as central to any tenure reform process. Cousins reiterates the point that for tenure reform to work, the exercise must seek legitimacy in the social realms and use rights must also be legitimated.

Ambiguities in land tenure arrangements may lead to conflicts over natural resources. Tenurial ambiguities and their potential in fuelling conflicts is highlighted by Shylock Muyengwa and Chaka Chirozva. Muyengwa's chapter presents a situation where issues over legitimacy to claims over land and natural resources create contested rights over ownership of high value resources. The chapter presents a new dimension in Zimbabwe's community-based natural resource management context in which ownership rights over resources are questioned by those living outside the designated area. The situation creates new challenges relating to reinterpretation of traditional systems of control, which are now overlaid by new discourses of politics, ownership and legitimacy.

Scenario planning

In Zimbabwe, local level scenario planning is evolving from the work that Murphree and his colleagues have been conducting with local communities in an attempt to make environmental management, planning and benefit sharing central to natural resources-based development activities. This effort is enshrined in various rural development documents under the rubric of 'participation,' popularised by Robert Chambers' 'Rural Development: Putting the Last First' (Chambers, 1983) and Cernea's 'Putting People First: Sociological Variables in Rural Development' (Cernea, 1991). Chambers later published another book highlighting the strengths and weaknesses of participation and indicating that participation as a rural development methodological tool requires modification: 'Whose Reality Counts? Putting the First Last' (Chambers, 1997). More recently, Cooke and Kothari's (2001) 'Participation: The New Tyranny' questions some of the assumptions that participation is always preferable in all situations.

The chapter by Mombeshora and colleagues presents attempts by a team of researchers to experiment on participation as a natural resources management development tool in a marginalised communal area, Mahuwe Communal Area, in Guruve District. It highlights the methodological thinking surrounding participation, which is reminiscent of the Campfire programme where local people were asked to participate in wildlife management as a way of reducing poaching (Anstey, and Mukamuri in this volume). However, what is common among what may be called the first generation of participatory rural development projects, involving local communities, is that local communities were being asked to participate in projects conceptualised and developed by external experts and development agencies.

Jeannette Manjengwa's contribution highlights, with examples from the District Environmental Action Plan (DEAP), how first generation participatory projects operated in a typical Zimbabwean context. First, she shows that DEAP was conceptualised as part of the World Conservation Strategy and the United Nations Conference on Environment and Development's Agenda 21. Secondly, she suggests that participation is always subject to other contexts and interests, particularly in relation to its implementation. First generation participatory projects were largely donor-driven and guided by what the author calls a 'one-off' approach. The projects largely failed to create a sense of local ownership of the activities by the local communities who were expected to benefit from them.

These shortcomings triggered the search for new approaches, one of which is presented by Manjengwa, of local level scenario planning, iterative assessment, and adaptive management, which aims to create local ownership of development initiatives, rather than reinforce vertical control. Central to scenario planning is engagement by invitation from interested communities wishing to conduct scenario planning, iterative assessments and adaptive management consistent with the outcome of assessments. In line with Simon Anstey's conclusion, the advent of scenario planning clearly shows the incremental process in acquiring skills and knowledge.

The community-based natural resource management debate in southern Africa cannot be complete without taking a look at the ongoing and potential land reforms in the whole region. Zimbabwe has been at the forefront in its endeavour to redress colonial land distribution imbalances between the African majority and European minority. Land reform in Zimbabwe, in particular, has brought to the fore discussions and real challenges for former conservancies, particularly in relation to their future existence and ownership structures.

References

Cernea, M.M. (ed.) 1991. *Putting People First: Sociological Variables in Rural Development*, (2nd edn). New York: Oxford University Press.

Chambers, R. 1983. *Rural Development: Putting the Last First*. Harlow: Longman.

— 1997. *Whose Reality Counts? Putting the First Last*. London: Intermediate Technology Publications.

Cooke, B. and U. Kothari (eds) 2001. *Participation: The New Tyranny*. London and New York: Zed Books.

2

Murphree's Laws, Principles, Rules & Definitions

Rowan B. Martin

Introduction

Marshall Murphree's 'laws' are rules linking people, conservation, sustainable use and development. Murphree himself did not call them 'laws' – the label was given to them by his admirers. In some of his writings, he enunciated principles which later assumed such status; elsewhere in his work, it has been left to his large readership to identify and confer the appellation on particular epigrammatic truths. The list of the principles has become so extensive that nobody can remember what, for example, is Murphree's 'seventh law'. This paper examines Murphree's publications, addresses and presentations from 1991 to 2005 and extracts from them a list of laws, principles, definitions, descriptions, critical insights and quotable quotes.

The work is not exhaustive. I had not been able to examine all of Murphree's papers. A comprehensive bibliography is given at the end of the chapter on those works which have been examined. The bibliography is restricted to Murphree's individual and joint papers; references to other authors are placed in footnotes on the relevant pages.

Definitions

Very early in the work, it became clear that some definitions were needed. The following, from *Webster's Dictionary*, has been chosen:

> Law: *Philosophy and Science*: A statement of an order or relation of phenomena which, so far is known, is invariable under the given conditions ... such laws are often specified by prefixing the name of the discoverer.

Thus my criterion for what constitutes a law is invariability in the context in which it is used.[1] It is also a 'high level' statement covering a range of situations, not a simple rule for a specific case. Of course a little latitude must be permitted. For example, Ohm's Law permits no latitude whatsoever (the relationship between voltage, current and resistance is fixed, precise and repeatable) but, in the description of what are now known as 'complex systems'[2] (Holling 2001), it would be unreasonable to except the same exactitude, especially because all the multitude of potential applications cannot be tested.

Having defined a 'law', a category is required for those statements, also of a general nature, which are less global in their scope and do not demand invariability. Webster's Dictionary defines a 'principle' (fourth definition) as: A fundamental truth; a comprehensive law or doctrine from which others are derived or on which others are founded; a general truth; an elementary proposition; a fundamental assumption; a maxim; a postulate.

From these two definitions, it would appear that a law and principle are equivocal. In the typology which follows, the distinction is that principles are useful for guiding policy or implementation whereas laws are simply a statement of fact requiring no application to make them useful.

Taking the typology further, whereas a principle emphasises the idea of a general application, a rule emphasises a more specific direction or regulation as in ' ... to follow certain principles of administration; to lay down certain administrative rules ...'

Some of Murphree's pronouncements fall in the category of definitions. Others could be described as maxims, aphorisms, axioms or epigrams. Where any of these are reproduced below, no attempt is made to categorise them.

It is not possible to create a flowing narrative out of the chosen subject matter. Murphree's text is lean, parsimonious and elegant with the result that every paper examined is rich in potentially quotable material.

Study approach

The simplest approach was to start at the beginning and work through Murphree's writings in chronological order extracting clauses, sentences and paragraphs that appear worthy of mention. Indeed, this is how the work began. The problem with this method is that the end result is a 'shotgun blast' of quotable quotes without any coherent theme. So I grouped the subject matter according to the following topics:

Natural resources management and sustainable use
Community-Based Natural Resources Management (CBNRM):
General
Policy and Tenure
Scaling-up
State protected Areas
Bureaucracy/Treaties
Science and General

Inevitably, I found many laws and principles which could be placed in more than one category because of the complexity of their content. Perhaps that is to be expected.

I have chosen to keep much of the introductory text relating to any 'law' or 'principle' since it is the rationale for the dictum. On examining the material, it became apparent that some laws or principles overlapped or are the same thing stated differently in two different publications. Accordingly, I presented the 'definitive' list of laws, principles, rules and definitions at the end of each subsection. In some cases I have taken the liberty of combining one or more statements and I have also made a few minor modifications to the original text to suit its presentation. Since it would be of very little use to anybody to refer to these laws and principles by numbers (e.g., 'Murphree's Seventh Law' or 'Murphree's Fourteenth Principle'), I have given each law and principle a title. In keeping with the spirit of this exercise, when I have been in doubt whether a statement is a law or a principle I have given the benefit of the doubt to the law.

This exercise yielded a total of 12 laws, 31 principles and 11 definitions. Some of the principles contain multiple parts and some rules are embedded amongst the principles. The breakdown of laws, principles and definitions is shown below.

Natural resources management 3 laws, 6 principles
CBNRM:

General	3 laws, 5 principles, 3 definitions
Policy and tenure	2 laws, 3 principles, 3 definitions
Scaling up	1 law, 3 principles, 1 definition
State protected areas	2 principles, 2 definitions
Bureaucracy treaties	6 principles
Science	1 law, 6 principles

The Laws, Principles, Rules & Definitions

The following boxes (Boxes 1–44) are a compilation of the laws, principles, rules and definitions. They do not require any explanation or analysis. Further reading can be obtained from the cited references in each box.

Natural resources management & sustainable use

Box 1 – Murphree's Law of Conservation in Africa
Re-inventing conservation in Africa – for that is the task in hand – was never going to be a quick job.

Source: Murphree (2001c: p. 296)

Box 2 – Murphree's Law of Conservation and Sustainability

Conservation is the same thing as sustainability and entails (Associated Rules):

- both biological and human sciences
- dealing with change
- considering resilience rather than stability
- viewing resilience as the product of negotiation over time.

Source: Murphree (2001f)

Box 3 – Murphree's Law of the Farmers First

Putting the farmers first is the formula for successfully linking wildlife conservation and sustainable rural development in Africa.

(Associated Rules)

- Attempts to maintain large wildlife populations, particularly of large mammal species, on land outside state protected areas which is ecologically and economically more suited to other forms of production under competitive marketing and tax structures are futile.

- The 'development to promote conservation' paradigm implicit in many programmes and projects is an inappropriate approach for the investments in sustainable use made by African farmers.

Source: Murphree (1996a)

Box 4 – Murphree's Principles of Costs and Benefits

People seek to manage the environment when the benefits of management are perceived to exceed its costs.

Source: Murphree (1991c)

Box 5 – Murphree's Principle of Resource Use and Resource Management

Wildlife and sustainable development are primarily about development rather than conservation.

Source: Murphree (1996a)

Box 6 – Murphree's Principle of Resource Use and Resource Management

Resource use without resource management is non-sustainable but, equally, any attempt to establish resource management without resource use is likely to be futile.

Source: Murphree (1991c)

Box 7 – Murphree's Principles of the Scope of Sustainability

Sustainable use issues are rarely confined to closed, biologically defined systems. Sustainability in the use of any species is usually embedded in larger ecosystem sustainability and this, in turn, is embedded in larger social systems with cultural, economic and political dimensions. Issues of sustainability cannot be adequately addressed independently of these macro structural components.

Source: Murphree (1996b)

Box 8 – Murphree's Principles of Regulation of Use

Regulation of use is an essential component for sustainability in use. Incentive is the fulcrum of regulation. Any regulatory system which relies primarily on negative incentives is, in the long term, in trouble.

Source: Murphree (1996b)

Box 9 – Murphree's Principle of Demand and Control

Sustainability will depend on the unfettered demand for the use of a resource and the controls which exist over that use.

Source: Murphree (1997)

Community-Based Natural Resources Management (CBNRM) – General

---

Box 10 – Murphree's Law of Evolving Community Conservation

The idea of community conservation is evolving and is not fixed ... individuals, groups and organisations compete or manipulate both the meaning that is invested in the term and the nature of its practice so as to achieve their personal, group or organisational goals.

Source: Murphree (2001a: p. 5)

Box 11 – Murphree's Law of the Core Objective of CBNRM

The core objective of CBNRM is increased communal capacity for adaptive and dynamic governance in the arena of natural resource use.

Box 12 – Murphree's Law of Effectiveness of Community Conservation

Ultimately the effectiveness of organisation in community conservation is determined by the will and capacities of communities themselves and cannot be imported from outside.

Source: Murphree (2001b)

Box 13 – Murphree's Principle of Rights and Responsibilities

Performance of community conservation initiatives will be determined by the degree to which they are able to reconcile conflicts created by property regimes that emphasise the responsibilities of communities but devolve few rights to them.

Source: Murphree (2001b: p. 31)

Box 14 – Murphree's Principle of Developing Resilience

'Best practice' in community conservation is not so much about transferring 'good' experiences from one project to another – rather it is about strengthening capacities and developing resilience of conservation agencies, communities and programme managers through the process of adaptive management where they experiment, learn and take decisions within the constraints under which they work.

Source: Murphree (2001e)

Box 15 – Murphree's Principles for Viable Communal Property Regimes

1. Effective management of natural resources is best achieved by giving focused value for those who live with them.
2. Tenure over natural resources should be delegated to the lowest level of social scale possible.
3. An internal legitimacy endogenously derived but also sanctioned by the state is likely to produce a more robust base for organisation.
4. Differential inputs must result in differential benefits.
5. There must be a positive correlation between the quality of management and the magnitude of benefit.
6. The level at which benefits accrue should be the level at which management occurs.
7. The unit of proprietorship should be the unit of production and management.
8. The unit of proprietorship should be as small as practicable within ecological and socio-political constraints.

(Associated Rules)

The relationship of Group Size to the Resource Base

   • Large groups with weak resource bases are unlikely to succeed.

Small, dispersed groups with large valuable resource bases will have difficulty acting in cohesion.

The Design of Small Local Jurisdictions

   • The fewer members the better.
   • The closer they live together the better.
   • The more they interact together on a daily basis the better.

Source: Murphree (1991c, 2001e: p. 294, 2000a)

Box 16 – *Murphree's Principle of Internal Conflict*

Community Conservation is no panacea for intra-communal differentiation or conflict.

Source: Murphree (2001e)

Box 17 – *Murphree's Principle of CBNRM and the Economy*

National macro-economic health and CBNRM success are closely linked.

Source: Murphree (2001b)

CBNRM general definitions

Box 18 – *Murphree's Definitions of Community, Cohesion, and Demarcation*

a) Community

'Community' can be defined functionally as a principle manifest in social groupings with the actual or potential cohesion, incentive, demarcation, legitimacy and resilience to organise themselves for effective common pool natural resource management at levels below and beyond the reach of state bureaucratic management.

Source: Murphree (2001b)

b) Cohesion

'Cohesion' is the social glue which persuades people, in spite of their differences, to act collectively to enhance mutual interest and represent it to others.

Source: Murphree (2001b: p. 26)

c) Demarcation

'Demarcation' is the definition of jurisdiction limits which reinforce authority and responsibility for the collective grouping and is necessary for efficient organisation.

Source: Murphree (2001b: p. 27)

Policy & tenure

Box 19 – *Murphree's Law of Dynamic Policy*

Policy is dynamic, and in constant and evolving interaction with implementation.

Source: Murphree (2001c: p. 38)

Box 20 – Murphree's Law of Conservation Policy in Africa

For generations, conservation policy in Africa has been socially illegitimate in the eyes of the continent's rural people. The task of creating a conservation policy that is embedded in African society, rather than imposed from above, will be the work of generations.

Source: Murphree (2001a: p. 7)

Box 21 – Murphree's Principles for Community Property Regimes

1. The era of externally-derived innovation in CBNRM should be brought to an end. The era of self-determined, tenurially robust communal natural resource management should be brought into being.

2. For long-term sustainability CBNRM requires a fundamental shift in national policies on tenure in communal lands. The core of the matter is strong property rights for collective communal units – not only over wildlife and other natural resources, but over the land itself.

3. The transition from 'community participation' to a strong communal property regime is not easy but it is the only approach which can effectively insert wildlife resources sustainably into African rural development.

4. Devolution of authority to communities or landholders for conservation and sustainable use of wild resources is a 'cardinal input'.

5. The smaller a property regime the more effective and efficient it will be.

(Associated Rules)
Sequencing Devolution

- Authority is a pre-requisite for responsible management and should not be held out as a reward for it.
- Devolution carries with it the responsibility for organisation, management, control, self-sufficiency and, above all, for developing resourcefulness.
- These attributes cannot be imposed, they must be developed experimentally in the local setting and without authority such experiments are defective.
- The stimulus for this development arises not from the anticipation of future entitlement but from the imperative of immediate empowerment.

Source: Murphree (1995b, 2002b, 1997b, 1996a, 2000a)

Box 22 – *Murphree's Principle of the Policy Grail*

Expectations for the present must be tempered by the recognition that common property resources are currently hostage to larger politico-economic realities. The grail of good common property policy and practice should still be pursued.

Source: Murphree (2000b)

Box 23 – *Murphree's Principle of Authority and Responsibility*

Authority without responsibility is likely to be dysfunctional or obstructive; responsibility without authority lacks the necessary instrumental and motivational components for its efficient exercise.

Source: Murphree (2000a)

Box 24 – *Murphree's Definitions*

a) Wildlife Ownership

Ownership is seldom, if ever, absolute. Rights are stronger the longer they have been in place and the fewer conditionalities are attached to them.

b) Politico-Legal Environment

By placing policy and practice before politics, CBNRM has been born in a politico-legal environment which, if not hostile, is hardly nurturing.

c) Implementational Stasis

'Implementational stasis' results when the state does not have the resources to effectively impose its policies, and communities do not have the resources to implement locally generated policy alternatives. This is a situation where the state is unwilling to surrender its technicist and prospective policy approaches while lacking the resources to make them effective, and the local community lacks the authority and incentives to create effective policies and regimes responsive to local imperatives.
Source: Murphree (1996a, 2002b)

d) Closing the Boundaries

Devolution involves the creation of relatively autonomous realms of authority, responsibility and entitlement, with a primary accountability to their own constituencies. Boundaries have to be closed through negotiated and reciprocal exclusion. Closing the boundaries is not an exercise in isolationism, rather it is a search for local regimes' independence within the large setting of interdependence at many scales.

Scaling up

Box 25 – Murphree's Law of Scaling Up

Scaling down to be sustainable involves scaling up.

Three themes emerge as principles for linking and matching functional ecological and jurisdictional scales:

The Principle of Jurisdictional Parsimony

Management institutions need to be matched to the specific requirements of the resources to be managed and should be no larger than necessary.

The Principle of Constituent Accountability

To reach the desirable situation where local groups influence the allocations of entitlements through the political process, local jurisdictions must become a significant political constituency of the state and one to which the state is accountable.

Devolution needs to focus on creating 'nested sets' of institutions at different levels of scale and involving federations of local organisations – rather than all-powerful authority.

Murphree's principle and rules on state protected areas.

The old notion of 'fortress conservation' is being displaced by new ideas of development through community conservation and sustainable use.

State-protected areas

Box 26 – Murphree's Definition of 'People and Parks' Project Failures

The proximate reasons for the failure of projects linking local people and state-protected areas are as follows:

- Cohesive communities have been hard to identify.
- Incentives for cohesion are absent or do not cover the transaction costs involved in developing or maintaining cohesion.
- The process requires time frames well beyond the impatient log frames of conventional donor project development.
- Conservationists have tended to 'colonise' and capture projects, and local actors have diverted projects away from their central objectives.

The ultimate and most fundamental reason for failure has been that the critical ingredient for project success, that of devolution of authority and responsibility, has been missing.

Source: Murphree 2002a

Box 27 – Murphree's Definition of 'People and Parks' Project Features

Governments (and NGO implementing agencies) have:

- retained ultimate power to shape objectives and control objectives and benefits;
- treated community involvement as the same thing as compliance;
- treated participation as the same thing as 'co-opting' communities;
- been reluctant, as politicians and bureaucrats, to surrender the power and control of access to resources essential for robust devolution.

As a consequence, most of the projects involving communities in natural resource management have simply become an exercise in aborted devolution.

Source: Murphree (2002a)

Bureaucracy/Treaties

Box 27 – Murphree's Principle of Protected Areas and Commons

Protected areas are no more than another form of 'commons' – areas set aside for a constituency which require protection through controls on their access and use.

Seen as an area of commons, a number of false perceptions need to disappear:

- Protected areas do not have to be managed by the state.
- They are not about use versus non-use.
- They are about regulated access rather than exclusion.

Source: Murphree (2002a)

Box 28 – Murphree's Law of the Bureaucrat's Behaviour

Power structures at the political and economic centre are not disposed to surrender their privileges and will use their power, including their abilities to shape policy and law, to maintain the monopolies of their position.

Those who hold power at the local level – traditional leaders, local officials and business people – are likely to use that power to capture new sources of income and resist any erosion of their position.

Source: Murphree (1998a, 2001e)

Box 29 – Murphree's Law of the Outcome of Establishment Incentives

Local incentives indicate devolution in proprietorship. Unfortunately, establishment incentives tend to resent it. These incentives include:

- the bureaucratic mind, disposed to the centralisation of authority;
- the technocratic mind disposed to see devolution as the surrender of professional management to the vagaries of cost/benefit decisions by unsophisticated peasants;
- the appropriative incentives of central political elite and their private sector allies.

Whatever the specific configuration of incentive, the result is that 'community-based' resource management initiatives turn out to be efforts to co-opt or bribe local peoples while authority still effectively remains firmly in state hands. This is institutionally fatal since authority and responsibility are separated.

Local incentives indicate devolution in proprietorship. Unfortunately, establishment incentives tend to resent it. These incentives include the bureaucratic mind, disposed to the centralisation of authority and the technocratic mind, which is disposed to see devolution as the surrender of professional management to the vagaries of cost/benefit decisions by unsophisticated peasants. They also include the appropriative incentives of central political elite and their private sector allies.

Source: Murphree (1997c)

Box 30 – Murphree's Definitions: Participation, Involvement & Decentralisation

Communally-based management regimes require far more than 'involvement', 'participation' and 'decentralisation'. 'Participation' and 'involvement' turn out to mean the co-option of local elites and leadership for derived programmes and 'decentralisation' turns out to mean simply the addition of another obstructive layer to the bureaucratic hierarchy which governs natural resource management.

Source: Murphree (1991c)

Box 31 – Murphree's Definition of Equity

Current usage of the term equity implies the elimination of gross disparities arising from situations or structures which concentrate and maintain power in the hands of a narrow band of elites.

'Equity' is thus a relative, dynamic and subjective concept arising from both material conditions and normative perceptions.

'Equity', in effect, becomes a synonym for 'legitimacy' – the legitimacy of structures and processes of entitlements, controls and obligations that hold a broad social consensus of normative support.

Source: Murphree (2002b)

Box 32 – Murphree's Principle of Re-examining International Conventions

International environmentalism has failed to reverse negative trends in the global environment. This is because:

- it has not seriously addressed the demand side of the resource equation; issues like population control and alteration of life-style aspirations are not politically expedient for powerful segments of its constituency;
- there are inadequacies in its conventions – its instruments of collective international husbandry and management of resources.

Manifestly, these have not adequately produced the effects for which they were created, and their design, their implementation and the role assigned to them bear re-examination.

They are extremely costly in time, effort and money and, unless they can be made to work, we should throw them out and start again.

Source: Murphree (1997b)

Box 33 – Murphree's Principle of Scale in International Conventions

Most environmental management requirements lie at lower levels and can be most efficiently dealt with at these levels. Increases in scale complicate communication and decision making and, beyond certain levels, regimes must bureaucratise with attendant costs.

Compliance inducement shifts from low-cost modes of moral and peer pressure to the high-cost methods of policing and formal coercion.

Increase in scale erodes the sense of individual responsibility.

Our conventions should be designed with these scale considerations in mind – place their priorities on issues requiring global action and refrain from intruding on the operations of smaller-scale regimes more suited to the management requirements of the resources they address.

If they do not, they can themselves become perverse incentives, resulting in the evasion of responsibility to achieve the results they advocate.

Source: Murphree (1997b)

Box 34 – Murphree's Principle of Incentive Compatibility

- Through policy, legislation and fiscal controls governments and international agencies can deny local people the organisational conditions necessary for the attainment of their conservation incentives.
- Through their in-place location and de facto managerial status, local people can render external initiatives futile.

Without incentive compatibility stasis occurs, since each party has an operational veto over the other.

The central challenge is, therefore, to transform such initiatives into sets of congruent, although not necessarily identical, incentives.

Source: Murphree (1997c)

Box 35 – Murphree's Principle of Hierarchy in Conservation Values

Intrinsic and existence valuations of biological diversity tend to be accorded a higher status at the international level than local and instrumental conservation incentives – which are regarded as lower level factors to be co-opted in the pursuit of the higher values.

This does not work.

Aside from their inherent merits local incentives have a powerful veto dimension.

Unless they are accommodated, international values and goals will be subverted by local responses ranging from defiance to covert non-compliance.

Source: Murphree (1997c)

Box 36 – Murphree's Principle of Socio-Ecological Topography

Social topography suggests 'small-scale' regimes while ecological considerations tend to mandate 'large-scale' regimes. When international treaties impose large-scale ecologically-determined project domains on local situations, they may force together social units which have not negotiated between each other or, worse still, cut through existing social units.

In so doing they concentrate on ecological sustainability at the cost of ignoring the institutional sustainability on which it depends.

The GBF and CBD should keep in mind that project approaches which start with a defined land area may not have as much potential as those which start with a focus on social units of organisation.

Source: Murphree (1997c)

Science & General

Box 37 – Murphree's Principle of Science as a Specialised Domain

The GBF and the CBD tend to regard science as a specialised domain outside the realm and mandate of local people, e.g., 'Governments should involve local people in decisions affecting use while continuing to base management decisions on science.'

Specifically, the GBF and the CBD should take pains to avoid the dichotomisations and condescensions of this stance and strive to build synergy between professional and citizen science.

Specifically, the GBF and the CBD should invest significantly in the facilitation of a new profile for the nature and role of science and its insertion into the policy and practice of sustainable use.

Source: Murphree (1997c)

Box 38 – Murphree's Law of the Study of Sustainable Use

Study of sustainable use entails more complex and less determinate conclusions.

In science there is an inverse relationship between exactitude and the number of relevant variables. This is used by critics to raise the canard that it is unscientific.

To the contrary, while good science regards exactitude as desirable it regards validity as necessary. Validity requires that analysis addresses all the relevant variables of the topic under consideration. In other words, eliminate or reduce the number of 'black boxes'.

Given the nature of sustainable use, its study can only be considered scientific if it is systemic.

Source: Murphree 1996b

Box 39 – Murphree's Principles of Science & Local Communities

Dealing with uncertainty is a continuing factor in the lives of local communities and risk aversion a pervasive feature of their farming strategies.

Their methodology – adaptive management – has the highest scientific credentials. It is elegant in its simplicity, robust in its empiricism and striking in its tight application to management decisions. It has huge potential for the development of locally-based environmental science which moves beyond issues of species off-take.

Such science, flexible in its foci and dynamic in its analysis, is far more important than the static domain of 'indigenous technical knowledge' – the box to which local insight and experience is condescendingly assigned.

Local communities have problems with the scientific environmental technicism of governments and international agencies.

They do not have the resources to conduct it themselves and its conduct by others involves a significant loss of control. They see it as a device which can be applied to stop use which their own science indicates is viable. And they have a healthy scepticism of its ability to produce the predictive certainties expected of it.

This perspective on professional science's epistemology and role is cognate to local science. In its applied form it has emerged regionally in new forms of resource and environmental management where uncertainty and surprises become an integral part of an anticipated set of adaptive responses.

Dissonance remains, however, where bureaucracies retain the expectation that science can provide a priori certainties.

Source: Murphree (1997c)

Box 40 – Murphree's Principle of Rural People Intrinsic Values

The intrinsic values that rural people hold for their environment are a cultural resource which is often ignored, or undermined, by external researchers and consultants whose personal values and training may lead them to believe that rural people see species and habitats purely in utilitarian terms.

Source: Murphree (2001a)

Box 41 – Murphree's Principle of Project Models

A clear practical lesson from current research is the need to avoid seeing the organisation of community conservation in terms of a 'Project Model'.

Source: Murphree (2001a)

Box 42 – Murphree's Principle of Engagement with Local Communities

Our methodology in dealing with local communities should be:

- invited rather than imposed;
- directed rather than directive;
- facilitative rather than manipulative.

It should represent professional science in the service of local civil science.

Source: Murphree (2001f)

Box 43 – Murphree's Principle of Natural Resource Mensuration

Accurate measurements of natural resources may be desirable in theory but, in practice, they are often infeasible and may undermine local natural resource management regimes.

Source: Murphree (2001a)

Box 44 – Murphree's Principle of Science Interacting with Policy

The powerful alliance between bureaucracy and science evident in environmental policy history has, at times, compromised an essential component of good science – the recognition of contingency and uncertainty in its findings.

Source: Murphree (2002b)

Murphree's Laws, Principles, Rules & Definitions applied to the Addis Ababa Principles for Sustainable Use

In the original abstract for this chapter, it was promised that the Addis Ababa Principles would be reviewed against Murphree's Laws – which were yet to be developed. In the event, the development of Murphree's laws and principles have occupied many pages of text and this chapter would become unwieldy were it also to contain a thorough review of the Addis Ababa Principles. Moreover, I have done a detailed review of these principles elsewhere.

Not unexpectedly, given Murphree's in-depth consideration of issues relating to the CBD, much of what is contained in the Addis Ababa Principles contravenes many of the laws and principles which have been put forward here. The first Principles (amongst a total of fourteen) illustrate the point very well.

The second paragraph of the preamble to the Addis Ababa Principles states:

'Sustainable use is a valuable tool to promote conservation of biological diversity.'

Murphree's Law of Conservation and Sustainability says that conservation is the same thing as sustainability.

Practical principle 1: Supportive policies, laws and institutions are in place at all levels of governance and there are effective linkages between these levels.

Rationale: There is need to have congruence in policies, and laws at all levels of governance associated with a particular use....

There are thousands of uses – are the proponents of the principle seriously suggesting that a policy and law is in place for every use? The principle requires supportive policies, laws and institutions ... perhaps all that is needed is devolutionary legislation.

... There must be clear and effective linkages between different jurisdictional levels to enable a 'pathway' to be developed which allows timely and effective response to unsustainable use....

Outside interventions to prevent unsuitable use need to be treated very carefully. A key aspect of devolution is that the users are allowed to make mistakes and learn from those mistakes. Outside intervention erodes the rights of those who have been empowered.

Both of these clauses contravene Murphree's Principle of Scale in International Conventions.

Practical principle 2: Recognising the need for a governing framework consistent with international and national laws, local users of biodiversity components should be sufficiently empowered and supported by rights to be responsible and accountable for use of the resources concerned.

At first sight this principle should be applauded. However, the seeds of disquiet are sown when:

(a) empowerment is constrained by and follows only after a governing framework consistent with international laws and national laws;

(b) empowerment is tempered by the word 'sufficiently' – which tends to imply 'enough empowerment and not more';

(c) local users are made accountable to some unspecified body for their use of resources.

Murphree's Principle of Hierarchy in Conservation Values applies.

The principle is further weakened by statements in the rationale and guidelines.

Rationale: Resource users should participate in making decisions...

If rights have been devolved, they will make the decisions!

Operational Guidelines

Where possible, adopt means that aim toward delegating rights, responsibility, and accountability to those who use and/or manage biological resources; review existing regulations to see if they can be used for delegating rights; amend regulations where needed and possible; and/or draft new regulations where needed. Throughout, local customs and traditions (including customary law where recognised) should be considered.

A curious sentence – local customs and traditions ... should be considered (in relation to delegating rights) – is a clear indication that the drafters of the principles are considering partial devolution at best. The remaining guidelines under Principle 2 reinforce the impression that local communities will be permitted to use natural resources only at the pleasure of higher authority.

Murphree's Principle of Rights and Responsibility applies to all the above.

Numerous other Operational Guidelines under the other Principles negate the intent of devolution expressed in Principle 2, e.g.:

- Require adaptive management plans to incorporate systems to generate sustainable revenue, where the benefits go to indigenous and local communities and local stakeholders to support successful implementation ... if rights have been devolved, benefits should automatically go to local entities.

- Include clear descriptions of their adaptive management system ... for whom are these plans intended ... which includes means to assess uncertainties ... adaptive management is primarily aimed at coping with uncertainties rather than assessing them.

- Respond quickly to unsustainable practices ... who responds?

- Investigate and develop means of ensuring rights of access and methods for helping to ensure that the benefits derived from using components of biodiversity are equitably shared ... surely this is a given under Principle 2?

- Link responsibility and accountability to the spatial and temporal scale of use ... who links?
- Define the management objectives for the resource being used ... who defines?
- Enable full public participation in preparation of management plans to best ensure ecological and socio-economic sustainability ... (a) This may be appropriate for a resource managed by the state but not for a devolved situation; (b) Public participation will not ensure sustainability.
- Set standards for resource management activities that promote interdisciplinary consultations ... sounds overly bureaucratic.
- Take account of socio-economic, political, biological, ecological, institutional, religious and cultural factors that could influence the sustainability of the management ... implies devolution will not take place.
- Seek guidance from local, traditional and technical specialists in designing the management plan ... yet under principle 2, rights have been devolved to these actors.
- Endeavour to have an independent review of harvests to ensure that greater efficiencies in harvest or other extractive uses do not have a deleterious impact on the status of the resource being used or its ecosystem ... this tells local communities they do not own the resource.
- Consider ways to bring uncontrolled use of biological resources into a legal and sustainable use framework, including promoting alternative non-consumptive uses of these resources ... (a) This appears redundant given the rationale for Principle 2; (b) Why should non-consumptive uses be promoted?
- Ensure that an equitable share of the benefits remains with the local people in those cases where foreign investment is involved ... if devolution occurs, this is up to the local people.
- Involve local stakeholders, including indigenous and local communities, in the management of any natural resource and provide those involved with equitable compensation for their efforts, taking into account monetary and non-monetary benefits ... Previous comments apply – but perhaps this guideline, in particular, illustrates a syndrome which assumes that the primary motivation for all actors is the conservation of biological diversity – instead of human development.
- In the event that management dictates a reduction in harvest levels, practicable assistance should be provided for local stakeholders, including indigenous and local communities, who are directly dependent on the resource to have access to alternatives ... clearly the state will manage the resource – this negates any prior statements about devolution.
- Ensure that harvest levels and quotas are set according to information provided by the monitoring system, not the economic needs of the

management system ... there is nothing in the principle or the rationale which warrants this sort of statement.

- Provide guidelines for resources managers to calculate and report the real cost of management in their business plans ... report to whom?

- Provide economic incentives for managers who have already internalised environmental costs e.g. certification to access new markets, waiver or deferral of taxes in lieu of environmental investment, promotion of 'green-labelling' for marketing ... it will not help the quest for sustainability to build subsidies into uses of biodiversity – by the same set of arguments that seek subsidies to be removed from land uses which destroy biodiversity.

- Ensure that resource users report to Government on their activities in a manner that facilitates broader communications ... is this intended to be a condition for devolution of resources rights or is it an indication of aborted devolution?

- Most of the above clauses conflict directly with Murphree's Principles for viable communal property regimes, Murphree's Law of the Farmers First and Murphree's Laws of Effectiveness of community conservation.

It becomes unnecessary to go further. By now the reader will have deduced that there is a large inconsistency between the doctrine preached by Murphree and the expression of these principles. Much of the conflict lies in the condescending and patronising tone of the statements. Murphree captures this when he says, 'The GBF and the CBD tend to regard science as a specialised domain outside the realm and mandate of local people ... Our language often betrays this, as when for instance we read the following criterion for "sustainable use", "Governments involve local people in decisions affecting the use while continuing to base management decisions on science", "The GBD should take pains to avoid the dichotomisations and condescension of this stance ..."' (included in the *Principle of Science as a Specialised Domain*).

In the Addis Ababa Principles, the proponents of 'Big Government' have triumphed over the advocates of 'Small is Beautiful'.

Conclusion

To claim that the above classification of the quotable quotes from Marshall Murphree work as laws, principles, etc. would be pretentious. It is imbued with subjectivity, and the decisions about where to place items are arbitrary. Marshall Murphree might be very uncomfortable with the outcome and might have selected an alternative list of topics, other titles for his dictum and better text to express them. However, I hope that readers have benefited from the richness of the content of his writing.

References

Compiled from Marshall Murphree's collection of papers and CASS List of Publications (January 1996): *Natural Resources Management Occasional Paper* series.

Murphree, M. 1995a. 'Optimal Principles and Pragmatic Strategies: Creating an enabling politico-legal environment for community-based natural resource management'. Paper delivered at a conference on the National Resources Management Programme, SADCC Technical Coordination Unit, Malawi, USAID-NRMP Regional, Chobe, 3 April.

— 1995b. 'The Sustainable Use of Wildlife Living Resources: The "Southern" Perspective'. Presentation at a conference entitled *Conservation of Southern Africa's Wild Living Resources: Exploitation sustainability and ethics*, University of Cape Town, 5 May.

— 1996a. 'Wildlife in Sustainable Development: Approaches to community Participation'. Presentation to the ODA, African Wildlife policy consultation, Sunningdale, UK, 18-19 April.

— 1996b. '*Ex Africa Semper aliquid novi*? Possibilities for linking African Environmental Scholarship, Policy and Practice'. Address delivered at a Pan African Symposium on the sustainable use of natural resources and community participation, Harare, 24-27 June.

— 1996c. 'Strategic Roots and Implementational Evolution'. Address delivered at a workshop entitled 'Enhancing Sustainability: Resources for our Future', World Conservation Congress, Montreal, 17 October.

— 1997a. 'Congruent Objectives, Competing Interests and Strategic Compromise: Concept and Process in the Evolution of Zimbabwe's Campfire Programme'. Paper presented at a conference entitled 'Representing Communities: Histories and Politics of Community Based Resource Management', Helen, 1-3 June.

— 1997b. 'In Search of Pragmatism: Efficiency in Coalitional Global Environmental Management'. Paper delivered at the Seventh Session of the Global Biodiversity, Kuala Lumpur, 24-26 November.

— 1997c. 'Synergising Conservation Incentives: Sociological and Anthropological Dimensions of Sustainable Use'. Paper presented at an STAP Expert Workshop on the 'Sustainable use of Biodiversity', Kuala Lumpur, 24-26 November.

— 1998. 'Incentives for Sustainability'. Address delivered at a workshop on 'Conservation, Sustaining Use of Species and Ecosystems', IUCN 50th Anniversary Celebration, Fontainebleu, 3-5 November, p. 15.

— 1999a. 'Enhancing Sustainable Use: Incentives, Policy and Science'. Working paper delivered at the Berkeley Workshop on Environmental Politics.

— 2000a. 'Boundaries and Borders: The Question of Scale in the Theory and Practice of Common Property Management'. Paper presented at the Eighth Biennial Conference of the International Association for the Study of Common Property (IASCP), Bloomington, Indiana, 31 May-4 June.

— 2000b. 'Community-Based Conservation: Old Ways, New Myths and Enduring Challenges', an address on Community-based Conservation - The New Myth?' Paper delivered at a Conference on African Wildlife Management in the New Millennium, College of African Wildlife Management, Mweka, 13-15 December, p. 16.

— 2001. 'Experiments with the Future'. Prologue to a *Seminar Property Resource Digest*, No. 60, pp. 1-3.

— 2005. 'Matching Management to Regime across the Protected Area Spectrum'. Presentation to the Ninth Meeting of SASUSG, Gondwana, 5 May.

Murphree, M. and E. Barrow (eds). 2001. 'Community Conservation: From Concept to Practice', in M. Murphree and D. Hulme (eds). *African Wildlife and Livelihoods: The Promise and Performance of Community Conservation*. Oxford: James Currey, pp. 24-37.

Murphree, M. and D. Hulme (eds). 2001a. *African Wildlife and Livelihoods: The Promise and Performance of Community Conservation* Oxford: James Currey, 336.

— 2001a. 'Community Conservation in Africa: An Introduction', in M. Murphree and D. Hulme (eds). *African Wildlife and Livelihoods: The Promise and Performance of Community Conservation*. Oxford: James Currey, pp. 1-8.

Murphree, M. and B. Jones. 2001. 'The Evolution of Policy on Community Conservation in Namibia & Zimbabwe', in M. Murphree and D. Hulme (eds). *African Wildlife and Livelihoods: The Promise and Performance of Community Conservation*. Oxford: James Currey, pp. 38-58.

— 2001b. 'Community, Council and Client: A Case study in Ecotourims Development from Mahenye, Zimbabwe', in M. Murphree and D. Hulme (eds). *African Wildlife and Livelihoods: The Promise and Performance of Community Conservation*. Oxford: James Currey, pp. 280-97.

Murphree, M. and D. Mazambani. 2002. 'Policy Implications of Common Pool Resource Knowledge: A Background paper on Zimbabwe'. Carried out as part of an initiative entitled 'Policy Implications of Common Pool Resource Knowledge in India, Tanzania and Zimbabwe', UK Department for International Development's Natural Resources Programme: Semi-Arid Production Systems (Project R7973), p. 127.

Taylor, M. 1996. *Community-based Natural Resource Management (CBNRM) – A Select Foundation Biography with Emphasis on Southern Africa*. Compiled for the Africa Resources Trust, Avondale, Harare, Zimbabwe.

— 1996. *A Select Biography relevant to Campfire (Communal Areas Management Programme for Indigenous Resources*. Compiled for the Africa Resources Trust and the Campfire Association, Harare, Zimbabwe.

3

Rethinking the Building Blocks: *A Critique of Demand Driven Decentralisation in Chizvirizvi Resettlement Area in Chiredzi Rural District of Zimbabwe*

Chaka Chirozva

Introduction

The world is characterised by the skewed distribution of power within and among various levels of social organisation, and decentralisation is a mechanism of aligning governmental powers among these different levels. (Murombedzi 1991; Murphree 1991; Ribot 1999). Although the merits of decentralisation are now more readily understood, efficiency, equity and democratic goals are not clearly evident. Decentralisation seeks to empower local bodies and communities by bestowing upon them 'bundles of entrustments' transferred from the central state (Ribot 1999). Such entrustments include regulatory and executive powers, responsibility and authority in decision making, institutional infrastructure and assets, and administrative responsibilities. In its most ideal form, decentralisation should result in devolution or democratic decentralisation in which entrustments are transferred to lower levels, and preferably elected authorities that are largely or wholly independent of central government (Bosuyt and Gould 2000). But in practice decentralisation often results in outcomes that are commonly referred to as de-concentration in that states extend themselves into the local arena by the transfer of some entrustments to local branches of government that remain responsible and accountable to central government (Agrawal and Ribot 1999; Ribot 1999). This is a weak form of decentralisation because the downward accountability relations from which many benefits are expected are not established as in democratic or political forms of decentralisation.

Although the ideal form may appear somewhat extreme, the common outcome of decentralisation raises questions of whether or not decentralisation as a policy strategy is desirable. As pointed out by Ruitenbeek and Cartier (2001: 4), policy makers are impatient and often seek a quick fix when things are better left to themselves. Their 'hands off' approach appears a crude but poignant reminder to environment and development practitioners to be more modest in their quest to effect change, because change cannot be invented; it is a pervasive and eternal feature of all social and ecological systems. And there is absolutely no reason to assume that peasant communities are so fatalistic and improvident that they are incapable of appropriately adjusting to changes in their everyday social and other environments. More often than not, most such people are adapting to change in ways that are more attuned to the prevailing challenges and opportunities, and what they do, or what they are capable of doing, is often a reflection of options and resources at their disposal. Such systems evolve naturally. It is in the face of such a truism that Ruitenbeek and Cartier (2001:17) strongly argue for non-interventionism, with the related foreclosure hypothesis being that 'premature introduction of external interventions could lead to system failure. This may occur because the introduction of such a process disrupts existing evolutionary processes within the system.'

Experiences with decentralisations appear to lend weight to this conjecture. For instance, in pointing out how most such interventions in southern Africa tend to turn into de-concentrations, Murphree (1991) observes that 'there is a tendency in bureaucratic hierarchies to seek power from levels above and a general reluctance to devolve such power to levels below'. Similar sentiments are echoed by Conyers (1990) and Murombedzi (1991), who point out that higher level actors tend to decentralise service type activities whilst retaining control of fiscal and production oriented activities. In supply led empowerment scenarios, state level and other external actors hold wide discretionary powers with respect to the form and extent of power to be given to actors on the fringes of formal systems of power, including local level bodies and communities. Mandondo (2001) articulates a language of alternatives and reversals in which he argues that decentralisation is likely to result in more thoroughgoing empowerment if it is demand driven. Such reversals and alternatives fall under the rubric of emancipatory approaches (Reason 1999), and have also been popularised as 'putting the last first' (Chambers 1983).

The ideals, in relation to everyday common outcomes of decentralisation, therefore implicitly justify a continuum of policy options that span from full-scale and wholesome intervention to non-intervention. There is mid-point logic of balances that occupies the centre of the continuum. Its basic argument is that no one among local communities, researchers and other stakeholders holds a monopoly of insight or is a priori exclusively endowed with superior qualities in terms of knowledge and skills; that none of the stakeholders will accept to be simply wished away through approaches that are not sufficiently inclusive; and that locals do not exist in isolation but are in fact subsets of over-arching systems with which they are intricately interconnected. The emerging discipline therefore emphasises integration across a variety of axes, including across stakeholders, disciplines, as well as across scales (Sayer and Campbell 2003).

In terms of methodology, this chapter uses empirical evidence from a decentralisation initiative that was largely demand driven to revisit the widely held view that decentralisation is likely to result in more thoroughgoing empowerment if it is demand driven. The chapter is based on a study that was conducted in the Chizvirizvi Resettlement Scheme which lies some 40km east of Zimbabwe's south-eastern Lowveld town of Chiredzi. The study was restricted to issues of land use planning, land tenure and settlement and resource access.

Study methodology

Interviews were conducted to collect primary data. Secondary data was obtained mainly from official documents. Informal discussions and formal semi-structured interviews were conducted with plot owners/farmers and people working in the area. Field level research was corroborated with interviews with relevant government officials such as the District Administrator, Agricultural Research and Extension (AREX) officers and the Malilangwe Conservation Trust, who had been involved in land use planning for the resettlement scheme. Data on conflicts were obtained from the chief's court sessions (*dare*) conducted every Wednesday of the week. In total 54 semi-structured interviews and three focus group discussions were conducted.

The Chizvirizvi community opted out of government initiated consolidated villages that were heavily congested to a system of more spacious self-contained 'private plots', which they planned for and implemented. The community made several other demands, including that they be conferred with legal titles over their plots; that there be fiscal accountability, and parity between taxation and service delivery by the Rural District Council, and that appropriate authority status over wildlife resources in their area be bestowed directly upon them, and not on the Rural District Council as has happened in other Campfire districts.

The history of land tenure & settlement in Chizvirizvi

Colonial land alienation and apportionment policies that were crafted in the early 1930s left a deep imprint on present-day patterns of land tenure and settlement in the Chizvirizvi area. The area adjoins a private wildlife conservancy and a state national park, the Malilangwe Conservancy and Gonarezhou National Park, respectively. The creation of these nature parks involved the eviction of communities and their relocation in the adjacent Sengwe Communal Lands. Over time, natural population growth resulted in inevitable population pressure in communal areas. Against a backdrop of population pressure, the key features of communal land tenure have remained largely intact despite the new political dispensation. Communal lands are legally state lands in which peasant communities enjoy rights based on usufruct. In practice, people enjoy de facto traditional freehold entitlement over their residential and arable plots, beyond which there are usually grazing, woodland and other commons, which people use and manage through various forms of collective or non-collective arrangements (Government of Zimbabwe 1994). During the late 1970s most communal lands, including Sengwe, became fragmented into zones of shifting control between the Rhodesian military and the mass mobilisation committees of the guerrilla movement. In response, the Rhodesian regime introduced protected villages (Lan 1985; Godwin 1996), a strategy aimed at creating buffers of uninhabited land to minimise contact between peasants and the guerrillas. The guerrillas depended on the peasants for material, moral and other forms of support (Lan 1985).

The abandonment of the protected villages after independence did not significantly alleviate population pressure within the communal land and this necessitated interventions to decongest the communal area in order to improve infrastructure and service provision. Colonial neglect of African reserves was the result of a fiscal apartheid in public sector capital investment policies (de Valk and Wekwete 1990). The bulk of the social and physical infrastructure investment was located in European areas to support a fledging capitalist economy, which was further supported by extensive subsidies and preferential marketing policies (Murphree and Cumming 1991; Scoones and Matose 1993; McGregor 1995). Under-investment in the African reserves reinforced the under-development of the peasant sector, which remained a source of cheap labour for the emerging capitalist economy. Over time the peasant sector had been weakened by the downstream effects of the communal tenure system under conditions of high population growth, including lack of collateral, subdivision into smaller and smaller holdings, low productivity and declining surpluses, and very low propensities to save and invest.

Decongestion and reconstruction and development policies in Chizvirizvi were implemented by a government resettlement scheme based on a system of consolidated villages. The scheme was established on land purchased by the government from the adjoining commercial farms. The consolidated villages were based on a system of land use planning that divided landscapes into three major categories: grazing areas, cropping areas and clustered villages located between the two. It was hoped that the centralised settlements would enhance peasant access to a variety of services, including water, electricity and road networks, as well as amenities such as schools, clinics, beer halls and grinding mills. In total, ten villages, each presided over by a village chairperson, were established, all falling under the control of a government paid resettlement officer.

Although modest progress was achieved in providing services and basic infrastructure within the consolidated villages, it was undermined by the failure of the plan to decongest settlement. People became disillusioned by this, and by the plan's propensity to worsen social ills – deprivation of individual and family freedom and autonomy, prevalence of misunderstandings and fights, jealousy, increases in theft, suspicions of witchcraft and increased incidences of adultery. Additional concerns included the degradation of woodlands around the consolidated villages. A five-member committee, later named the Chizvirizvi Development Committee, was set up to articulate these concerns. The committee was exclusively males. As pointed out in the literature, gender is an axis through which privileged access to resources is often entrenched and reproduced, with men being more privileged in most of cases (Fortmann and Nabane 1992). Consultations within the committee led to the broaching of a vision of settlement based on self-contained plots as opposed to the crowded cluster villages.

Towards a new vision of tenure, settlement & resource use

Given the community's concerns over congestion and environmental degradation, the Chizvirizvi Development Committee solicited the support of the Department of Natural Resources for a more dispersed resettlement scheme to be based on a system of individual plots in which the plot holders would be ultimately responsible for most resources within and around their plots. Similar support was solicited from the Ministry of Lands and Agriculture in 1989. Although both these government agencies were supportive of the idea, rampant destruction of the natural resources in areas close to the clustered settlement continued unabated. The support nevertheless encouraged residents to put in place temporary mechanisms to apprehend violators and protect their resources. Such measures included the collective monitoring and policing of resource use.

At the local level the Committee enlisted the support of the local chief and the chairpersons of the ten villages in endorsing the proposed plans, which were subsequently submitted to government through the Provincial Lands Office. Although the community received a favourable response in 1995, it was indicated that the government did not have funds to support the implementation of the plan. Through his links with the Zimbabwe Farmers Union, the chairman of the Committee was able to meet with the Minister of Agriculture to open avenues for funding. Although no financial support could be obtained from the ministry, the committee was able to secure ministerial endorsement to enable access to alternative funding, including donor support. On the advice of the Chiredzi District Administration the community's donor outreach strategy laid emphasis on building lasting partnerships with local potential donors. Building strategic partnerships appears to have been key as the community forged ahead with its vision of decentralised land use planning and conservation of natural resources.

Following a request for funding, the Malilangwe Trust organised a multi-stakeholder meeting that included experts from Zambia, Malawi, South Africa and the USA. The Trust subsequently donated funds for surveys, mapping and demarcation of plots. After concerted efforts to secure technical support from the district and provincial agricultural extension agencies, a survey team was eventually assigned to the area in June 1999. The survey work started later that year, with logistical support being mainly provided by the Malilangwe Trust, and the community providing labour. After completion of surveys and demarcation, plots were allocated in March 2000, witnessed by the District Administrator, the Member of Parliament and representatives from the President's office.

The range of district and national partnerships appears to have been key in planning for and implementing the vision. But conceptual and theoretical debates about state-local relations tend to dichotomise the two as disparate entities, with the state's presence at the local level often considered at best as intrusive, and at worst as inefficient, unaccountable, insensitive, obtrusive, and hegemonic (Phimister 1988; Murombedzi 1991). Distrust of the state's local presence is rooted in Africa's historical processes. Outside imposition has tended to reinforce the view of governments as imperial organisations aspiring to control the entire national jurisdiction (Scott 1998). Moreover, partly because of their quest to exert enduring and far-reaching political control, governments have indeed aspired to establish single centre administrations. Thus, over the years, state visions of the appropriate way to manage resources have generally been implemented in peasant areas through a centrally directed structure and process. Supporters of decentralisation often advocate empowering local communities by pushing back and scaling down the state's role – 'rolling back the state'. However, this solution seems based on certain unrealistic assumptions: that the state has the political willingness to agree to a roll-back; that communities have the know-how and wherewithal to step in and fill the gaps left by this rolling back; and that communities, a priori, have qualities that the state lacks in terms of accountability, representativeness and efficiency (Hesseling 1996). Evidence from Chizvirizvi indicates that though the land use planning initiative was community driven, it drew on the support of various other actors at scales that transcend the local, including the district, the national and indeed the international levels. Effective empowerment therefore appears to need to preserve a role for upper-level (non-local) actors, especially in providing political legitimacy and technical, as well as financial, support.

The practical political economy of land allocation in Chizvirizvi

A total of 293 plots, each measuring 85 hectares, was allocated from the then consolidated resettlement scheme, some farmers in villages 6 and 10 being allocated more than 85 hectares to compensate for the poor soils. Allocation

Table 1: A breakdown of ownership of plots in Chizvirizvi by gender

Gender of Plot Owner	Frequency (n = 293)	Frequency of Ownership as % of Total
Male registered ownership	231	79
Female registered ownership	51	17
Inherited from father	9	3
Inherited from mother	2	1
Total	293	100

Source: Agricultural Research and Extension (AREX) Office, Chiredzi, and Chaka Chirozvdi Notes 2005

was done through a raffle, but two of the villages declined to take part, preferring to remain in the consolidated village. The chief was exempted from the process as a sign of respect, and he was allocated a larger plot encompassing his original homestead. Two plots were additionally given to the chief to allocate to nominees of his own choice. Local leaders who oversaw the allocation devised a secretive and clandestine way of exemptions in order to raise funds for the logistical costs associated with the process, including the provision of food. Households that contributed funds for this purpose were secretly allocated cards prior to the public raffle, and through this arrangement were able to gain privileged access to prime plots. Patterns of ownership were markedly skewed along gender lines, with only a very small proportion of women obtaining plots that were registered in their names.

Decentralisation is often portrayed as a one-off allocation process involving transfers from one level, often the state, to another, usually the community. The implicit assumption is that resource use and other relations in community settings become more egalitarian, and that empowerment is almost guaranteed once powers are retired to that level. But as is evident in the above narrative, ownership relations engendered by a community driven initiative encompass elements of both equity and imbalance. For instance, the raffle appears to have been premised on equity considerations, whilst allocation to the chief and his network of colleagues, though a gesture of respect, could arguably be seen as entrenching elite domination. Mandondo (2001) argues that in order to resolve the dilemma of community marginalisation through decentralisation there is a need to address intra-community inequalities of access to resources.

As a sign of gratitude for support rendered, the community reserved a quota of six plots that were to be allocated to the District Administrator (DA), an agricultural commodity provider employee, Malilangwe Trust, Agritex and other relevant service institutions. Most of these individuals were interested in obtaining their own plots within the scheme. Just as most researchers see a dichotomy between the local and state levels and other external actors, the communities themselves show a sense of partnership with other actors beyond and among themselves.

Hence, narratives of communities portray them within the context of social and political continuums that they are linked with; such links cannot be simply wished away. Communities do not embrace approaches that sever them from broader social and political systems of which they are part. It is important to rethink and reconfigure the building blocks even in such instances where decentralisation is demand driven. Multiple actors enter the arena and each struggles for control over access to and use of resources particularly forests, land and wildlife. Although this narrative portrays the land allocation process as having been largely consensual, this was not quite the case. The next section will consider the micro-politics surrounding the process.

The micro-politics of land allocation in Chizvirizvi

First preference to take up the new plots was given to people formerly residing in the government initiated consolidated villages. Some of these people were initially reluctant to move because they had made infrastructural investments at their homesteads; however, they joined the last-minute rush for plots when evidence emerged of the good harvests secured by the pioneer group of settlers. An array of power-plays was engaged as people asserted claims to the land. A group of teachers at a local school was one strong constituency that had been left out of the initial allocation. They are reported to have clandestinely instigated the local village worker to mobilise people in two of the villages to revolt against the scheme, purportedly because they had been allocated infertile plots. In the hope of limiting the ensuing conflict, the District Administrator unilaterally took over control of the unassigned plots, but his custodianship did not last long, neither did it dampen the conflict. Realising the futility of intervention, the DA later capitulated and re-vested such control in the committee that had hitherto overseen the allocation process.

In August 2000, the land allocation committee was approached by a group of 16 liberation war veterans, who felt that they were also being left out of the entitlement process. The chairperson of the land committee decided to enlist the support of the chief in deciding how best to handle the issue. For fear of squaring up against the veterans, it was quickly decided that they be allocated land. But the problem was how to allocate the seven then remaining plots among the 16 veterans. With initial concurrence of the veterans, it was decided that the plots be allocated through an elimination raffle; although this was done with the initial support of all concerned, the losing veterans did not honour the result, most of them opting to grab plots that had already been allocated to other people.

Conflicts in Chizvirizvi revolve around boundary disputes and the gender dimensions of entitlement to land by way of inheritance. Although the conflicts mostly pit local peasants against each other there were instances in which others became involved. A national AREX official was embroiled in a boundary dispute with his peasant neighbour, and the resolution of the conflict is still pending in the chief's court at the time of writing. The general law is that the spouse should inherit a plot on the death of a partner, with the children taking over if both the mother and father die. Despite such arrangements conflict over plots still arise depending on the nuance and entitlement and peculiarities of intra-household relations. Conflicts over land and resources often cascade to higher levels, where customary, elected and other leaders vie for influence and control over the whole resettlement domain. Thus, over the years, Chizvirizvi has come to typify what could be described as the 'waxing and waning' as well as the 'emergence and submergence' of typical rural institutions.

Alliances between champions of development, as represented by the resettlement committee, and the 'more legitimate' traditional leaders appear to have emerged by the turn of the century, But the emerging configuration of institutions did not translate into an enduring monopoly of power and influence. People in Chizvirizvi now more readily attest to the benefits of their land use planning initiative, including, in general, bigger and better plots, greater autonomy, and distance from suspected bewitchers. Notwithstanding the bottom-up manner in which this decentralisation initiative was implemented, all is not bliss and harmony in Chizvirizvi. Orienting change in the bottom-up direction appears pivotal, but such interventions still need adequate follow-up if they are to result in genuine empowerment. Whether it be bottom-up or top-down, decentralisation appears to need robust efforts to remove the conditions that may, from time to time, detract from the attainment of enduring empowerment. Such decentralisations should be seen as processes, not as events, and there is a need to continuously negotiate the terrain where contests over resource control unfold. This calls for skills in conflict resolution, but caution needs to be exercised because such conflicts are often tools and weapons through which the poor and marginalised insert themselves into political processes (Scott 1985). There is, however, no reason to assume that the local poor and powerless can act alone in effectively staking their claims given the preponderance of elite influence. The next section considers resource use relations within and between plots and the adjoining Sengwe Communal Area.

Resource access & use relations

Outside access to grazing and other woodland resources in resettlement plots was a highly contentious issue. Plot owners want to exclude outsiders whilst neighbouring communal areas, on the basis of historical claims, want a continuation of open-access use regimes. The contested nature of resources within Chizvirizvi is thus a major source of conflict, with plot owners generally under siege from tenure contests and pressure from adjoining Sengwe communal area farmers. The views of those asserting use pressures varied from extremist arguments against the compartmentalisation of land and resources, with proponents insisting on a reversion to the then existing open access utilisation regimes, to moderate viewpoints emphasising the need for dialogue and mutual use regimes together with related win-win obligations. In other cases, acquiescent viewpoints were also held and these tended to emphasise the need to respect the entitlement and ownership of the plot owners. On the other hand most plot owners argued for exclusion management, with most of them advocating for the fencing off of their properties, together with the need to re-erect the boundary fence between the whole resettlement area and the adjoining communal areas. Most people recognised the limitations of such an option in terms of cost, and also in terms of effectiveness, since an earlier fence had been vandalised, and most plot owners saw the conferment of formal title as a key part of the incentive structure for enhancing exclusion management.

Despite these conflicts, there are also reciprocal arrangements relating to the use of resources. In general the northern part of the scheme is drier and less fertile – with less arable land, but more wooded and endowed with better grazing resources. The reverse generally tends to obtain in adjacent communal areas as well as in southern parts of the resettlement scheme. Disparities in the spatial distribution of resources generally necessitate the need for reciprocity. Reciprocal resource use relations are mostly forged at a personal and informal level – people from the drier north negotiate for access to arable land, thatching grass and water from those in the southern parts of the scheme and from adjoining communal areas, with the latter groups usually seeking to have access to grazing resources, firewood, *mopane* worms and poles from the former.

These narratives would seem to have serious implications for the extent to which solutions to dilemmas of resource access can be crafted, particularly in situations of conflict. There appears to be no simple solution to the above problems of access when considered in relation to scale, but what appears to be evident is the need for parsimony with an emphasis on forging solutions that match the scale of the problem. There are two possible options. Firstly, to leave things as they are at the inter-personal scale where people come up with arrangements for mutual use. Secondly, to facilitate multi-stakeholder dialogue with appropriate groups where problems appear to cascade over larger spatial and social scales. Given the polarity of opinion in some instances, particularly that obtaining between communal area and Chizvirizvi scheme residents, neutral arbitration may be needed, a role that can be usefully taken up by external actors. Such arbitrators often turn out to be those whom the anti-state fringe of the environment and development research movement is quick to vilify.

Conclusion

I have argued that empowerment that is demand driven stands a better chance of being based on people's felt needs and priorities than the top-down and supply led alternatives. However, even if empowerment is demanded, relations in decentralised arenas are seldom egalitarian. Regardless of their orientation, environmental decentralisations are best not conceived as one-off events in which power is abstracted from one level to be retired to another level. Such interventions should be regarded as continuous processes in which the dilemma of community marginalisation from the centre of power is tackled in tandem with intra-community impediments to such empowerment.

Earlier hypotheses posited whether it is best to intervene fully, a little or not at all in environment and development processes that subsume a decentralisation agenda. Subsequent findings and analyses have largely supported a mid-point logic of integration and multi-stakeholder partnership in which the community should be the locus of initiative and change. This is best done within a framework in which other stakeholders play a more supportive role of fostering conditions that enhance that attainment of thoroughgoing empowerment, or dismantling those that detract from its attainment. Contrary to the anti-state passion of some sections of the environment and development research movement, the logic of integration and partnership sees a role for state level and other external actors particularly in providing the political legitimacy that community driven initiatives are so utterly in need of. In addition, this often provides a countervailing source of information, skills and ideas through which ideas can be scrutinised and improved. No one side has a monopoly of insight. In a similar vein, these decentralisation interventions should be seen as ways of providing co-ordination, especially where community problems appear to cascade beyond the level at which communities themselves can address them. The state thus provides neutral arbitration in instances where community-level polarisation stalls the scope for progress.

Finally, in considering the scope for extrapolation and scaling up, no context is exactly the same as another – what worked for Chizvirizvi may not necessarily work elsewhere, and vice versa. Notwithstanding context specificity, it is argued that the demand driven approach to transacting rural empowerment constitutes a far better option than top-down, supply led, and sadly seldom successful ways of doings things. In decentralised interventions it is important to continuously rethink and reconfigure the actors, powers and accountability arrangements that are found and look at options to converge interests.

References

Agrawal, A. and J.C. Ribot. 1999. 'Accountability in decentralisation: A framework with Asian and African cases', *Journal of Developing Areas*, 33, pp. 473-502.
Bosuyt, J. and J. Gould. 2000. 'Decentralisation and poverty reduction: elaborating the Link-

ages', *Policy Management*, Brief no. 12. Maastricht: European Centre for Development Policy Management.

Chambers, R. 1983. *Rural Development: Putting the Last First*. London: Longman.

Conyers, D. 1990. 'Decentralisation and development planning: a comparative perspective' in P. de Valk and K.H. Wekwete (eds). *Decentralisation for Participatory Planning: Comparing the Experiences of Zimbabwe and other Anglophone Countries in Eastern and Southern Africa*. Brookfield: Avebury Press, pp. 15-33.

de Valk, P. and K.H. Wekwete (eds). *Decentralisation for Participatory Planning: Comparing the Experiences of Zimbabwe and other Anglophone Countries in Eastern and Southern Africa*. Brookfield: Avebury Press, pp. 15-33.

Fortmann, L. and N. Nabane. 1992. *The fruits of their labours: gender, property, and trees in Mhondoro District*. Harare: Centre for Applied Social Sciences Publications, University of Zimbabwe.

Godwin, P. 1996. *Mukiwa: A White Boy in Africa*. New York: Atlantic Monthly Press.

Government of Zimbabwe. 1994. *Report of the Commission of Inquiry into Appropriate Agricultural Land Tenure Systems*. Harare: Government Printers.

Hesseling, G. 1996. 'Legal and institutional incentives from local environmental management' in H.S. Marcussen (ed.). *Improved Natural Resource Management: The role of Formal Organisations and Informal Networks and Institutions*, Occasional Paper No. 17, Roskilde: Roskilde University Press.

Lan, D. 1985. *Guns and Rain: Guerrillas and Spirit Mediums in Zimbabwe*. London: James Currey.

Mandondo, A. 2001. 'Situating Zimbabwe's natural resource governance systems in history', Centre for International Forestry Research Working Paper 32. Bogor: Indonesia Centre for International Forestry Research.

McGregor, J. 1995. 'Conservation, control and ecological change: the politics and ecology of colonial conservation in Shurugwi, Zimbabwe', *Environment and History*, 1, 257-79.

Murombedzi, J. 1991. 'Decentralising common property resources management: a case study of the Nyaminyami District Council of Zimbabwe's wildlife management programme', Paper No. 30. London: International Institute for Environment and Development.

Murphree, M. W. 1991. *Communities as institutions for resource management*. Harare: Centre for Applied Social Sciences Publications, University of Zimbabwe.

Murphree, M.W. and D.H.M. Cumming. 1991. 'Savanna land use policy and practice in Zimbabwe', paper presented at the United Nations Educational Scientific and Cultural Organisation (UNESCO) Conference on Economic Driving Forces and Constraints on Savanna Land Use, Nairobi, January.

Phimister, I. 1988. *An Economic and Social History of Zimbabwe 1890-1948: Capital Accumulation and Class Struggle*. London: Longman.

Reason, P. 1999. 'Integrating action and reflection through co-operative inquiry Management Learning', *The Action Dimension in Management: Diverse Approaches to Research, Teaching and Development*, 30, 2, pp. 207-27.

Ribot, J. C. 1999. 'Decentralization, participation and accountability in Sahelian forestry legal instruments of political-administrative control', *Africa*, 69, pp. 23-65.

Ruitenbeek, J. and C. Cartier. 2001. 'The invisible wand: Adaptive co-management as an emergent strategy in complex bio-economic systems', Occasional Paper No. 34, Bogor: Indonesia Centre for International Forestry Research, 51.

Sayer, J.A. and B.M. Campbell. 2003. 'Research to integrate productivity enhancement, environmental protection, and human development', in J. A. Sayer and B. M. Campbell (eds), *Integrated Natural Resource Management: Linking Productivity, the Environment and Development*. Bogor: CABI Publishing in Association with the Centre for International Forestry Research, pp. 1-14.

Scott, J. C. 1998. *Seeing Like a State: How Certain Schemes to Improve the Human Condition have Failed*. New Haven: Yale University Press.

— 1985. *Weapons of the Weak: Everyday Forms of Peasant Resistance*. New Haven: Yale University Press.

Scoones, I. and F, Matose. 1993. 'Local woodland management: constraints and opportunities for sustainable resource use', in P.N. Bradley and K. McNamara (eds) *Living with Trees: Policies for Woodland Management in Zimbabwe*. Washington DC: World Bank, pp. 157-98.

4

Beacon & Barometer:
CBNRM & Evolutions in Local Democracy in Southern Africa

Simon Anstey & Liz Rihoy

Introduction

'We are resolved to be cheated no longer, nor be held under the slavish fear of you no longer, seeing the Earth was made for us as well as for you: And if the Common Land belongs to us who are the poor oppressed, surely the woods that grow upon the Commons belong to us likewise. If we lie still, and let you steal away our birthrights, we perish ... though we have paid taxes, given free quarter and ventured our lives to preserve the Nations freedom as much as you, and therefore by the law of contract with you, freedom in the land is our portion as well as yours, equal with you. Therefore we require, and we resolve to take both Common Land and Common woods to be a livelihood for us, and look upon you as equal with us.'
(An extract from 'A Declaration from the Poor and Oppressed People of England', Gerard Winstanley et al. (1649))

This declaration comes from around 360 years ago in the period of the English Revolution, when supporters of Parliament had just 'liberated' England from the efforts of Charles I to institute an unpopular (religious) ideology and an absolute form of monarchy against the broad will of the people. However, the leaders of the Parliamentary faction had then gone on to utilise their new elite status to attempt a land and resource grab of state and common land – the above declaration being a reaction to this and addressed to the new elite. It was a reaffirmation from those who had fought in this 'liberation war' of their rights to land, but not only to the land itself. It explicitly linked their land proprietor rights to the management and benefits of resources on those lands (communal land). The Declaration was not however a call for devolution or decentralisation; it had in its basis no sense of local democracy or natural resource management and rights as being a function of a downward extending state or public hierarchy. It 'required' and 'resolved' the restitution of land and resources on the basis of a belief in equality and a mutually binding contract of rights. It did so with reference in its text to the extensive history of local self-government embodied in the Common Law and framed by custom and precedent.

What does Winstanley's demand for rights and benefits from communal land and resources have to do with CBNRM or evolutions in local democracy in southern Africa in 2007, or in a celebration of Marshall Murphree's scholarship?

On the latter aspect, this chapter will draw out constant themes that relate to local or rural democracy and natural resource governance, justice, and the use of political philosophies and governance frameworks that have historical weight as well as operational purpose. Over ten years ago Murphree (1995) noted the close inter-relationship of local democracy, tenure rights, and local political activism:

> 'In the context of CBNRM, tenurial rights will make the difference between rural democratic representation and the *persistence of perpetual adolescence for rural peoples in national structures of governance* ... optimal conditions for CBNRM require strong tenurial rights, this requires fundamental devolution of power, one which politicians are unlikely to make unless there is a strong political reason to do so. This reason can only lie in a *strong, politically potent constituency demand* that this takes place ... this is the rural resource-managing communities themselves'. (emphasis added).

His scholarship subsequently drew on the governance declarations of Abraham Lincoln and the Gettysburg Address in his analysis of '*conservation for the people, with the people and by the people*' (Murphree 1998). In his 2000 paper on scale and boundaries, one that shifted CBNRM debates beyond the stalemate of focus on the pervasive experience in southern Africa of 'aborted devolution', he drew on the ideas and practical governance experiences of the eighteenth-century political philosophers of America in their evolutions of federal government in tackling interactions between jurisdictional scales and institutions in governance. In this paper (Murphree 2000a) the emphasis was that devolution in natural resource governance is not an exercise in isolationism, but a process of finding local regime inter-dependence within the larger setting of inter-dependence at many scales. The key elements were:

- *Principle of Delegated Aggregation* – local jurisdictions *delegate upwards* aspects of their responsibility and authority to collective governance of larger scope in which they continue to play a role.

- *Principle of Constituent Accountability* – each institutional tier above the community level is *accountable downwards* to the constituency that empowered it.

These principles and ideas relating to CBNRM governance share many elements with those of Madison, Adams or de Tocqueville regarding the challenges faced in a more purely political field, and the options of retaining a considerable degree of self-government at a local scale that formed the federal USA, the basis of the Bill of Rights and the American Constitution (see Siedentop 2000).

Regarding the relevance of Winstanley's Declaration of 1649 to CBNRM and evolutions in local democracy in southern Africa now, the first aspect worth noting is the link between land tenure, resource tenure and rights of use, and that the contest over these between local and centre remains remarkably comparable over time and place. As will be explored in further sections, the need to align land and resource rights (rather than separate or partial entitlements) and the challenges of achieving these rights in the existing political space are as relevant to local voices in north Mozambique and south-east Zimbabwe today as to those of the 'poor and oppressed of England' 360 years ago. This suggests that scholar-practitioners in CBNRM in southern Africa are not facing a unique challenge or novel experiment with success and failure outcomes determined within time frames of five or ten years. They face a wider and iterative process of local democracy and resource rights, and have historical experiences to draw upon. The current narratives and theoretical underpinnings of *democratic decentralisation* and devolution are less likely to be similar, but there are almost certainly local parallels between 1649 and 2007 regarding natural justice; and the years of struggle in this region were not endured to achieve a second-class status and build a nation safe for elites.

Against this background, and its premise that CBNRM is a process of applied and incremental experiments in democracy, this chapter explores the role of CBNRM as both a *beacon* for catalyzing wider aspects of democratic governance in Africa in practice (land reform, shifting democracy to lower than national scale), and a *barometer* for tracking their progress.

It does so first by exploring the complexities that have emerged around narratives, processes and definitions of democratic decentralisation and devolution in natural resource management – the *de-processes*. It does this because, whatever the differences in the meanings ascribed to these two related concepts and despite the considerable emphasis on them of donors, governments and those promoting or implementing local scale natural resource management, the stark feature is that to date both have been honoured more in the breach than in the practical application. The section looks at whether this stalemate, in what is widely regarded as a prerequisite of powers and authority for CBNRM, is specific in context or representative of a broader democratic stalemate (a crisis in rural governance and in the *democracy of the base*).

This leads to the second section of short case-studies looking at contrasting local scale experiences, one in Mozambique and the other in Zimbabwe. With very different national contexts and timeframes in which the experiences are unfolding, with shared crises in external and internal *enabling environments*, this section explores how, despite imperfections in devolution-decentralisation, often surprising changes are occurring. The aim is to illustrate, through the very different settings, that an emphasis on *devolution now* or *decentralisation best* analysis could usefully shift to a more nuanced acceptance that issues, context and circumstance should be allowed to determine the use of structure. Or to put in another way, not letting theoretical narratives get in the way of common sense, and staying true to local diversity as enriching scholarship.

The concluding section revisits the beacon-barometer metaphor and suggests that what CBNRM in southern Africa has the potential to offer is a contribution towards deepening African democracy in the twenty-first century.

Hatching out in a rough neighbourhood – decentralisation and devolution

Democratic decentralisation and devolution have contested meanings, as is often the case with key elements of complex development or academic narratives (see Roe 1991). Before discussing the various definitions used in the southern African CBNRM context, it is worth noting that both incorporate a 'chicken and egg' dilemma of theory with limited feedback from practice.

As Murphree (2000b) noted in the context of southern Africa, 'CBNRM has not been tried and found wanting, it has been found difficult and rarely tried', because the prerequisite of devolution of proprietary rights from the centre for CBNRM to effectively function has been notably absent. Murombedzi (2003) sums up a broad body of regional analysis by noting that most CBNRM initiatives which characterise themselves as 'devolved' 'reflect rhetoric more than substance' and that in reality they continue to be 'characterised by some continuation of substantive central government control and management over natural resources rather than a genuine shift in authority to local people.'

Larsen and Ribot (2005) note that democratic decentralisation in natural resource management is 'barely happening', despite considerable investment and the fact that decentralisation has become a truly global movement and a favoured narrative of donor agencies. All the case-studies in their global research highlight problems with power transfer from central government to local entities and/or accountability from such entities to constituents. Democratic decentralisation of natural resources is caught in an 'if then' proposition – if the institutions are right, then the outcomes will be positive. They note that, 'We cannot yet say whether these "if then" propositions are right because ... decentralisations are not getting to "if".' (Larson and Ribot 2005).

Ribot (2002) is a widely quoted source of definitions and descriptions of democratic decentralisation and related concepts within the 'decentralisation' narrative.

In further clarifying definitions of decentralisation, Ribot (2005) notes that 'theorists define decentralisation as the transfer of powers from central government to lower levels *within* government's political-administrative hierarchy' (emphasis in original). Murphree (2000) provides a definition (and distinction from democratic decentralisation) in the more widely southern Africa CBNRM use of a devolution narrative; he interprets devolution as 'the creation of relatively autonomous realms of authority, responsibility and entitlement, with a primary accountability to their own constituencies'.

While there is considerable overlap (and potential for confusion) in these

---

> *Box 1 – Ribot's (2002) definition of decentralisation*
>
> **Decentralisation** is any act in which a central government formally cedes powers to actors and institutions at lower levels in a political-administrative and territorial hierarchy.
>
> **Democratic decentralisation** occurs when powers and resources are transferred to authorities representative of and downwardly accountable to local populations. Democratic decentralisation aims to increase public participation in local decision making. Through greater participation, democratic decentralisation is believed to help internalise social, economic, developmental and environmental externalities; to better match social services and public decisions to local needs and aspirations; and to increase equity in the use of public resources.
>
> **Privatisation** is the permanent transfer of powers to any non-state entity, including individuals, corporations, NGOs and so on. Privatisation, although often carried out in the name of decentralisation, is not a form of decentralisation. It operates on an exclusive logic, rather than on the inclusive public logic of decentralisation.

terms and their definitions, there are some critical differences. The devolution narrative is concerned with 'relatively autonomous' entities that can encompass bodies holding for example land or resource title and legal entity status (such as trusts or cooperatives) and that do not have to be within a government political-administration hierarchy. The democratic decentralisation narrative theorises that this approach to natural resource management operates on an exclusive logic and endangers the emergence, cohesiveness and effectiveness of elected local governments in consolidating local interests in the political-administrative hierarchy (Ribot 2002). It consigns devolution in the southern Africa CBNRM usage, as beyond the pale of democratic decentralisation and into the category of 'privatisation'. Case-studies in Ribot and Larsen (2005) and Ribot (2005) point to the dangers of elite capture of natural resources in conditions with weak elected local government, a proliferation of local institutions and a growth in state use of 'traditional' authority in local governance.

However, there is also clearly emerging a more nuanced and less doctrinal approach to options for local scale management of natural resources. This is both in the 'beyond devolution' shifts in southern African scholarship emphasising jurisdictional scales in inter-dependant institutions for natural resource governance, and in recent writings on the general decentralisation narrative. For example, Ribot (2007) takes a more pragmatic approach to proliferating local entities than in his earlier work:

> Competition between different entities can be divisive, or it may lead to more efficiency and better representation all round. It can undermine the legitimacy of local democratic authorities while producing conditions for elite capture, or it may produce a pluralism of competition and cooperation that helps establish and thicken civil society.

Larsen's (2005) studies in Guatemala, where democratic decentralisation had largely stagnated due to central government resistance, argue for re-thinking decentralisation models and especially recognising the importance of decentralisation from below, and its informality and dynamism. After seven years of largely failed efforts to develop elected local government through democratic decentralisation reforms in Mozambique, Baptista-Lundin (1998) notes (apparently without intentional irony) that 'there seems to be a need to think about inverting the democratisation process, to attempt to let it develop from the bottom'.

Perhaps there are some underlying factors which have made these *de-processes* of democratic decentralisation and devolution complex to the point that stalemates are reached in the efforts to apply them.

Epistemologies in this context may help – or to put it another way, in the beginning was the word and then the deed. The '*de-*' functions as a prefix with its etymology based on the Latin roots of '*from, down, away*'. Such words inevitably thus act to privilege the centre as a starting point, and create a 'mental model' around which central power and authority are the negotiating start and control the direction and speed of the process. In privileging the centre they reinforce a bureaucratic view of the state and a subject rather than citizen approach to democracy. It's hard to get to the *deed* (effective local democracy, empowered citizenship, self government) if the *word* privileges and hands out discretionary control to the centre.

Finally, the notion that 'a central government formally cedes powers to actors and institutions at lower levels in a political-administrative and territorial hierarchy' appears rather empty of historical precedent or applied political philosophy; especially considering the political histories of those countries that have been bankrolling this narrative or constituting its main theorists and proponents.

If democratic ideas have been profoundly influenced (see Lewis 2003) by political philosophies that start with the inalienable rights of citizens to life, liberty and property, and if government's legitimacy and prime function, based on the consent of the governed, is to defend such rights, then the *aborted devolution* and generally observed absence of progress in *democratic decentralisation* bring into sharp focus the claim to legitimacy of resistant government and central elites.

From this perspective, refusing to facilitate the powers and authority required by local government or local natural resource institutions to work effectively, is also inherently to declare oneself illegitimate to govern. It is difficult to avoid that political philosophy and logic by claiming bureaucratic complexity, hierarchical delays or the inability of rural citizens to manage their rights and responsibilities. That one can do so (and clearly and persistently get away with it) in the context of devolution-decentralisation narrative is indicative of its flaws. To put it crudely – the inalienable rights-consent of governed is a model based on a transparent citizen-state contract with penalty and revoking clauses; the top-down decentralisation-devolution model acts as an open-dated cheque held in a central government safe, and one critically lacking the co-signature of the citizen.

In this sense, one shift beyond devolution-decentralisation for CBNRM scholarship is simply to be aware of epistemological constraints and wary of development narratives with weak historical precedence and little supporting ballast from political philosophy. One fruitful option seems to be to better understand what Ake (2000) has called the 'democracy of the base' in Africa and in the context of what Turner (2004) calls a regional 'crisis of rural governance', namely, how in different contexts, circumstances and facing different issues, the structural challenges arising out of the apparently stalemated devolution-decentralisation discourse are being addressed locally. As Rihoy and Maguranyanga (forthcoming) state:

> Attention has to be paid to the political landscape of CBNRM, and innovative and strategic political manoeuvring, dialogue and engagement with government bureaucrats, politicians and other relevant stakeholders – particularly local communities, local political economic elites and traditional authorities.

The next section addresses the issues, context and circumstances through two brief case-studies of local initiatives in Mozambique and Zimbabwe, and some 'strategic manoeuvrings' by rural practitioner-scholars.

Chipanje Chetu & Mahenye – contrasts & congruence in adaptive governance

> It is at the local level where bargains are made, deals negotiated and politics practised ... With multiple and competing lines of authority, the local political context is key, and is often ignored in the standard models and assessments of decentralization policies. (Norfolk 2004)

In looking at two cases studies of local evolutions, one in Sanga District in northern Mozambique and one in Mahenye Ward in south-eastern Zimbabwe, it is first useful to have a background on some key national differences in land and resource tenure and local government.

National specifics & histories
Land tenure

Mozambique, unlike Zimbabwe, did not have in colonial times a dualistic land tenure structure that included 'native reserves' or 'Tribal Trust Lands', nor after independence was communal land tenure a feature of the rural landscape. The post-independence government nationalised all land, and it remains constitutionally the property of the state, which grants user rights to other entities. The key element of land tenure development was the evolution in the 1990s of policy and law (GOM 1997) that not only provided options for granting private land use rights for up to 100 years, but also provided self identified 'local communities' with land use rights in perpetuity, and without the necessity for registration of title, based on oral testimony of their having at least ten years of occupancy. Title to the land (or DUAT) could be granted to local communities defined as:

> A grouping of families and individuals, living in a circumscribed territorial area at the level of a locality or below, which has as its objective the safeguarding of common interests through the protection of areas of habitation, agricultural areas, whether cultivated or fallow, forests, sites of socio-cultural importance, grazing lands, water sources and areas for expansion (Law 19/97 Article 1/1).

The local community in land law terms is thus a fully recognised private body with legal status that holds actual private use rights to a resource and can enter into legally binding contracts. The critical point is that in Mozambique both private and local community land use rights are equal rights in law. This is unlike the differential land rights and legal status of communal and private tenure in Zimbabwe (see Chitsike 2000), which leaves local communities in a legal limbo, with circumscribed rights and no independent institutional status – essentially a perpetuation of 'rural adolescence'.

Resource tenure

The past ten years have also seen considerable policy and legal reform in the wildlife and forestry sector in Mozambique. A general policy was published in 1996, a new Forestry and Wildlife Law in 1999 (Law 10/99) and regulations to implement them were enacted in 2002 (Decree 12/2002). However, if the land process stressed ownership, a basis of equal rights between community and private interests, the wildlife and forestry process has stressed participation in a co-management approach in which the state is regulator. It has introduced a level of confusion regarding the nature of the community as an entity, as it treats the community as a form of public body that has a legitimate interest in resource management, rather than a private body (as in the Land Law) that holds actual private use rights to a resource (see Norfolk 2004 and Tanner et al. 2006). Communities' benefits from resources are envisaged as indirect – dependent on receiving a portion (20 per cent) of the state taxes charged, for example, on timber extraction or sport hunting.

In Zimbabwe there has been less legal reform, but existing legislation has been adjusted to permit greater devolution of appropriate authority – to manage and benefit from, at least, wildlife resources – to the elected local government level of the Rural District Councils (RDCs), if not to the originally envisaged private legal and local scale entity of community cooperatives or trusts (see Chitsike 2000; Rihoy and Maguranyanya forthcoming). Economic benefits for local communities arise not from portions of state taxes, but from portions (50+ per cent) of the contracts between the RDCs and private hunting or tourism companies. The significant economic returns in the Zimbabwean case have meant that this aspect (rather than proprietorship) has formed the locus for the greatest contestation, particularly between the producer community (village-ward) and the RDC. Put simply, a kind of stalemated 'semi-adolescence' in the Zimbabwe case, and 'full adolescence' in the current but still rapidly evolving Mozambique reforms and implementation.

Local government

Zimbabwe and Mozambique have very different historical experiences with local government. Zimbabwe has a history of elected structures, stretching from village to ward to district (RDC) (see Chitsike 2000 for details), and an embedded practice of accountability and authority in rural governance – even if actual experience has been varied or imperfect. Mozambique, in both colonial and post-colonial eras, has by contrast had a vacuum of elected rural local government and, in much of the rural areas, decades of weak or non-existent state administration below district level (Buur and Kyed 2005). As in the other sectors, there have been considerable efforts in Mozambique since the end of the civil war in 1992 to reform policy and legislation relating to local government, and in particular following the powerful donor funded narrative of 'democratic decentralisation'. However, implementation and results have been very slow to materialise and remain politically highly contested. Contradictions have also arisen between the rights and autonomy basis of local communities in the land law, and upwardly accountable state administration structures in still generally unelected forms of rural local government. As observed by Norfolk (2004) this has been:

> ... a parallel process through which the government has been reinstituting the institution of 'indirect rule' through 'community representatives'. The decree (15/2000) essentially re-appoints the traditional chiefs as legally-recognised representatives of community groups .... The definition of a local community in the regulations to the decree varies from that in the Land Law and is strictly related to territorial administrative divisions: district, administrative post and locality. Community representatives of these groups are therefore state-appointed, state remunerated and of a public character, whereas local community groups in terms of the land law are private land-holding entities.

In summary, rural Zimbabweans have, relative to their Mozambique counterparts, a very different lived experience of formal structures of local democratic governance, different expectations of it and different options to make use of its institutions when engaging in political manoeuvring. This will become clearer in the contrasting case-studies discussed below.

A few additional country features need mentioning first. In terms of CBNRM programmes, Mozambique has not evolved within a consistent investment framework or on the basis of a developed market context. Initiatives, whether national or local in scope, have rarely benefited from investments of more than three years in a highly project specific environment of donor, NGO or govern-ment activity. This stands in contrast to 20 years of a national programme in Zimbabwe (Campfire) and of considerable focused investment (Rihoy and Magurunyanya, forthcoming). Nor has CBNRM in Mozambique benefited as in Zimbabwe from an established and innovative private sector (such as in wildlife and tourism) offering demand, capacity and marketing services to CBNRM.

In terms of general political and economic status the two countries present considerable contrasts. Mozambique currently has a generally stable political climate and a rapidly growing economy, albeit against a background of great instability in the period from the 1970s to the early 1990s. Zimbabwe has experienced since the late 1990s a political and economic crisis that remains in stalemate and that affects, and is mirrored with distortions by, all levels from the very local to the national and including the CBNRM sector (see Rihoy et al. 2007 for discussion).

Chipange Chetu CBNRM, north Mozambique

'The rain falls on both cemeteries and villages, but it is the village that goes forward.' (Mwenye Pauila, 21 June 2000, North Sanga)

The following study is drawn from Anstey (2000 and 2005) and related doctoral research. Chipanje Chetu (*'our wealth'* in the local language of Chi-Yao) is a CBNRM initiative started in late 1999 in northern Mozambique in an area covering around 6,500 km^2 which has remained up to the present a zone with a very low population density, relatively rich natural resources and remoteness from government administration.

The broad goal of the initiative was to test in practice the possibilities of the new and still emerging reforms in land, resource and local governance, with the aim of transferring the rights and responsibilities for land and resource management to local communities to gain an output of improved livelihood based on sustainable use of natural resources.

The experience in reality was, and remains, far less structured than such a project logical framework or the formal institutions or the text of national laws and policy might suggest. Chipanje Chetu has more accurately been a process of 'muddling through' in a context of local politics, resilient but complex customary institutions, weak but often predatory formal institutions, key but often unpredicted actors, disputes and collisions over authority, power and money, and breakthroughs and breakdowns. It is no clearer today than five years ago where the process will end, and perhaps the only certainties are that:

- the question of 'whose wealth?' is now firmly on the agenda;

- it has forced new political relationships and negotiations more directly between government and active citizens;
- this dynamic is rooted at the local scale.

Probably the most significant process and institutional change in this 'muddling through' towards local democracy was the realisation by the community of the title to the land (or DUAT) covering over 650,000 ha in the north of Sanga District. The title process was initiated in 1999 and by 2002 the land demarcation, and agreement amongst the communities involved and with neighbouring communities, had been completed. The DUAT was granted in March 2003, signed by the chosen representatives of the five villages (the traditional authorities or *Mwenyes* were selected by the communities for this role) and counter-signed by the relevant district officials. It was a major step forward as it was not only the largest community title to land in a CBNRM programme in the country, but also the single largest community title of any kind in Mozambique.

However, the process faced many obstacles and required considerable manoeuvrings within both the community and the institutions and actors outside. The Yao people of the area have a form of matrilineal social system which functions most effectively at the very local scale of a hamlet or small village, with customary governance systems ineffective and highly contested at any higher scales. Reaching agreement over boundaries and shared land and other resources over 650,000 ha and almost 3,000 people, and consensus over representation in the DUAT title and related institutional structure, required considerable development of intra-community trust. Key actors within the community (a locally respected Muslim cleric) and outside it (trusted government and NGO staff) had to act as 'honest brokers' in breaking deadlocks that stalemated progress. Achieving consensus in borders, resources and representation was thus as much a local socio-political breakthrough for the community as was gaining the title itself. Outside the community there were also challenges of bureaucratic obstruction, rent-seeking or lack of knowledge of the land law provisions by the provincial and district authorities responsible for the process of granting the DUAT title. These required the agency of key actors including the provincial head of wildlife and forestry and the Governor of the Province of Niassa. In short, the apparently technical process of land titling was a deeply political activity – not surprisingly, given that its outcome, the DUAT, is a radical transfer of power and authority to a local autonomous entity creating very new power relations between local and centre, community and government.

It is perhaps equally unsurprising that this DUAT has since 2003 faced concerted efforts to cancel it. Stratagems to have it revoked have included, for example, efforts by a government minister involved in a private sector enterprise to gain an exclusive tourism concession over the area on the basis that the community DUAT should be set aside due to alleged procedural mistakes made in its issuance. Such pressures have required further manoeuvrings, counter-stratagems and resistance efforts – most powerfully from the community itself. These have included appealing directly to the Niassa Provincial Governor (a presidential appointee and member of cabinet and thus with considerable party and administrative powers), more subtle local party politics and making their case to the national media.

Resource benefits in the form of cash dividends (mainly from a sport hunting lease) have had an important role also in the dynamics of political change. Initial efforts to generate resource based cash income for the community via a pilot sport hunting lease became deadlocked, first by the lack of a local entity (prior to the DUAT) able to enter a financial arrangement, and secondly by the absence of regulations authorising how the 20 per cent of the government taxes due to the community in the new Forest and Wildlife Law could be dispersed. Again the key actors in breaking this stalemate were the provincial head of forestry and wildlife and the Provincial Governor of Niassa. The former had the authority for contract issuance on a pilot basis and drafted a memo for the latter concerning local revenue distribution of the taxes. Strategically turning a blind eye to the Wildlife and Forestry Law, the proposed distribution was: 80 per cent of the trophy fees to accrue to the community (57 per cent for direct cash dividend, 23 per cent for local management costs), the balance to a district administration fund, and – most notably – nothing to central government. The Governor used his wide discretionary powers to sign this into effect and for three years (until the light was seen by central government) it was able to provide at least locally significant income. The local income in turn was a factor in encouraging the community to take on the risks and social costs being incurred internally during the complex DUAT process.

The benefit distribution model had one other politically salient feature. It encouraged a more positive interaction by the district administration, particularly given the District Administrator's gatekeeper status in signing off on the still evolving DUAT. Up to this point the relationship between this initiative and the district administration had been at best lukewarm – partially because 80 per cent of those arrested for illegal meat hunting recorded during the early years of Chipanje Chetu were involved in some way with staff members of the administration. To change the question of who 'owned' the wildlife in the district – was it an unofficial perk for badly paid bureaucrats, or a community owned resource? – called for balancing acts, not just confrontation. With a portion for district income in the pilot phase and the interest of the Provincial Governor (their ultimate boss) clearly evident, a positive partnership was able to see the DUAT to conclusion.

These developments largely took place before 2004; more recent information is patchy, but suggests that local politics continue to defy neat structural analysis. The process and institutions that have emerged in this local context retain their dynamism. What is certain is that, with loss of donor funds and most NGO support in 2002, the further realisation of the DUAT possibilities and other progress towards local democracy and resource rights is being done in the local political context, using local political skills.

Mahenye Campfire programme, south-eastern Zimbabwe

Vanhu varwadziwa, havana kwavanochemera

(People are not happy, but they don't know where to complain)

The following discussion summarises Rihoy et al. (2007) and related doctoral studies.

Mahenye Ward in south-eastern Zimbabwe, in Chipinge District. It covers only 210 km² with a population of less than 1,000 households but its influence over the past two decades on the practice of CBNRM nationally, regionally and internationally belies its size or remoteness. In the early 1990s Mahenye was the reference point for a widely influential publication – *The Lesson from Mahenye: Rural Poverty, Democracy and Wildlife* – that drew on the Campfire and pre-Campfire initiatives of the ward and its people to articulate the links between local democracy, development and natural resources (Murphree 1995). Positive lessons were still being drawn from Mahenye until the late 1990s, reflecting continued progress in local institutional development and economic diversification.

The Mahenye Campfire Committee (MCC) was established in the late 1980s linked upwards to the Rural District Council, which holds Appropriate Authority as the legal entity for Campfire. The operations of the MCC are governed by 'bye-laws' developed following lengthy consultations with the general community, traditional leadership and local Campfire leadership. While neither the MCC nor the bye-laws have formal legal status they were strongly legitimised by use, precedent and acceptance by the various Campfire related bodies. The bye-laws outline the objectives of the institution, the roles, responsibilities and terms of the office bearers and general members, and stipulate means through which accountability to the broader membership are to be assured. The institutional linkages and networks between authorities and across jurisdictional and functional scales were also well developed over this period and broadly followed the principles of upward delegation and downward accountability. During the early 1980s the primary decision making institutions were those of the traditional authority working in a closely coordinated relationship with the democratically elected 'modern' political and development institutions such as the Ward Development Committees (WADCOs) to the higher scale of the Rural District Council. In the 1990s, by virtue of its elected basis and local development importance, the MCC also became a powerful institution. Strong linkages existed between the MCC and 'national players' such as

NGOs (WWF, Zimbabwe Trust, University of Zimbabwe CASS), the national Campfire representative and advocacy body (Campfire Association) and the state wildlife sector.

In terms of economic benefits one of Mahenye's progressive attributes, compared to most Campfire wards, was its revenue diversification during the late 1990s from sport hunting into joint enterprises in the eco-tourism sector. In summary, the evolutions of CBNRM institutions and economic arrangements from the late 1980s to the late 1990s largely concurred in practice (if not formal legal arrangements) with devolutionary principles. The MCC was a transparent, democratically elected body with considerable if not full devolved authority and a clear accountability to a constituency of local members. In addition there was evidence of the equally important dynamics for CBNRM of linkages and delegated functions upwards from the producer community and MCC level to district and national agencies, NGOs and the private sector.

However the positive perspective was replaced in the mid 2000s by a situation of crisis and stalemate in Mahenye CBNRM that was apparently as intransigent as the wider national political and economic crisis. Since 2000 there have been significant shifts of power within and between institutions in Mahenye, one outcome of which was the dramatic demise of Campfire in the view of the overwhelming majority of local inhabitants and summed up as follows by one woman in 2005:

Campfire used to be for all the people, now it's a family business.

The demise of Campfire in Mahenye and the MCC, and dramatic falls in the value of household dividends, coincided with – and were strongly influenced by – four related local events:

- the death of the highly respected old Chief Mahenye in 2001 and replacement by his son, the current Chief;
- the explicit instructions of the new Chief to change MCC office bearers following the flawed MCC elections of 2001, including the direct appointment (not election) of the Chief's younger brother as Chairman;
- the election of a new Councillor for the Ward;
- the re-tendering of the hunting concession that led to ongoing conflict and the widespread belief amongst most local stakeholders that the operators were un-transparently bidding for the concession and were competing amongst each other in their attempts to illicitly 'buy off' the Chief and MCC to ensure that they were treated preferentially.

The combination of these events created a local governance regime of elite capture in which power and authority were concentrated and accountability to the community constituency massively reduced. The MCC bye-laws were openly flouted and the complex interaction between local institutions broke down. Linkages between local and national levels, such as the 'honest brokers' and Campfire Association, also largely ceased to function. Finally, both national economic challenges (especially rocketing inflation) and corruption in local financial management within the MCC meant that economic benefits in terms of cash dividends to households were negligible.

Interviews within Mahenye indicated both a clear appreciation of the complexities of the stalemate, and options that might be applied to emerge from it. Whilst the RDC was widely distrusted on the grounds that it has its own agenda in relation to the safari operations and securing its own revenue, there was nevertheless clear recognition within Mahenye that the RDC had a legal responsibility to step in to break the local stalemate and had the political agency and state-party linkages to do so. A broadly reflective view was:

> The RDC is the only one that can help us to do this [sort out our problems], they are legally responsible as the holders of AA, and they must accept their responsibilities.

In the last quarter of 2005, an Annual General Meeting was held of the Mahenye Campfire Committee:

> Tempers flew. People accused each other of lying. There were veiled threats of violence. Most villagers present made open submissions that there were institutional problems troubling Campfire. With the assistance of the Rural District council, local elections were held and a new committee was elected. These local elections entirely removed the previous committee and traditional leadership from Campfire. Campfire is now being run in line with the provisions of the Mahenye Campfire bye-laws.

Despite the problems faced by Mahenye, this evidence suggests that Campfire's long history in the area has had a positive impact in terms of empowering local residents, providing them with incentives, knowledge and organisational abilities to identify and address problems and constraints, and identify where external interventions are required. Rihoy et al. (2007) concluded that Mahenye evolutions illustrated:

> that CBNRM is a political process and that implementers and policy advocates need to appreciate local power relations and the local political landscapes in the quest for better governance.

Conclusion: CBNRM – beacon & barometer?

> While the masses want concrete economic and social rights, it [electoral democracy] offers them only abstract political rights; while they want empowerment and more control over their lives and destiny, it offers them ritual participation; while they want self realisation in recreating the principles of democracy anew in their cultural and historical setting, it offers them alienation by reducing democracy to a historical practice. (Ake 2000)

This quote from the late Claude Ake presents a critique of the current governance evolutions in Africa – a stalemated phase focused on electoral democracy with abstract political rights and little opportunity to be grounded in locally appropriate historical and cultural contexts. He goes on to argue the need for a 'democracy of the base' with concrete social and economic rights. He sees a way out from what Ostheimer (2001) calls the 'permanent entrenchment of democratic minimalism' via the reinvigoration of democracy itself from this new base, and concludes:

> It would appear that it is in the lowly and struggling regions of the world, such as Africa, that the historic mission of democracy will be finally vindicated or betrayed.

This chapter has explored the evolution of CBNRM as contributing in southern Africa to address current constraints on the dispersal of power and authority to the rural scale and for propelling concrete rights and processes linking rural citizen to central scales.

It has looked at two case-studies in very different historical and cultural contexts – one in a near vacuum of formal rural institutions and upward institutional links but with a clear citizen-state contract (DUAT), and the other with a deeper rooting in local government linkages and CBNRM networks but with weaker formal land rights. Both are in positions where the props of donor funding and NGO support have largely disintegrated. Both equally show the ingenuity, maturity and political skills of rural people in breaking through stalemates and deadlocks in local democracy when land and resources are at stake. The studies have aimed to illustrate that an emphasis on 'devolution now' or 'decentralisation best' analysis could usefully shift to more nuanced acceptance that issues, context and circumstances should be allowed to determine the use of structure. This is especially so when the structural features of decentralisation-devolution narratives shares similar weaknesses to that of Ake's electoral democracy.

The paper concludes that CBNRM does act as a barometer tracking how local democracy is emerging, but perhaps its greatest possibility still lies in its capability to function as a beacon illuminating concrete land and resource rights and local institutional options in the path towards the reinvigorating possibilities of the 'democracy of the base'.

References

Ake, C. 2000. *The Feasibility of Democracy in Africa.* (Dakar: CODESRIA, Africa Book Collective).

Anstey, S.G. 2005. 'Governance, natural resources and complex adaptive systems: A CBNRM study of communities and resources in northern Mozambique', in V. Dzingirai and C. Breen (eds), *Confronting the Crisis in Community Conservation: Case-studies from Southern Africa.* Durban: UKZN Press.

— 2000. 'History matters: Institutional change and CBNRM in Sanga District Northern Mozambique'. Paper presented at the Eighth Conference of the International Association for the Study of Common Property, Bloomington, June.

Buur, L. and H.M. Kyed. 2005. 'State recognition of traditional authority in Mozambique', Discussion Paper 28. Uppsala: Nordiska Afrikainstitutet.

Chitsike, L.T. 2000. 'Decentralisation and devolution of Campfire in Zimbabwe', Working Paper 107/2000. Harare: University of Zimbabwe.

Larson, A.M. 2005. 'Formal decentralisation and the imperative of decentralisation from below: A case study of natural resource management in Nicaragua', in J. C. Ribot and A. M. Larson (eds), *Democratic Decentralisation through a Natural Resource Lens*. Oxford: Routledge.

Larson, A.M. and J.C Ribot. 2005. 'Democratic decentralisation through a natural resource lens: An introduction', in J.C. Ribot and A.M. Larson, *Democratic Decentralisation through a Natural Resource Lens*. Oxford: Routledge.

Lewis, J.E. 2003. *The New Rights of Man: An Anthology of the Events, Documents and Speeches that Have Shaped Western Civilisation*. London: Robinson.

Murombedzi, J. 2003. 'Revisiting the principles of CBNRM in Southern Africa', in *NACSO Proceedings of the Regional Conference on CBNRM in Southern Africa: Sharing Best Practices for the Future*. Windhoek: NACSO.

Murphree, M.W. 1995. 'The lesson from Mahenye: Rural poverty, democracy and wildlife conservation', *Wildlife and Development Series*, 1. London: International Institute for Environment and Development.

— 2000a. 'Boundaries and borders; the question of scale in the theory and practice of comon property management'. Paper presented at the Eighth Biennial Conference of the International Association of Common Property (IASCP), Bloomington, Indiana, 31 May.

— 2000b. 'Community conservation: old ways, new myths and enduring challenges'. Paper presented at a Conference on African Wildlife Management in the New Millennium, Mweka, College of African Wildlife Management, 13-15 December.

Norfolk, S. 2004. 'Examining access to natural resources and linkages to sustainable livelihoods: A case study of Mozambique', FAO LSP WP 17, Access to Natural Resources Sub-programme.

Ostheimer, A. E. 2001. 'Mozambique: The permanent entrenchment of democratic minimalism?', *African Security Review* 10, 1, pp. 15-34.

Ribot, J.C. 2005. 'Institutional choice and recognition: Effects on the formation and consolidation of local democracy'. A Natural Resource and Democracy Concept Paper, Washington, World Resource Institute.

— 2002. 'African decentralization, local actors, powers and accountability. Democracy, Governance and Human Rights', Working Paper 8, Geneva, UNRISD.

Ribot, J.C and A. M. Larson. 2005. *Democratic Decentralisation through a Natural Resource Lens*. Oxford: Routledge.

Rihoy E.C., C. Chirozva and S. Anstey. 2007. 'People are not happy - Speaking up for adaptive natural resource governance in Mahenye', CBNRM Paper 31. Cape Town, University of the Western Cape.

Rihoy, E.C. and B. Maguranyanga. (in press). *Devolution and democratisation of natural resource management in Southern Africa: A comparative analysis of [the] CBNRM policy process in Botswana and Zimbabwe*. Cape Town: PLAAS, UWC.

Roe, E. 1991. 'Development narratives or making the best of blueprint development', *World Development*, 23, pp. 1065-69.

Siendetop, L. 2000. *Democracy in Europe*. London: Penguin Books.

Tanner, C., S. Baleira, S. Norfolk, B. Cau and J. Assulai. 2006. 'Making rights a reality: Participation in practice and lessons learned in Mozambique', LSP Working Paper 27, Rome, FAO Livelihood Support Programme, FAO.

Turner, S. 2004. 'A crisis in CBNRM? Affirming the commons in southern Africa', Paper presented at the Tenth IASCP Conference, Oaxaca, 9-13 August.

5

Global-local linkages
The meanings of CBRNM in global conservation politics
Rosaleen Duffy

Introduction

This chapter will analyse the global context for natural resource management, and will highlight how even the most 'local strategies' are interlinked with global networks and affected by the wider global context. This is apparent in the ways that Community Based Natural Resource Management (CBNRM) has been adopted, adapted and promoted by global networks. It is clear that conservation does not exist in a bounded locality, but engages with global interest groups and is informed by international approaches to environmental management, especially in the arena of wildlife conservation. Sub-Saharan Africa has been the site of multiple forms of interventionism which reveal the global patterns that inter-link the continent with the rest of the world. In the realm of natural resource management these global patterns of interventionism are manifested in diverse ways. Environmental interventionism can take expected forms such as the impact of global conventions (notably CITES and the Convention on Biodiversity) on national and local level wildlife policy making; similarly it can take the form of the influence of global wildlife NGOs which provide funding for particular forms of wildlife management or run global campaigns against practices they regard as threatening to wildlife and biodiversity. However, the global context of wildlife conservation also plays out in less expected ways, which have an equally important impact on the livelihoods and environmental practices at the 'local' level. The increasing patterns of co-operation between environmental NGOs, state agencies, the private sector and International Financial Institutions (IFIs) produces new challenges for thinking about the role of local communities in wildlife management. In particular, this chapter will analyse the meanings of CBNRM, community empowerment, local participation and proprietorship in the context the changing roles and powers of global networks involved in what seem to be 'local' natural resource management strategies.

CBNRM: expanding out from Campfire

CBNRM constitutes one of the major developments in the field of conservation, and during the 1990s it was taken up and promoted by a wide range of organisations at the global, regional, national and local scales. At the time it seemed to offer a workable and more socially just alternative to the 'fortress conservation' approach which was based on the idea of separating wildlife and people through the creation of strict people-free protected areas. Furthermore, it had the added advantage that it seemed to 'pay its way' through careful development of sustainable use of wildlife (through production of meat, skins, ivory, or the sale of wildlife as sport hunting trophies and for photographic/cultural tourism). As a result it was attractive precisely because, in financial terms, it was not 'donor dependent', unlike some other forms of wildlife conservation in sub-Saharan Africa. It resonated with the new-found faith in local communities and individuals as 'rational' resource managers, which neatly fitted with the fashion for decentralisation and participatory development.

One of the earliest examples of CBNRM was the Communal Areas Management Programme for Indigenous Resources (Campfire) in Zimbabwe, which arguably provided a model for conservation and development practice that was used as a template in sub-Saharan Africa and beyond (Hutton, Adams and Murombedzi 2005: 345). Consequently it attracted international attention as a programme that was at the forefront of what seemed to be an innovative and workable approach to negotiating the potential conflicts between people and wildlife and between sustainability and development. For donors, NGOs and national governments alike, CBNRM presented a more socially and politically acceptable rationale for conservation in the context of the creation of new 'democracies' in Africa in the 1990s (*ibid.*: 344). Traditionally, wildlife conservation and rural development have been considered as conflicting goals (Brockington 2002; Wolmer 2007). This is because there was an assumption that conservation required existing areas of land for wildlife to be maintained, if not expanded, whereas development meant industrialisation or the expansion of land available for crops and livestock. This conflict between conservation and rural development was most sharply demonstrated by the national parks systems of sub-Saharan Africa. The establishment of national parks in the colonial and post-independence periods had resulted in communities being moved from their land, excluded from the new parks and denied access to the wildlife and grazing areas that they once enjoyed (Brockington 2002; Adams and MacShane 1992). However, the failings of this exclusionary approach are well documented, not least the injustices associated with eviction of communities to make way for parks, and the continued resistances by communities against their exclusion (for example see Brockington and Igoe 2006). Therefore CBNRM, and Campfire in particular, appeared to offer a workable solution to this conflict.

During the 1990s Campfire became internationally renowned for its efforts to reconcile the needs of conservation and development. It was promoted as a model programme for CBNRM that included local control over tourism developments. Begun in 1986, it aimed to ensure that the rural communities living in Zimbabwe's semi-arid and marginal Communal Areas were able to capture the benefits from wildlife utilisation, in all its forms. It is often suggested that Campfire began as an idea hatched by a group of white liberals in the Zimbabwean Parks Department which Murphree referred to as the 'khaki shorts brigade' of wildlife enthusiasts; in developing Campfire, this group rapidly found themselves at the forefront of debates about rural development (Murphree 1995). Despite this perception and its association with the Parks Department, it was quickly embraced by a number of rural districts. The legislative changes in the post-independence period provided the context for the development of CBNRM in Zimbabwe. Once Zimbabwe gained independence in 1980, the 1975 Parks and Wildlife Act looked discriminatory and colonial, therefore the amended 1982 Act allowed District Councils in the Communal Areas to be designated as an appropriate authority to manage wildlife. This legislative change allowed the concept of Campfire to be further developed during the 1980s, but the first Campfire areas were only established in 1989 in Guruve and Nyaminyami. Campfire was intended to strike a workable and ethical balance between wildlife conservation and meeting the basic needs of rural people. Furthermore, during the 1990s Campfire provided the key argument for the Parks Department's controversial approach to wildlife based on sustainable utilisation; and it was especially important on the international stage as the major justification for Zimbabwe's stance on reopening a limited ivory trade in order to capture the full economic value of elephants (see Duffy 2000).

However, the ways that CBNRM has been taken up and expanded to numerous contexts by multiple organisations means that in some ways it has been the victim of its own success. It could be argued that the intentions of the original promoters of Campfire and of CBNRM were to provide a more socially just and practically workable approach to conservation and rural development; but over the last 20 years the concepts and practices of CBNRM have been picked up and expanded so that they have become the depoliticised 'catch-all' justification for conservation schemes. In this way CBNRM has shifted from being an *approach* to conservation to being a *component* of conservation schemes; it can thus be used to legitimate conservation initiatives in ways which mask potential problems, dynamics and challenges. Therefore, while many projects are criticised for engaging in 'green-washing' to satisfy environmental concerns, it could be argued that they run the danger of 'participation-washing' to answer the concerns of local communities; however, these projects do not do very much beyond engaging in rhetoric on participatory development and developing 'partnerships'. Global organisations, including donors, IFIs and NGOs have all used CBNRM as part of their justification for conservation schemes, especially ecotourism initiatives and large-scale trans-frontier con-servation areas (TFCAs). This then means that it is important to interrogate what is meant by terms like 'community based', 'participation' and 'partner-ship' in this new context. This chapter will now turn to an examination of the relationships between CBRNM and the international context of NGOs, IFIs and donors. It will then analyse how CBNRM has been used to justify the development of tourism in sub-Saharan Africa and the shift from CBNRM to Trans-boundary Natural Resource Management (TBNRM).

CBNRM & global networks

Despite the assumption that CBNRM is the most localised form of decen-tralised natural resource management, it has been increasingly taken up and promoted by global networks of NGOs, donors and IFIs. CBNRM has proved to be highly attractive to global organisations, which took it up, modified it and expanded its application. This is especially the case with the World Bank and conservation oriented NGOs, which have gained influence since the 1990s. A specific vision of good conservation practice and CBNRM have been transmitted through global environmental NGOs such as Wildlife Conservation Society, African Wildlife Foundation, World Wide Fund for Nature-International (WWF-International) and Conservation International to the wider donor community, and ultimately to national governments. For example, the African Wildlife Foundation claims that the core sentiment of its mission statement is 'Together with the People of Africa' and that it engages with communities in 'conservation enterprise' where communi-ties are encouraged to develop commercially viable enterprises that conserve wildlife while improving the livelihoods of people.[1] WWF-International also advertises its commitment to community conservation as an approach which recognises the need to improve rural livelihoods.[2] Equally, while Conservation International states that it puts 'science' at the centre of its strategy, it also points to the importance of partnerships with local communities to make conservation strategies work.[3] This apparent commitment to a community based approach to conservation has also been taken up by the World Bank, for example in engaging communities with Fynbos conservation in South Africa.[4] It seems, then, that global organisations are keen to demonstrate their community-friendly credentials as part of a justification for their support for

---

1   http://www.awf.org/section/people, accessed 16 August 2007.
2   http://www.panda.org/about_wwf/where_we_work/africa/what_we_do/cbnrm/index.cfm, accessed 14. August 2007.
3   http://web.conservation.org/xp/CIWEB/strategies/, accessed 14 August 2007.
4   http://web.worldbank.org/WBSITE/EXTERNAL/OPPORTUNITIES/GRANTS/DEVMARKE TPLACE/0,,contentMDK:20215186˜menuPK:214469˜pagePK:180691˜piPK:174492˜theSit ePK:205098,00.html. accessed 14 August 2007.

conservation. Environmental NGOs have had an increasing impact on global definitions of 'good conservation practice'. Their ability to disseminate environmental information through the media and campaigning activity has been used to embarrass governments and international organisations, as well as to heighten awareness about key issues (Keck and Sikkink 1998; O'Brien et al. 2000: 109-23). NGOs might be expected to operate in contestation with the World Bank; however, they have developed a very close relationship, working to achieve common (often neoliberal) goals in the form of economic liberalisation alongside environmental protection (for further discussion about the impact of the global civil society on World Bank policy see O'Brien et al. 2000; Goldman 2001). For example Brockington and Igoe (2006) argue that there has been an expansion in the number of protected areas globally at precisely the same time as capitalism has become the dominant global force. In many ways, we would expect preservation of environments, and conservation more generally, to be in conflict with the expansion of capitalism. However, what we see is a counter-intuitive relationship between IFIs, donors, environmental NGOs and national governments to push forward economic liberalisation, political liberalisation and good governance agendas alongside specific forms of environmental conservation which are often justified as socially acceptable through including a component of CBNRM (Duffy 2006; also see Zimmerer 2006; and Goldman 2001).

One of the questions about CBNRM in the current neoliberal global context is how global organisations like NGOs and IFIs can develop genuine partnerships with local communities involved in conservation schemes. Harrison suggests that their influence is extended through a politics of 'post conditionality' characterised by terminology such as participation, stakeholders and partnership, rather than through the formal conditionalities that accompanied loans and aid in the 1980s and 1990s (Harrison 2004: 71). In line with this, local communities engaged in CBNRM are increasingly incorporated into new networks of actors, including NGOs, IFIs, international organisations, bilateral donors and private companies. This then raises the question about how genuine these partnerships with global organisations are and what impact these relationships have on how communities engage with and regard more recent forms of CBNRM.

While the influence of global environmental NGOs has assisted in expanding CBNRM, they are also a potential threat to community based approaches to conservation. The ways in which global donors and NGOs maintain a powerful position can be seen very clearly in the ways that the NGOs in particular are engaged in framing and defining the terms of environmental policy making. One key example of their importance as knowledge brokers is the role of Conservation International and the Wildlife Conservation Society in a partial resurgence of the 'fortress conservation' narrative. Conservation International developed out of WWF because it wanted to break away from WWF-US and WWF-International which had clearly embraced community conservation approaches as the way forward for the South. Conservation International wanted to pursue conservation programmes that 'put the science first' and move away from community conservation which it regarded as not as effective (see Chapin 2004 for further discussion). One way that this outlook has translated into practice is through Conservation International's funding of the creation of both publicly and privately owned protected areas in what it defined as 'biodiversity hotspots' around the world, financed through its Global Conservation Fund.[5] Brockington argues that there is a specific vision of the African environment that has driven conservation. The premise is that people have harmed the environment, a view supported by scientific interpretations of environmental change, a romanticised view of a stunning wilderness and an aura of extraordinary biodiversity (Brockington 2002: 3; also see Hutton, Adams and Murombedzi 2005). While this narrative has been challenged by influential work on the need to integrate people and environments for conservation (see Hulme and Murphree (eds) 2001), the vision of the human-free African wilderness remains a powerful one. Consequently, for many donors, saving African environments means that they have to become free of people. As a result of this shift in thinking back towards separation of people and wildlife, justified through appeals to scientific rationality, the commitment to CBNRM has been downplayed from being an *approach* to conservation to becoming a *component* to justify and legitimate interventions to create new protected areas or interventions to conserve specific species (for further discussion see Hutton, Adams and Murombedzi 2005).

CBNRM, global networks & new directions in community tourism

Despite the changes in fashions in conservation approaches, the relationship between IFIs, NGOs, donors and national governments is particularly clear in the ways that CBNRM is often bound up with plans to develop ecotourism in the south. International environmental NGOs have been key actors in promoting community based ecotourism and their involvement is indicative of changes in global politics. In theoretical terms, forms of CBNRM which are based on ecotourism and sustainable harvesting of forest products do not challenge the dominant view of powerful global actors; they resonate with the claim that developing the market value of nature will 'save it' and equally will provide a pathway out of poverty. This cross-cutting and contradictory discourse on preservation and community conservation is also interspersed with a clear commitment to neoliberal principles that equally resonate with donor and NGO agendas. As with many conservation programmes in protected areas, much of the discussion about saving the environment has been intimately tied

5   http://www.conservation.org/xp/gcf/where/, accessed 13 August 2007.

up with the idea that conservation would eventually have to pay its own way; a common argument put forward by donors, global environmental NGOs and local organisations alike is that once the environment is secured, or 'saved', it will attract global business in the form of ecotourism or adventure tourism. One of the core justifications for ecotourism is that nature can be conserved and saved precisely because of its 'market value' to ecotourists willing to pay to see and experience specific landscapes. While supporters of ecotourism development argue that natural resources, landscapes and wildlife have intrinsic, cultural and ecological values, they also point to their economic value which can be harnessed through the introduction of market based mechanisms (see McAfee 1999). In effect, wildlife and landscapes can be sold in multiple ways: as images, products and destinations.

Ecotourism suffers especially from being promoted as a kind of magic bullet which can simultaneously hit multiple targets; it is also intimately bound up with CBNRM, since the empowerment of local people is a core component of the definition of ecotourism: the International Ecotourism Society defines ecotourism as 'responsible travel to natural areas that conserves the environment and improves the well being of local people'; for the International Ecotourism Society, it 'should provide financial benefits and empower local communities'.[6] As a result it has been promoted by a range of organisations including the United Nations, The World Bank, national governments and environmental NGOs as a means of achieving sustainable development for North and South alike. At the 2003 World Parks Congress in Durban, South Africa, the World Conservation Union (IUCN) passed a recommendation that tourism (and especially ecotourism) was key to the conservation of biodiversity and maintenance of protected areas (IUCN 2003). This fits neatly with the wider context of economic conditionalities that encourage liberalisation of economies and the development of so-called 'comparative advantage' in tourism. In terms of debates about the South, tourism is regularly presented as an engine of development. A recent special issue of *Africa Insight* was devoted to tourism, under the headline: 'Tourism: Africa's key to prosperity. The African Continent needs to conserve its natural heritage while creating a future for its people. Tourism can do both.'[7] 2002 was declared the International Year of Ecotourism by the United Nations, which focused attention on this growing niche market. Furthermore, the World Tourism Organisation also claims that ecotourism can contribute to heritage conservation in natural and rural areas, as well as improving living standards in them.[8]

One example of this is in Madagascar, where a number of community based

6   http://www.ecotourism.org/webmodules/webarticlesnet/templates/eco_template.aspx?articleid=95&zoneid=2, accessed 14 August 2007
7   *Africa Insight*, vol 33, no.1. June 2003.
8   UNWTO (2003) *UNWTO Assessment of the Results Achieved in Realising Aims and Objectives of the International Year of Ecotourism 2002* (UNWTO: Madrid). p.2 at http://www.world-tourism.org/sustainable/IYE/IYE-Rep-UN-GA-2003.pdf, accessed 5 July 2007.

eco-tourism schemes have poverty alleviation as one of their objectives. The influence of international environmental NGOs in pushing forward the ecotourism and CBNRM agendas is very clear. The Wildlife Conservation Society has been heavily involved in what it calls 'transfer management', whereby it acts as a 'go-between' or facilitator in relations between rural communities and national or international organisations, including the World Bank. The Society has emphasised the need for local communities to be involved in managing natural resources in their area, including the development of ecotourism.[9]

In line with the positions of international environmental NGOs, donors have also supported the notion of transforming natural resources into marketable goods. Once again, CBNRM has been used as part of their justification for the development of markets for forest products. For example, the French Government has expressed an interest in developing markets in sustainably harvested forest products for the tourist trade in Madagascar. In particular, they have tried to develop orchid cultivation for communities surrounding Ranomafana National Park. Since Madagascar is the site of numerous rare and highly prized orchids the assumption is that orchid collectors and tourists would be willing to buy plants to take home as souvenirs; the hope was that local communities would be engaged in collecting orchid specimens from the forest, then cultivating them for sale at the entrance of the park.[10]

The notion that communities can manage natural resources and develop ecotourism fits very well with neoliberal views about regulating, organising and implementing methods of conservation that include extending the market as the most efficient manager of natural resources. In particular, it intersects with the argument that decentralised networks of 'stakeholders' can govern resources, rather than having them left in state hands. This in turn fits with the agendas of IFIs and NGOs that claim to engage in participatory methods of development and conservation with local communities. As such, the notion that ecotourism provides a community oriented and participatory approach to producing economic development in a sustainable way is a very powerful argument, and one that presents a significant challenge to its critics. Ultimately for local communities, it is often very hard to resist schemes to develop it in the poorest areas of sub-Saharan Africa. This is especially the case in areas with no alternative means of generating income, because of their remoteness or seeming lack of economic development. In the end, then, local communities are persuaded to accept conservation and ecotourism schemes that are wrapped in a CBNRM rationale. In addition, Neumann argues that the threat of violence can also be behind claims that conservation must be enforced by

9   Interview with Lantoniaina Antriamampianina, Director of the Terrestrial Programme, Wildlife Conservation Society, Antananarivo, 24 March 2004.
10 Interview with Jean Jean-Luc Francois, Conseiller de Cooperation Adjoint Developpement Rural, Environnement, Infrastructures, Ambassade de France, Antananrivo, 1 April 2004; also see interview with Benoit Girardin, Charge d'Affairs, Swiss Embassy, Antananarivo, 3 May 2006.

communities or state agencies in order to serve the 'greater public good' that is economic development through tourism (Neumann 2000: 222-35). Neumann suggests that local participation and communities are central elements to a new approach to conservation; however, in practice the new schemes resemble traditional colonial conservation strategies. It is clear that communities are expected to demonstrate their stewardship capacities in order to qualify for land entitlements and the right to be deemed appropriate resource users and managers. Within this set of arguments, there is also a clear process of the extension of state control through the use of communities in surveillance of their own members and those of neighbouring communities. In this sense communities can become the eyes and ears of the state in remote locations where conservation schemes are implemented (*ibid.*: 222-235). Neumann argues that the idea of 'local people' is rarely rigorously examined and communities are regarded as homogenous units that are not stratified by gender, class or ethnicity. However, it is clear that conservation schemes often favour one section of a community over another. Notions of local benefit sharing and participation may not be the same as the power to control, use and access resources which many communities really seek (Neumann 2000: 237; also see Duffy 2000: 89-113).

CBRNM has not remained static in conceptual or practical terms; its adoption and promotion by a growing range of organisations means that it has been continually transforming. Originally, it was associated with local level, small-scale wildlife based tourism which only required basic facilities and accommodation. However, new forms have developed recently which mean that it now intersects with luxury-end ecotourism. As part of this, the debates about the importance of engaging local communities in the participatory management of wildlife and other natural resources have also been taken up by the private sector. This is very visible in the proliferation of new luxury ecotourism resorts that define themselves as private sector, profit-driven companies, but which also market themselves as playing a key role in local community development. These luxury resorts are intended to tap into a new and growing market for ethical travel that offers high-end luxury experience which does involve community participation and development. In general community-based ecotourism has been associated with basic accommodation and facilities, and it has been aimed at independent and low budget travellers who do not expect (or want) high-end facilities. The development of new luxury lodges which blend community based conservation initiatives is a significant new departure. For example, in Madagascar, the Ministry of Culture and Tourism has been especially keen on allowing private luxury eco-lodges to form the centrepiece of the Malagasy ecotourism.[11] This is partly in recognition of a lack of capital available for investment from Malagasy individuals and businesses.

11 Interview with Jean Jacques Rabenirina, Minister of Culture and Tourism, Ministry of Tourism, Antananarivo, 30 March 2004.

One very interesting example of a privately owned but community-oriented ecotourism initiative is the resort of Anjajavy, in north-eastern Madagascar, which is marketed to 'high end/luxury' ecotourists. Its combination of luxury ecotourism with community development has attracted the attentions of the global media, including the BBC.[12] While Anjajavy is owned by South Africans, all the staff are from the neighbouring community, and the income from the resort has been used to build a clinic and a school in the area. The Anjajavy resort offers trips to the village of Ambodro Ampasy to see the dispensary and primary school established by the Ecole du monde NGO, as well as the craft shop set up by the Association des Amis d'Anjajavy. Their promotional information reassures visitors: 'You can take part in the village's development and help the local populace by purchasing Malagasy handicrafts made on site by the villagers.'[13] The Anjajavy project is indicative of new directions in CBNRM. It is a privately owned and run luxury lodge which goes one step further in terms of community engagement: rather than simply offering employment, it is involved in community development projects and poverty alleviation on a wider scale in the local area. In terms of marketing, the owners draw attention to the ways that in choosing to holiday there, ecotourists will be directly contributing to poverty alleviation, community development and conservation in the surrounding area. This effectively blends the approach of luxury nature-based tourism with elements of the rationale for community based ecotourism which are centred on poverty alleviation and environmental conservation. This is beneficial for some but raises questions about the meanings and purposes of partnership in this context. It may well mean that the development of private luxury eco-lodges that have a community rationale merely offer communities 'more of the same' rather than developing and offering pathways for them to develop initiatives that operate on their own terms. There is the danger of replicating the problems associated with mass tourism and conventional forms of tourism where operators (often foreign owned) make the greatest level of profit while local communities benefit in a very minimal way through employment in menial tasks rather than taking a central role as managers, owners and tour operators.

From CBNRM to TBNRM

The importance of interrogating the precise meaning of global-local partnerships in conservation and CBNRM is particularly important in the more recent development of large ecosystem scale conservation initiatives. One key

---

12   Interview with Clement Ravalisoana, President of the Professional Association of Tour Operators in Madagascar, Antananarivo, 19 April 2004.
13   http://www.anjajavy.com, accessed 15 August 2007; see also pers comm. Nivo Ravelojaona, Director, Za Tour, Antananarivo, 27 April 2004.

aspect of the post-Cold War neoliberal order is the important of decentralisation and pluralisation of governance; CBNRM provides a perfect fit because of its emphasis on networks of non-state actors, particularly local communities. In some ways then, the development of large, ecosystem-scale protected areas would seem to be in conflict with such notions of localisation and decentralisation. However, regional 'ecosystem scale' conservation initiatives have in part been justified through a commitment to CBNRM. By the late 1990s there was a sense within the regional and global conservation community that CBNRM rationale was yesterday's news; instead there was a need for a new set of arguments and rationales to continue conservation activity by those same organisations, but with a new mission. The emergence of transboundary natural resource management (TBRNM) was a direct result of the feeling that CBNRM was no longer *the* fresh and exciting argument to use to draw in financial support from major donors. For example, the IUCN Regional Office for Southern Africa (IUCN-ROSA) and the Ford Foundation were leading exponents of CBNRM in the 1990s, but in 2002 they identified TBNRM as a 'cutting edge development' that could be replicated elsewhere in the region (IUCN-ROSA 2002: 2). TFCAs in southern Africa clearly involve partnerships and networks of global, local, public and private actors which create direct networks that link global organisations to local interest groups and organisations. In southern Africa, discussions over the establishing and implementing TFCAs are often conducted between local communities, local and global NGOs, and IFIs such as the World Bank.[14] A critical element in justifying the switch to transnational conservation areas is that communities should participate in TFCA management and derive benefits from them, including tourism revenues and sustainable use of resources which fits well with current neoliberal thinking about the transformation of natural resources into commodities (see Buscher and Webster, 2007; Hughes 2006 for further discussion).

The ways that local communities are encouraged to be involved in the governance of the TFCAs are indicative of the proliferation of forms of power and authority that lie outside the realm of the state, and fit with neoliberal ideas about decentralisation and empowering non-state actors. One of the criticisms of TFCAs is that far from being a force for decentralisation through a commitment to CBNRM, they allow for a greater degree of centralisation of power and authority. TFCAs can be regarded as a means by which global actors can recentralise control over resources and people from the global level and concentrate power in the hands of a narrow network of international NGOs, IFIs, global consultants on tourism and community conservation, and bilateral donors. Neumann argues that global conservation strategies tend to gloss over the magnitude of political change involved, and instead invest international conservation groups and states with increased authority to monitor

---

14   Meeting of the Campfire Service Providers, Chimanimani Hotel, Chimanimani (Zimbabwe), 16 February 2000.

rural communities (Neumann 2000: 220-22; and see Neumann 1998). Indeed, one of the consultants for the Mozambican side of the Great Limpopo Transfrontier Park had expressed concerns that the whole project was jeopardised by pressures from the implementing agencies. For example, because the Peace Parks Foundation[15] had raised millions of dollars for creating the transfrontier reserve the donors now expected to see an instant park; he suggested that in the zeal to create the park, it was being rushed through without adequate community consultation; he futher argued that Mozambique was not ready to receive and manage translocated surplus elephants from the Kruger National Park in South Africa.[16]

In many ways, TFCAs can be regarded as Wolmer suggests, as the latest in a line of top-down, market oriented environmental interventions by international bureaucracies (Wolmer 2003: 7). For instance, in April 2003 a decision was taken to remove a 20-kilometre section of fence between the eastern boundary of the Kruger National Park and the Limpopo National Park in Mozambique.[17] The decision was criticised as hurried, and was designed to force through an initiative ahead of time, resulting in a complete lack of consultation with the communities on the Mozambican side where at least 6,000 people live with their cattle.[18] The South African Minister of Environmental Affairs and Tourism, Valli Moosa, was heavily criticised in 2002 for promising an 'instant Kruger' in the Limpopo National Park in Mozambique when he announced that delivery times for the transfrontier park were to be cut in half and a minimum of 1,000 elephants should be herded into Mozambique to kick-start the venture. It was reported that the 30,000 Mozambican villagers living in the proposed transfrontier park only heard of it when 30 elephants were delivered from South Africa. This resulted in threats that the wildlife would be killed in response to the lack of consultation and to demonstrate that the villagers would not move from the area. The Peace Parks Foundation stressed that the decision to release the elephants was not deliberately timed to coincide with the 84th birthday of its Director, Anton Rupert, but was instead approved by a ministerial committee.[19]

The anxiety surrounding the importance placed on global-local partnerships is linked to this concern about increasing levels of external control. The concern in communities is that TFCAs represent the latest in a long history of bad experiences with national and international environmental schemes, and

---

15 See the Peace Parks Foundation website for further information on their mission and activities. http://www.peaceparks.org, accessed 13 August 2007.

16 *Mail and Guardian*, 16 December 2002. *Poaching stymies superpark.*

17 Peace Parks Foundation, *Great Limpopo Transfrontier Park – current status.* See http://www.peaceparks.org/content/newsroom/news_pop.php?id=67, accessed 14 January 2004. For current information on the role of the PPF in the Great Limpopo parks, see http://www.peaceparks.org/tfca.php?pid=1&mid=147#current_projects, accessed 18 August 2007.

18 *Mail and Guardian*, 16 December 2002, *Poaching stymies superpark.*

19 *Mail and Guardian*, 26 April 2002, *Mega park threatened.*

this means that communities are often wary of involvement in such initiatives. The funders, NGOs and state agencies driving the establishment of TFCAs have been criticised for their lack of consultation with communities. Leonard Seelig of the Peace Parks Foundation suggested that many communities who lived beside protected areas were suspicious of transboundary conservation because of the long history of exclusion of local people from parks.[20] Wolmer suggests that the fashionable language of 'stakeholders', 'partnerships' and 'capacity building' has allowed for an unhelpful and depoliticised discussion of the role and dimensions of community involvement in TFCAs. Instead, the new focus on TBNRM and the shift away from CBNRM are directly linked with, and neatly serve, the interests of numerous stakeholders, not necessarily communities, in the transfrontier reserves (Wolmer 2003:19; also see Harrison 2004). The role of some NGOs has been controversial, and in many ways the use of NGOs in the implementation of global conservation schemes can often add just another layer of bureaucracy that 'stakeholders' have to negotiate (see Neumann 2000). In line with these criticisms, IUCN-ROSA indicated that transfrontier reserves were in danger of reinforcing the status quo, or even worsening land disputes with communities through the gazetting of new national parks such as the Limpopo National Park in Mozambique (IUCN-ROSA 2002: 6-7).

Conclusion

CBNRM has presented a significant challenge to more traditional ways of thinking about conservation, especially the assumption that conservation is best served by the strict separation of wildlife and people. During the 1990s CBNRM became the main counter narrative to such 'fortress conservation' approaches, and seemed to offer a more socially just, ethical and workable solution to conservation and rural development. However, in some ways it has become the victim of its own success; the ways in which CBNRM has been taken up by a wide range of global actors and been redefined and reconfigured to suit the interests of global networks means that it has moved far from its original focus. The ways that global networks of NGOs, IFIs and donors have adopted and adapted the meanings of terms like 'participation', 'local communities', 'partners' and 'stakeholders' means that the CBNRM rationale can often end up being a mere component of conservation programmes rather than being an alternative approach to conservation in practice. The rationale for CBNRM has been so easily adopted and adapted because it was dependent on ideas of decentralisation, participatory development and partnership with local communities, which intersected perfectly with global interest in decen-

---

[20] Interview with Leonard Seelig, Micro Development Programme, Peace Parks Foundation, Somerset West (South Africa), 16 March 2000.

tralisation, liberalisation, the rollback of the state and the transformation of environmental resources into globally marketable goods (usually through the development of tourism). Therefore, top-down and neoliberal environmental interventions can be justified and legitimated through their use of CBNRM; in effect, CBNRM can often be just the 'wrapping' that is used to silence critics of new conservation schemes and to reassure local communities that NGOs, IFIs and donors are not engaged in old style conservation.

References

Adams, J.S. and T.O. 1992. *The Myth of Wild Africa: Conservation Without Illusion*. New York: W.W. Norton and Company.

Brockington, D. 2002. *Fortress Conservation: The Preservation of the Mkomazi Game Reserve, Tanzania*. Oxford: James Currey.

Brockington, D. and J. Igoe. 2006. 'Eviction for Conservation: A Global Overview', *Conservation and Society* 4, 3, pp. 424-70.

Buscher, B. and B. Webster. 2007. 'Whims of the Winds of Time? Emerging Trends in Biodiversity Conservation and Protected Area Management', *Conservation and Society* 5, 1, pp. 22-43.

Castree, N. 2008. 'Neoliberalising nature: the logics of deregulation and reregulation', *Environment and Planning A* 40(1), pp. 131-52.

— 2003. 'Commodifying what nature?' *Progress in Human Geography* 27, 2, pp. 273-92.

Chapin, M. 2004. 'A Challenge to Conservationists', *World Watch Magazine*, 17, 6.

Duffy, R. 2000. *Killing for Conservation: Wildlife Policy in Zimbabwe*. Oxford: James Currey.

Duffy, R. 2006. 'NGOs and Governance States: The Impact of Transnational Environmental Management Networks in Madagascar', *Environmental Politics*, 15, 5, pp. 731-49.

Goldman, M. 2001. 'Constructing an Environmental State: Eco-governmentality and Other Practices of a 'Green' World Bank', *Social Problems*, 48, pp. 499-523.

Harrison, G. 2004. *The World Bank and Africa: The Construction of Governance States*. London: Routledge.

Hughes, D.M. 2006. *From Enslavement to Environmentalism: Politics on a Southern African Frontier*. Washington DC: University of Washington Press.

Hulme, D. and M. Murphree (eds). 2001. *African Wildlife and Livelihoods*. Oxford: James Currey.

— 1999. 'Communities, wildlife and the 'new conservation' in Africa', *Journal of International Development* 11, 3, pp. 277-85.

Hutton, J., W.A. Adams and J.C. Murombedzi. 2005. 'Back To The Barriers? Changing Narratives in Biodiversity Conservation', *Forum For Development Studies* 2, pp. 341-70.

IUCN-ROSA. 2002. 'Rethinking the Great Limpopo Transfrontier Conservation Area and TBNRM Developments in Southern Africa'. Discussion paper for a collaborative workshop to establish current baseline data and current research efforts for TBNRM management in Southern Africa, Southern Africa Wildlife College, Hoedspruit, South Africa, Harare, IUCN-ROSA.

Keck, M.E. and H. Sikkink. 1998. *Activists Beyond Borders: Advocacy Networks in International Politics*. New York: Cornell University Press.

McAfee, K. 1999. 'Selling Nature to Save it? Biodiversity and the Rise of Green Developmentalism', *Environment and Planning D: Society and Space* 17, 2: pp. 133-54.

Murphree, M. 1995. 'Optimal Principles and Pragmatic Strategies: Creating an Enabling Politico-Legal Environment for Community Based Natural Resource Management (CBNRM)'. An address to the Conference of the Natural Resources Management Programme, SADC Technical Coordination Unit, Malawi, USAID-NRMP Regional, Chobe, 3 April.

Neumann, R.P. 1998. *Imposing Wilderness, Struggles Over Livelihood and Nature Preservation in Africa*. Berkeley: University of California Press.

— 2000. 'Primitive Ideas: Protected Area Buffer Zones and the Politics of Land in Africa' in

V. Broch-Due and R. A. Schroeder (eds), *Producing Nature and Poverty in Africa*. Uppsala: Nordiska Afrikainstitutet, pp. 220-42.

Neumann, R. 2001. 'Disciplining Peasants in Tanzania: From State Violence to Self Surveillance in Wildlife Conservation', in N.L. Peluso and M. Watts (eds), *Violent Environment*. New York: Cornell University Press, pp. 305-27.

O'Brien, R., A-M. Goetz, J.A. Scholte, and M. Williams. 2000. *Contesting Global Governance: Multilateral Economic Institutions and Global Social Movements*. Cambridge: Cambridge University Press.

Schoon, M. 2006. 'Neo-Imperial Conservation: The Relationship between South Africa and its Neighbors in Transboundary Protected Areas'. Paper presented at the annual meeting of the International Studies Association, San Diego, California, 22 March.

Wolmer, W. 2003. 'Transboundary Conservation: the politics of ecological integrity in the Great Limpopo Transfrontier Park'. Sustainable Livelihoods in Southern Africa Research Paper No. 4, Institute of Development Studies, Brighton.

— 2007. *From Wilderness Vision to Farm Invasions: Conservation and Development in Zimbabwe's South-East Lowveld*. Oxford: James Currey.

Zimmerer, K. S. 2006. 'Cultural Ecology: at the interface with political ecology – the new geographies of environmental conservation and globalisation', *Progress in Human Geography*, 30, 1, pp. 63-78.

6

Rural Institutions
Challenges & Prospects for their Active Participation in Natural Resources Governance in Zimbabwe

Billy B. Mukamuri

Background & introduction

The last two and half decades have been characterised by numerous academic studies on rural institutions and their prospective roles in the governance of locally available natural resources: flora, fauna and aquatic resources. Academic staff members associated with both the Centre for Applied Social Sciences (CASS) and the Institute for Environmental Studies (IES) conducted studies on wildlife and woodland conservation, respectively. Central to these two research institutions, both located at the University of Zimbabwe, has been the question of how rural people, in collaboration with their respective institutions, both manage and benefit from locally available natural resources. Special recognition went to CASS, under the visionary leadership of Professor Marshall Murphree, for championing proprietorship of wildlife resources based in communal areas from the state to local communities, with the view that this would create incentives for people to manage and conserve wild animals instead of viewing them as a menace. With the launch of the Communal Area Management of Indigenous Resources (Campfire) programme in the mid 1980s, rural communities in areas that had been accorded Approved Campfire status started benefiting from financial dividends emanating from safari hunting, and meat from wild animals killed under Problem Animal Control (PAC). Implementation of Campfire also benefited communities through construction of schools, clinics, grinding mills, community halls and other facilities. In addition, a small unit based in CASS specifically looked at fish, especially in Lake Kariba. Fish are important in both economic and dietary terms. Studies looked at questions surrounding equal access to fisheries among established fishing companies largely owned by whites and big private companies, and emerging small fishing companies owned by black Zimbabweans and rural communities living adjacent to the lake (Hobane 2003; Malasha 2005; Nyikahadzoi, 2006).

IES on the other hand, took the lead in bringing to light the immense socioeconomic benefits rural people derived from indigenous woodlands. These included shade, honey, birds, mice, ants, caterpillars etc. More important values derived from woodlands included timber, firewood for both domestic use and brick moulding, crafts (for selling in urban and international markets) and implements for domestic use. IES also brought to light the increasing role indigenous trees are playing in complementing the ailing health delivery system. One such study found that 95% of African survey respondents used traditional medicines largely derived from woodlands (Mukamuri and Kozanayi 1999).

Apart from academic work that has been going on at the University of Zimbabwe, local and international NGO have taken a lead in the promotion of wildlife and woodland resources as rural development tools, largely to address environmental degradation and poverty. For example, Environment and Development Activities in Zimbabwe (ENDA), an international and locally registered organisation, started in 1987 to work with local communities in regeneration and replanting indigenous trees in homes, fields and grazing areas. The project also encouraged woodland management by communities. In addition, it had a strong bearing on engaging local traditional and modern institutions in mobilising community support and participation (Mukamuri 1995). Other locally based NGOs, with the support of international donors, have promoted the marketing of products (e.g., jam, dry seeds of *Berchemia discolor*, baskets and hats made from *Adansonia digitata* [baobab] fibre, and crafts) derived from indigenous plant species and to an extent they participate in international trade fairs to promote such products. Huge amounts of funds have been channelled towards research on identifying, processing and marketing. Another local NGO, Environment Africa, has embarked on a project to produce *Warburgia salaturis*, locally known as Muranga, an endemic tree widely believed to have important medicinal properties, at a commercial farm.[1]

The engagement of local communities in woodland management has gone beyond NGOs; state institutions have also recognised the importance of the work. For example, the state's Forestry Commission (FC) started in the late 1980s to engage communities in what has become known as Joint Forestry Community Management programme (JFM). The initiative engages communities neighbouring state forests in the management of those forests. This is supposed to be a symbiotic activity in which the state benefits by way of reduced veld fires and poaching for timber while people benefit by having access to non-timber forest products such as grass for thatching, honey, mushrooms, medicines and controlled grazing.

The above examples highlight the contribution academics have made towards understanding the benefits that local people derive and can potentially derive from natural resources. The programmes being initiated by vari-

---

1   The first lot of commercially planted warburgia totaled 10,000 seedlings. An additional number of about 100 seedlings were planted in small-scale farms around Mt. Selinda area, eastern Zimbabwe.

ous actors, including local communities, state institutions (Parks and Wildlife Authority and Forestry Commission), international and local NGOs point to a significant paradigm shift in terms of how natural resources management has been viewed and practiced in Zimbabwe, dating back to the colonial era and up to the mid 1980s. For example, the introduction of Campfire by the National Parks and Wildlife Authority and JCP initiatives by the Forestry Commission marked a new and promising era characterised by less state involvement in the management of wildlife and woodland resources. Despite the contributions academics and development practitioners have made in initiating bottom-up strategies, they are still far from solving problems such as failure of beneficiary communities in Chivi and Zvishavane to continue with ENDA's initiative of planting indigenous trees in spite of all parties involved recognising their roles. Another challenge has been posited by communities in conjunction with their respective institutions to challenge the continued hegemony imposed by RDCs, safari hunters and, to a limited extent, National Parks and Wildlife Authority, particularly with regard to benefit sharing and major decision making in Campfire areas.

Traditional institutions & the Zimbabwe context: past & present

Pre-colonial traditional institutions comprised chiefs and their respective headmen. Evidence suggests that these were largely self-contained homogenous groups, tied together by totemic belonging. The chiefdoms tended to be independent, with little or no political authority over one another (Malasha 2003). However, with the advent of British colonial rule in 1896, chiefs as institutions remained independent units but got a new dimension of reporting to a central state, through district native administrators. In addition, chiefdoms were reconfigured particularly after the enactment of the Land Apportionment Act (1930). This is the period when the regime moved large populations of people to new areas as it started to create large scale farms for white settlers. People who were forcibly moved to other chieftainship areas created a social grouping known as immigrants. Immigrants largely do not share totems with members of the ruling elite. Social relationships between the two have however developed over time through marriages and kinship ties. What is more important is that in many instances immigrants have managed to create their own areas of localised control, by attaining the roles of kraal-heads (*sabhuku*). This has generally been achieved through demographic increases of different clans forming villages. Normally, authority to create a village is granted by the state if the number of households reaches 300 or more. This strategy is largely used by aspiring kraal-heads in order attain power and control over resources, e.g., land, gifts and food relief. The process of creating a new village is often associated with conflicts and tensions as it is usually interpreted as intransigence or secession by the incumbent kraal-head.

Zimbabwe's independence in 1980 ushered in a new dimension to the traditional leadership system in rural areas. In 1982, Robert Mugabe, then the Prime Minister, issued a decree to create Village Development Committees (VIDCOs). The VIDCOs were intended to be the major conduits of government initiated development projects. However, they became a major source of conflict at the village level as they were interpreted by traditional leadership as usurping their power. More important was that immigrants who had taken up leadership during the war of liberation occupied most of the VIDCO positions (Mukamuri 1995).

The new dispensation brought in active involvement of Rural District Councils (RDCs), traditional leadership structures (kraal-heads, headmen and chiefs) and lower level state sanctioned institutions such as the VIDCOs and Ward Development Committees (WARDCOs) (Nhira 1994). The new context has produced challenges which past and current research has not been able to address adequately. The policy framework to improve the positioning of rural institutions in terms of meaningful participation and benefit sharing from locally available natural resources is in place but challenges continue to persist unabated. This chapter argues that rural institutions are still very weak and lack the sophistication and tools to face the challenges presented by the new demands emanating from a new environmental management and development order. Rural institutions' attempts to participate in natural resources and proposed solutions are viewed in this chapter as great strides in addressing the governance issues and constraints currently bedevilling Zimbabwe's rural and natural resources development landscape.

There is strong recognition, almost a consensus, in the available literature that local level institutions represent the best platform for long term and sustainable management of natural resources. Even the government has recognised and endorsed the idea through recommendations made by the Commission of Inquiry into Appropriate Agricultural and Land Tenure Systems. The objective of the commission was to investigate appropriate institutional arrangements for the management of resources in communal areas. To reinforce the current paradigm, its 1995 submission recommended increased emphasis on traditional authorities as the stewards over communal natural resources. In addition, it recommended state withdrawal from managing communal resources and that full rights be given to village communities and their respective committees. According to Rukuni (1998), management of communal grazing areas and other natural resources would be improved by strengthening village-level institutions.

This chapter recognises and supports the popular view that local-level institutions are the best in terms of fostering locally responsive common pool resources. However, and despite the wide recognition that rural institutions are important, what needs to be taken cognisance of is that they are operating in a superficial context, characterised by a less African, and rather more western, socio-political and economic environment dating back to the colonial period (Murombedzi 1990). In addition, rural institutions, particularly traditional ones, are increasingly functioning in a fast developing and globalising environment and their adaptation at a commensurate pace is unlikely without dynamic interventions. Furthermore, are village level institutions in the best position to be able to take up this challenge?

Understanding rural institutions

Any attempt to understand challenges and opportunities for rural institutions to actively participate in natural governance issues requires knowledge of what they are and how they relate to governance issues. It becomes therefore imperative to define concepts related to institutions and governance, and to bring out concrete examples from case-studies.

Another challenge is to remove rural institutions' failure to take the lead in managing natural resources as embedded intrinsically within them and ignore the extrinsic factors that may be part of the larger governance and macro-economic environment. The matter needs to be viewed in a longer historical fashion. This requires looking at the performance and characterisation of institutions through various stages of development, and this is possible given that CASS and others have conducted studies dating back to the pre-colonial era (Latham 2007). The colonial era requires serious consideration because it represents a critical phase in the development of Zimbabwe's rural institutions. Research studies conducted during the independence era are very informative on the performance and dynamics of rural institutions as they grapple with developmental and political issues.

Rural institutions: some theoretical perspectives

Rural institutions: governance as co-management

Scholars concerned with natural resource and management issues have largely borrowed their conceptualisation of co-management from the literature on governance. Governance has been defined as the 'structures and processes of power and authority, co-operation and conflict, that govern decision making and dispute resolution concerning resource allocation and use, through the interaction of organisations and social institutions' (Woodhouse 1997: 540).

When examining how governance is operating in a typical communally owned natural resource regime one needs to examine how rules are made and enforced 'for setting the rules for the exercise of power and settling conflicts over such rules' (Hyden 1989). Governance as co-management has been interpreted as 'a middle range management option situated somewhere between state and community management' (Mohamed 2001). According to Pomeroy and Berkes (1997: 466), governance as co-management, 'covers various partnership arrangements and degrees of power-sharing and integration of local and centralised management systems'.

In addition, governance within co-management arrangements entails a considerable degree of responsibility by users of a particular resource and does not mean token consultations by outsiders (Jentoft 1989; Mohamed 2001). Governance includes various degrees of participation and decision making by resource users. This represents a dramatic paradigm shift from the instructive, or top-down, as characterised by state driven conservation, to a bottom-up and cooperative user driven strategy (Mohamed 2001). Co-management also entails negotiated rights and responsibilities by both users and outsiders. Barrow and Murphree (1998: 15) view the objective of participatory or decentralised management as establishing 'local responsibility for the management of such resources so as to achieve conservation as well as community objectives'. Finally, the nature of partners does not limit the existence of co-management initiatives; it is open to business arrangements made between representative sectors of the community (Mohamed 2001).

Institutions & Design Principles

Both rationalism and functionalism seem to inform most thinking with regard to institutions. For example, Ostrom (1987: 262) postulates that '... it is possible for those involved in a commons dilemma to arrive at a set of rules that enables them to keep total use within the limits of sustainable yield.' This supposes that human beings are rational and are capable of developing rules that make them live within the confines of a society or community, and marks a direct contradiction to Hardin's 1968 'Tragedy of the Commons' motif, whereby human beings sharing commons are guided by greed, rent-seeking and all other forms of self-interest. In 1990, North produced what are now popularly known as Design Principles:

1. *Clearly defined boundaries*: individuals or households who have rights to withdraw resources from the CPR must be clearly defined, as must be boundaries of the CPR itself.

2. *Congruence between appropriation and provision rules and local conditions*: appropriator rules restricting time, place, technology and quality of resource unit are related to local conditions and to provision rules requiring labour, material and/or money.

3. *Collective choice arrangements*: most individuals affected by the operational rules can participate in modifying the operational rules.

4. *Monitoring*: monitors who actively audit CPR conditions and appropriator behaviour are accountable to the appropriators.

5. *Graduated sanctions*: appropriators who violate operational rules are likely to be assessed graduated sanctions depending on the seriousness and content of the offence, by other appropriators.

6. *Conflict resolution mechanism*: appropriators and officials have access to low-cost arenas for resolving conflicts.

7. *Minimal recognition of rights to organise*: the rights of appropriators to devise their own institution are not challenged by external government authorities.

8. *Nested enterprises*: appropriation provision, monitoring, enforcement, conflict resolution, and governance activities are organised in multiple layers of nested enterprises (North 1990).

Underlying the Design Principles are notions of legality and organisation. Although Design Principles are widely accepted, they remain irrelevant if aspects of governance or co-management, organisation and legality are negated, or simply highlighted and not acted upon. Increased organisation is likely to lead to institutions being more effective, so is the legality access. Inclusion of the legality aspect could probably reverse what Matose (1994) refers to as the 'criminalisation' of people's livelihoods when referring to state rules governing access to natural resources by communities living adjacent to Protected Forests.

In terms of functionalism, society was capable of self-regulation through traditions, norms and other social control mechanisms to maintain a balance between nature and societal needs of natural resources; people lived in harmony with nature. The problems characterised by the present environmental degradation are largely attributed to colonisation and the associated weakening of traditional authority. It also appears from the literature that institutions are largely defined by rules. For example, Ostrom (1987) defines common pool institutions surrounding communally held natural resources as '... the rules in use by a community to determine who has access to common pool resources, what use units authorised participants can consume at what times and who will monitor or enforce these rules. Hence an institutional arrangement refers not only to a constituted body of persons but also to a prescribed constitution to guide its activities.' The increased role of rules in shaping institutions brings us close to what could be described as game theory, which translates to viewing natural resources sharing by communities as a game and the referees being the institutions. Games can only be played where there are laid down rules.

For reasons important for this chapter, Shanmugaratnam (1994) has gone further by introducing the notion of 'organisation' and 'legality' within the definition of an institution. His definition is that it is '... a social organisation which through the operation of tradition, custom or legal constraint tends to create durable and routinised patterns of behaviour'.

The notions of organisation and legality as embedded within the concep-tualisation of institutions are both important and interesting. Though not used in the same sense, I am not sure organisation is important for institutions to be able to tackle some of the challenges they are currently facing, be it at local or other levels. Secondly, 'legality' ensures that everyone is treated fairly and penalties are given to defaulters and deviants. Two questions arise: how organised are rural institutions in Zimbabwe, and how legal are they? The answer to both could be the same: there is less and less of both organisation and legality. If organisation and legality are crucial in terms of capacity building at the local level there is need to take our institutional analysis to the larger macro-economic and political levels (Murphree 1990; Murombedzi 1996). I view legality and organisation as key ingredients in giving people guaranteed proprietorship over their natural resources. Proprietorship here relates issues as use rights, mode of usage, full access to agreed benefits and rules of access.

Rural institutions: the challenges for woodland management in Zimbabwe

Rural institutions and their relationship to woodland management cannot be discussed without reference to the existing legal instruments. Woodlands in Zimbabwe fall under the Forestry Commission, a parastatal that was created by the colonial government in 1948. It has now been broken down into components, the State Forests division and the Forestry Company of Zimbabwe, which is the commercial division. Over the years, it has been conducting tree growing promotions, and more recently promoting planting of both exotic and indigenous trees. The legislative context of the Forestry Commission in its engagements with communal people has been the Communal Forest Produce Act (1987).

Despite the existence of the Act, studies have indicated that it was introduced to stop harvesting of commercially important hardwoods in Zimbabwe's Matebeleland North Province where vast amounts of *Pterocarpus angolensis* and teak exist. The Act has not been effective in controlling harvesting of other tree species in other parts of the country (Matose 1994). Following the realisation that no single legislative mechanism could stop the poaching of firewood and other resources in Protected Forests, the Forestry Commission began experimenting with the Joint Forestry Management model, especially in areas involving neighbouring communal areas and state forests. Results from studies continue to show that rural people are not making meaningful decisions over access to and use of those resources. Joint Forestry Management has also shown hegemonic tendencies by central state agencies. A recent study by Sithole-Campbell (2003) shows that communal women have been forced to exchange firewood for 'sex', an apparent show of failure by communal people to effectively assert their needs within the Joint Forestry Management regime. Matose (1994) further points to continued 'criminalisation' of local practices by state officials, even within the framework of the Joint Forestry Management regime. Management of woodlands has largely been skewed in favour of state institutions, that is, as far as access, decision making and management are concerned.

All stakeholders accept that trees and woodlands are important and highly valued in Zimbabwe's rural areas. For example, trees have been found to be important for use as timber, firewood, medicines (Mukamuri and Kozanayi 1999), windbreak, soil erosion control, and social (Hamudikuwanda et al. 2001) and livestock fodder (Scoones 1990). A number of trees have been described as sacred and therefore highly revered by people living in communal areas of Zimbabwe and these include many trees that produce edible fruits (Wilson 1989; Mukamuri 1995).

Studies on woodlands management in typical communal settings have shown that multiple approaches are needed to foster an effective management regime (Nhira and Fortmann 1993). This scenario is aggravated by the existence of a plethora of nested interests, institutional hierarchies and poorly defined boundaries (Mandondo 1998). However, many authors have been attracted by the existence of territorial and local cults which purport to be protecting the environment (Schoffeleers 1982; Wilson 1986; Mukamuri 1987; Spierenburg 1995; Dzingirai and Bourdillon 1998). Increased focus on traditional religion and environmental or woodlands management was premised on the hope that since territorial cults have been instrumental in mobilising resistance against the colonial state, then they would form the alternative model for sustainable woodlands management. Territorial cults have been known to be closely associated with some of the remaining sacred groves (*marambatemwa*) found in many parts of the country. More important was their close association with rainfall, and hence going against their rules was often thought to bring droughts and other pestilences (Schoffeleers 1982). Forest-related rules included banning the cutting of certain tree species, especially fruit-bearing ones. For example, in most parts of Zimbabwe, trees such as *Parinari curatelifolia, Azanza garkeana, Lannea spp, marula, Uapaca kirkiana, mukute* are not allowed to be cut, largely because of the fruits they bear. Widely protected non-fruit-bearing trees in southern Zimbabwe include *Parinari curatelifolia, Gardenia globiflora and Pseudostlylus maprofolia* (Matose 1991). The importance of ritual beliefs to the management of woodlands is better appreciated by bringing to light the creation of AZTREX in 1988, which was formed by a group of people comprising chiefs, spirit mediums and ex-combatants calling themselves traditional ecologists.

Literature on religious cults and their purported importance in the protection of trees and woodlands largely ignores the institutional forces at play on the ground. For example, most of the so-called sacred groves have vanished due to increasing pressure on forests for firewood and other local needs. In recent years pressure on woodland resources has been driven not only by population pressure, but by the commercialisation of wood products such as artefacts (Braedt and Standa-Gunda 2000). Further weakening of the traditional religious cult system has been promulgated by modernisation tendencies, especially the adoption of Christianity and other western religious beliefs, as well as persistent droughts (Mukamuri 1990). Fourtmann (1995) identifies other factors leading to the breakdown of sacred or traditional controls as immigration by outsiders, market forces, economic hardship, education and modernity (Fortmann and Nabane 1992). The issue of migrants is particularly important in terms of the emergence of roadside wood-based product markets; these have presented a major challenge to rural institutions regarding where the markets are located and where the timber is harvested. Most of the wood carvers and vendors are not locals and hence they have openly challenged the authority of the local leadership structure (McGregor 1989; Mukamuri 1995a, 2003).

NGOs have played a critical role in trying to promote planting and management of indigenous woodlands in Zimbabwe. In 1988, ENDA initiated, with funding from Ford Foundation, a project aimed at planting and managing indigenous woodlands in the Chivi and Zvishavane Districts of south-central Zimbabwe. Seedlings, fencing and extension services were provided free, and communities selected woodlot sites in places of their choice, including grazing areas, homes and arable fields. Seedlings were also planted at schools and clinics in the project areas. Success was greater in individual plantations than in public ones. For public plantations, mobilising was conducted through local leadership, VIDCOs and traditional leaders. One of the major outcomes of the project, in terms of our understanding of how rural institutions operate, was the open hostilities between state-sanctioned and traditional institutions. Added to this was the fact that most of the VIDCO positions were occupied by immigrants, people who moved into the area following the implementation of the Land Apportionment Act of 1930. Most VIDCOs were formed by individuals, and not by a committee as suggested by the title. No re-election or replacement of old members of VIDCOs was ever recorded and other members of the village knew little about who was in the committee. These anomalies made VIDCOs illegitimate and superficial, making planning through them very difficult, if not impossible (Mukamuri 1995a). In addition, boundaries were hard to draw, as people accessed resources from one village despite being registered in another. Location of the household did not coincide with the family's participation in the activities of the domicile village. Social and productive networks rarely followed the location of the household.

During the implementation of the project, a parallel study was conducted into the function of rituals and ritual beliefs, and the possibility of incorporating them into a community based conservation model. The main focus of the studies was rainmaking ceremonies, locally known as *mitoro*, which were conducted annually. People would be asked to contribute finger millet for beer brewing and the headman would provide a goat for ritual slaughter during the

ceremony. Although people were very happy to attend the rainmaking ceremonies, little interest was shown in making contributions, and headmen had
no power to punish people who did not contribute. In other circumstances
rainmaking ceremonies were used to show allegiance to different traditional
leaders as one succeeded another. Some traditional heads were also known to
have created their own rainmaking ceremonies and shrines in order to promote
a personal following. In short, rainmaking ceremonies can be divisive rather
than unifying within a given community, and support for them is waning.

Although not the subject of this chapter, a leaf on institutional dynamics
in Zimbabwe can be drawn from the new resettlement areas. Newly resettled
areas are largely characterised by an institutional vacuum. In most of these
former large scale commercial farms, taken over by the government from 2000,
large populations of people with diverse backgrounds and origin, largely from
urban areas, moved in. In what is reminiscent of the VIDCO vs kraal-heads
debacle discussed above, conflicts are arising as to who has control over other
settlers and natural resources (Marimira 2003). Open conflicts are rampant
between war veteran leaders and self-appointed kraal-heads, the latter coming
from neighbouring communal areas. The result has been increased poaching
of wildlife and trees, the latter largely for sale in neighbouring urban areas
(Mukamuri 2003). Attempts are being made by certain individuals to re-intro-
duce traditions such as sacredness, and rules forbidding the killing of certain
wildlife species and the cutting down of specific tree species, but these emerging leaders find their legitimacy questioned and sometimes openly challenged
by other settlers who have had no strong rural backgrounds and who rarely
adhere to African traditional values (Mukamuri 2003).

Rural institutions & challenges in the management of wildlife resources: the case of Campfire

Murombedzi (1990: 6) has argued that:

> It goes without saying that the success of Campfire will, in the final analysis, be
> determined by the extent to which the programme is able to create viable local
> management institutions.

He was corroborating what Marks (1984) identified as central to the attempts
to bring about sustainable natural resources management in small-scale
rural communities such as Zimbabwe's marginalised communal areas. Marks
argued that:

> ... decisions affecting wildlife survival and the welfare of small-scale rural
> societies, often existing on the same terrain, are increasingly made in
> bureaucratic institutions far removed from the consequences of their actions
> ... the survival of biological resources, such as wildlife, is best managed at the
> local level. In this view, the welfare of indigenous peoples and the management
> of their resources are linked directly (Marks 1984: xiii).

Marks further asserts that:

Once in place, protective laws and institutions obtained their own momentum and continue today to the point where, as a strategy, they have reached the limits of traditional skills and resources. (Marks 1984: 12)

In what could have been pressure to devolve wildlife management from the state to the local level, the government decentralised management of communal area wildlife to Rural District Councils by giving them 'Appropriate Conservation Status'. Appropriate Status was accorded mostly to those districts neighbouring National Parks and other wildlife areas. The umbrella programme for coordinating this shift in wildlife management and benefit sharing was Campfire. According to the Zimbabwe Trust (1990), the initiative was meant to bring about local participation in the management of wildlife and to allow revenue generated from these activities to benefit local communities.

Campfire had considerable success in increasing household incomes, reducing poaching and changing the way most people viewed wild animals. Before Campfire, wildlife was considered a nuisance to human beings (Mukamuri and Mavedzenge 1997). Negative perceptions were largely due to wild animals destroying crops and in some cases human lives. According to Murphree (1991) and Murombedzi (1992) Campfire succeeded in areas where there were high wildlife numbers, agriculturally marginal areas and low human populations.

Campfire recognised the need for local people and their respective institutions to engage in negotiations. The negotiations should have been conducted with the respective local authorities, RDCs, and should have determined issues related to benefit sharing (Child and Peterson 1998). The biggest snag was the reluctance of RDCs to devolve real proprietorship over the resources, resulting in the programme benefiting RDCs more than the communities. Nor have local communities been accorded the chance to fully participate in discussions on management and benefit sharing (Murphree 1990; Murombedzi 1992). However, Child and Peterson (1998) suggest that the early days of Campfire were progressive in meeting the goals of the programme: devolving management and benefit sharing to the local communities. What appears to be happening is that current macro-economic hardships are further curtailing the ability of cash-strapped RDCs to meet their goals. Most stories coming out of the Campfire districts show a continuous institutional evolution in that certain district officials have developed conflicts of interest by being both executives or representatives, and also safari operators. This is disturbing, but is also academically enriching in the sense that as people expected communities to develop institutions to further their interests, a new and opposing institutional framework is emerging. Communities have generally failed to challenge this status quo, even though in most cases only a handful of individuals are involved.

The country's economic system is also not helping the situation. Communities and RDCs continue to lose money because of the dual exchange-rate system. Proceeds from safari hunting and trophies are paid in hard currency, while RDCs are paid in local currency at the official exchange rate (US$1.00: Z$250, whereas the parallel rate is now [June 2007] over Z$200,000). Discussions about whether RDCs can open foreign currency denominated bank accounts are only beginning to emerge, but the question remains as to how this will translate into meaningful benefits to the marginalised communities. Without proper institutional rearrangements by all stakeholders involved in the Campfire programme, local communities will continue to be estranged from the real benefits.

Rural institutions: lessons & recommendations

This chapter has pointed to a disturbing but not yet hopeless situation regarding rural institutions in Zimbabwe, particularly those presiding over woodlands and wildlife resources. Evidence so far presented indicates that rural institutions are still far from meeting the criteria of co-management, and exercising authority over the access to and use of natural resources (Woodhouse 1997: 540). There is little evidence that rural institutions are heavily involved in setting rules and settling conflicts over rules (Ostrom 1987; Hyden 1989), and there are few good examples of partnership arrangements, power sharing and integration with state-sponsored institutions such as RDCs (Pomeroy and Berkes 1997). There is little in practice to show that local institutions have been accorded full responsibility, particularly in the case of high value resources such as wildlife and commercially important tree species (Jentoft 1989; Barrow and Murphree 1998; Mohamed 2001). Most of the problems emanate from the entrenched position in which rural institutions have found themselves. They have been subjected to a more sophisticated and legally protected system of governance, largely characterised by state sponsored Rural District Councils which are more organised and more sophisticated (Murombedzi 1990).

Lessons from literature show that in a typical Zimbabwean social forest, boundaries are not clearly defined. The Campfire programme challenges this assertion because it is hard to link the boundary of a mobile CPR (e.g. elephants) to a fixed community (e.g. a ward or village). The issue of rules and their policing by local institutions has been discussed above, largely pointing to lack of coordinated rule formation by local institutions, particularly over wildlife. Collective choice arrangements, though beneficial if in place, are largely lacking, particularly in matters related to local and state interface such as Campfire. The lack of participation by communities in quota setting of wildlife resources clearly shows that they are not yet involved in the active monitoring of their resources. Since the rules are not clear, it is difficult to see how communal people can offer graduated sanctions to violators; in most cases, as with Campfire, violators are legally and politically more powerful than local-level institutions. So far, the playing field is largely dominated by the RDCs in Campfire, a small elite within the system and safari operators who deliberately ignore local calls for increased benefit sharing and participation in management of natural resources. Nested enterprises are limited to the shortlist of the privileged and powerful.

It would be naïve to think that weaknesses in rural institutions are wholly a result of the way state institutions interface with rural ones. Contextual dynamics also shape this scenario. For example, internal conflicts affecting traditional leaders emanate from the colonial system of governance that created a dualistic and naturally conflicting environment. This was further fuelled by the post-colonial government when it superimposed the VIDCO system. Macro-economic forces, especially economic structural adjustment programmes introduced by the International Monetary Fund and the World Bank, undermined the role of the traditional leadership system as more people diversified from agriculture and began following other livelihood options. Agriculture continues to lose its position as the major rural livelihood option because of increased costs of production and falling real incomes derived from it. Land is gradually losing its economic value, and hence the power of the traditional leaders who traditionally allocated it. Dynamism in culture has also contributed to the demise of the rural institutions. With education and Christianity taking a strong footing, rural people have started to disdain African traditional values; fewer and fewer people believe that traditional systems bring rainfall, much less that certain tree species are sacred.

Rural institutions, and especially traditional leadership systems, need some kind of cautious modernisation in line with changing global management trends. Their administrative outlook needs to be harmonised in a codified fashion. A plebiscite system of appointing various committees under the traditional leaders might be premature, but it is nevertheless worth consideration. This could be accompanied by strong capacity building efforts to transform their efficiency, effectiveness and responsiveness. However, all of this requires support to transform rural institutions into legal and organised platforms of governance. In addition, committees – or more prudently, legal community trusts – can be formed to function as caretakers of specific natural resources and community interests. With proper legislative support, I perceive these trusts or committees can challenge prevailing hegemonic tendencies. Zimbabwe can also learn from other regional examples where community trusts for natural resources have been in place and are working well. Meanwhile, effort needs to be redirected towards those religious aspects and beliefs that can be central in mobilising communities for natural resources management. For RDCs to be responsive to local needs, as they are supposed to be, steps could be taken to ensure that office bearers work in a fiduciary manner, and avoid conflicts of interests.

References

Barrow, E. and M. Murphree. 1998. 'Community conservation from concept to practice: a practical framework', Working Chapter 8, in *Community Conservation in Africa*. University of Manchester: Institute for Development Policy and Management.

Berkes, F. 1997. 'New and not-so-new directions in the use of the commons: co-management', *The Common Property Digest*, 42, pp. 5-7.

Braedt. O. and W. Standa-Gunda. 2000. 'The sustainability of markets in forest products: the case of woodcrafts in Zimbabwe', *International Tree Crop Journal* 10, pp. 367-84.

Child, B. and J.H. Peterson (eds). 1991. 'Campfire in rural areas: the Beitbridge experience', Occasional Paper-NRM Series, CPN 1/91. Harare: Centre for Applied Social Sciences Publications, University of Zimbabwe.

Dzingirai, V. and M.F.C. Bourdillon. 1998. 'Religious ritual and environmental control in the Zambezi Valley: the case of Binga', Occasional Paper-NRM Series. Harare: Centre for Applied Social Sciences Publications, University of Zimbabwe.

Fortmann, L. and N. Nabane. 1992. 'The fruits of their labour: gender, property and tree resources in Mhondoro District', Occasional Paper Series. Harare: Centre for Applied Social Sciences Publications, University of Zimbabwe.

Hamudikuwanda, H., K. Marovanidze and P.H. Mugabe. 2001. 'A comparison of governance of some community based woodland and wetland projects with grazing schemes in Masvingo Province, Zimbabwe', Commons Southern Africa Occasional Chapter Series. Harare: Centre for Applied Social Sciences/PLAAS.

Hyden, G. 1998. 'Governance issues in Conservation and development', http:www.cdf.ufl.edu/cdf/gov-hyden.htm.

Jentoft, S. 1989. 'Fisheries co-management: Delegating government responsibility to fishermen's organisations', *Marine Policy*, April, pp. 137-54.

Latham. J. 2007. 'Nyika Vanhu: the land is the people', PhD thesis, University of Zimbabwe.

Malasha, I. 2003. 'Fisheries co-management: a comparative analysis of the Zambian and Zimbabwean inshore fisheries of Lake Kariba', PhD thesis, Harare, University of Zimbabwe.

Mandondo, A. 1997. 'Trees and spaces as emotion and norm laden components of local ecosystems in Nayamaropa Communal Lands, Nyanga District, Zimbabwe', *Agriculture and Human Values* 14, pp. 353-72.

Marimira. S.C. 2003. 'An analysis of institutional and organisational issues on fast track resettlement', an MSc thesis submitted to the Centre for Applied Social Sciences, Harare, University of Zimbabwe.

Matose, F. 1994. 'Local people's uses and perceptions on forest resources: an analysis of a state property regime in Zimbabwe', MSc thesis submitted to the Faculty of Graduate Studies, Edmonton, University of Alberta.

— 1992. 'Villagers as woodland managers', in G.D. Pierce and P. Shaw (eds), *Forestry Research in Zimbabwe*, Proceedings of the Anniversary Seminar, Forestry Advances in Zimbabwe. Harare: Forestry Commission.

Mohamed, N. 2001. 'Co-Governing natural resources in southern Africa: lessons from fisheries co-management, Malawi & Conservation co-management, South Africa', Commons Southern Africa Occasional Paper Series. No. 4.

Mukamuri, B.B., B.M. Campbell and G. Kowero. 2003. 'Local Organisations and Natural Resources Management in the Face of Economic Hardships: A Case Study from Zimbabwe'. In G. Kowero et al. (eds), *Policies and Governance Structures in Woodlands of Southern Africa*. Indonesia: CIFOR.

— 1995a. *Making sense of social forestry: a contextual and critical study of forestry projects in Zimbabwe*. Acta Tamperensis: University of Tampere.

— 1995b. 'Local environmental conservation strategies: Karanga Religion, Politics and Environmental Control', *Environment and History* 1, pp. 63-71.

— 1990. 'Karanga Religion and Environmental Protection', in P. Virtanen (ed.), *Conservation and Woodland Management in Zimbabwe*. Tampere: University of Tampere.

— 1987. 'Karanga Religion and Environmental Protection', BA (Hons) thesis. Harare, University of Zimbabwe).

Mukamuri B.B. and W. Kozanayi. 1999. 'Institutions surrounding the use of marketed forest products: the cases of *Berchemia discolour, Warburgia salutaris and Adansonia digitata*', IES Working Chapter 17. Harare: Centre for Applied Social Sciences Publications, University of Zimbabwe.

Mukamuri B.B. and T. Mavedzenge. 1997. *People and Big animals: an evaluation of the Campfire Project in Guruve District.* Harare: CIRAD.

Murombedzi, J.C. 1996. 'Wildlife in sustainable development', Occasional Chapter-NRM Series. Harare: Centre for Applied Social Sciences Publications, University of Zimbabwe.

— 1991. 'Decentralising common property resource management: a case study of the Camp-fire project', Occasional Paper-NRM Series. Harare: Centre for Applied Social Sciences Publications, University of Zimbabwe.

— 1990. 'The need for appropriate local level common property resource management institutions in communal tenure regimes', Occasional Paper-NRM Series. Harare: Centre for Applied Social Sciences Publications, University of Zimbabwe.

Murphree, M.W. 1991. 'Communities as institutions for natural resources management', Occasional Paper-NRM Series. Harare: Centre for Applied Social Sciences Publications, University of Zimbabwe.

— 1990. 'Decentralising the proprietorship of wildlife resources in Zimbabwe's Communal Areas'. Harare, Centre for Applied Social Sciences, University of Zimbabwe.

Nhira, C. and L. Fortmann. 1993. 'Local woodland management: realities at the grassroots', in P.N. Bradley and K. McNamara (eds), *Living with trees: policies for forestry management in Zimbabwe.* World Bank Technical Report No. 20, Washington D.C.

Nhira. C. 1994. 'Indigenous woodland usage and management in Kanyati Communal Area, Zimbabwe, with special reference to common property regimes', PhD thesis, University of Zimbabwe.

North, D. 1990. *Institutions, Institutional Change and Economic Performance.* New York: Cambridge University Press.

Ostrom, E. 1990. *Governing the commons: the evolution of institutions for collective action.* New York: Cambridge University Press.

— 1987. *The theory of collective action.* New York: Cambridge University Press.

Pomeroy, R. and F. Berkes. 1997. '"Two to Tango": the role of government in fisheries co-management', *Marine Policy* 21, 5, pp. 465-80.

Rukuni. M. 1998. 'Land reform in Zimbabwe: dimensions of a reformed land structure'. Paper presented to the Centre of African Social Studies, University of London and Britain Zimbabwe Society, 11 March.

Schoffeleers, M. 1982. *Guardians of the Land.* Gweru, Mambo Press.

Scoones, I.C. 1990. 'Livestock populations and the household economy: A case study from Southern Zimbabwe'. PhD thesis, University of London.

Spierenburg, M. 1995. 'The Mhondoro Cult in the struggle for control over land in Dande (Northern Zimbabwe): social commentaries and the influence of adherents', Occasional Paper-NRM Series. Harare: Centre for Applied Social Sciences Publications, University of Zimbabwe.

Wilson, K.B. 1989. 'Trees in fields in Southern Africa', *Journal of Southern African Studies* 2, pp. 369-83.

Woodhouse, P. 1997. 'Governance and local environmental management in Africa', *Review of African Political Economy*, 24, 74, pp. 537-47.

7

More than Socially Embedded
The Distinctive Character of 'Communal Tenure' Regimes in South Africa & its Implications for Land Policy

Ben Cousins

Introduction

Controversies over land tenure reform in post-apartheid South Africa resonate strongly with those raging elsewhere in Africa. This chapter focuses on a recent South African law, the Communal Land Rights Act of 2004, and relates debates around the Act to long-standing arguments on the nature of land rights and authority over land in Africa, and on state policies to reform 'customary' land tenure. Given that compulsory and systematic individual titling is no longer seen as an appropriate policy in African contexts by most policy analysts, the central issue in tenure reform in many parts of Africa (and elsewhere) is how to recognise and secure land rights that are clearly distinct from 'Western-legal'[1] forms of private property but cannot be characterised as 'traditional' or 'pre-colonial', given the impacts of both colonial policies and of past and current processes of rapid social change.

The policy challenge is to decide what kinds of rights, held by which categories of claimants, should be secured through tenure reform, and in what manner, in ways that will not merely 'add to possibilities of manipulation and confusion' (Shipton and Goheen 1992: 318). The difficulties are underlined by consideration of the record to date, in which reform efforts have not taken sufficiently into account the reality of how tenure regimes operate in practice, leading to a variety of unintended consequences (Shipton 1988; Berry 1993). Securing the land rights of women and other vulnerable categories and interest groups has proved particularly difficult. The analytical challenge is to characterise complex and dynamic realities using appropriate concepts and theories, which might inform the design of policies and laws.

Another key issue is authority over land matters and the design of appropriate institutional frameworks for land administration. Power relations are key to understanding how tenure regimes work in practice, since 'struggles over property are as much about the scope and constitution of authority as

---

1 Daley and Hobley (2005: 8) suggest this useful term for the dominant notions of private property.

about access to resources' (Lund 2002: 11). In particular, the powers and functions of 'customary authorities' in relation to land are highly controversial and widely debated. A particularly contentious issue, which the South African case clearly illustrates, is demarcation of the jurisdictional boundaries of 'customary authorities', which has important implications for how land rights are defined and administered as well as for broader questions of local governance (see Lenz 2006 for an instructive Ghanaian case).

I argue in this chapter that the character of land tenure regimes in the 'communal areas' of South Africa are dynamic and evolving regimes within which a number of important commonalities and continuities over time are observable in many, but not all, circumstances. Some key underlying principles of pre-colonial land relations are identified, which informed adaptations of tenure regimes in the colonial era and in the subsequent period when policies of segregation and apartheid were pursued, and continue to do so in many areas today. Exploring the policy implications of this analysis, I suggest that the most appropriate approach to tenure reform in South Africa is to make socially legitimate occupation and use rights, as they are currently held and practised, the point of departure for both their recognition in law and for the design of institutional frameworks for mediating competing claims and administering land.

Tenure reform in post-apartheid South Africa

Contemporary forms of 'customary' or 'communal' land tenure in South Africa can be understood only in the context of a centuries-old history of land dispossession and state regulation, together with a variety of local responses, ranging from high profile rebellions to 'hidden struggles' (Beinart and Bundy 1987) that shaped the outcomes of these interventions to a degree. This history has involved major modification and adaptation of indigenous land regimes, but seldom their complete destruction and replacement. Conquest and settlement in the colonial period, followed by twentieth-century policies of segregation and apartheid, saw white settlers and their heirs take possession of most of the land surface of South Africa. State policies attempted to reconfigure the livelihood and land tenure systems of the indigenous populations in ways that served the interests of the dominant classes. African 'reserves' were created as a way to contain resistance and to facilitate the supply of cheap labour for the emerging capitalist economy. They also functioned to lower the cost of colonial administration through a system of indirect rule, within which traditional leaders undertook local administration on behalf of the state – often in a highly authoritarian manner, termed 'decentralised despotism' by Mamdani (1996).

The large-scale dispossession of land that took place means that programmes of land redistribution and restitution are the key focus of South

African land reform policies in the post-apartheid era. The third leg of land policy is tenure reform, which aims to secure the land rights of farm workers and labour tenants living on privately-owned large scale commercial farms and of residents in the 'communal areas', or former reserves. These constitute around 13 per cent of the land area of the country but are home to a large proportion of the country's population – perhaps 20 million, or around 43 per cent of the total.

There is widespread overcrowding and forced overlapping of rights in these areas as a result of a history of forced removals and evictions of black South Africans from white-owned land, and uncertainty as to the legal status, content and strength of these rights. Administration by traditional leaders often involves corruption in relation to land (Levin 1997; Ntsebeza 1999; Claassens 2001). The land administration system in many 'communal' areas is now near collapse. Permission to Occupy certificates (PTOs) may or may not be issued to occupiers of land, procedures to allocate land vary widely and are often ad hoc, and registers of rights holders are seldom kept up to date (MacIntosh, Xaba and Associates 1998; Turner 1999; Lahiff and Aphane 2000). Lack of clarity on land rights constrains infrastructure and service provision, and there are tensions between local government bodies and traditional authorities over the allocation of land for development projects (e.g. housing, irrigation schemes, business centres, and tourist infrastructure – see Peires 2000). Women's land rights are more insecure than those of men, and are often seen as 'secondary' in character, given that women's access to land is obtained only via their husbands or other male relatives (Meer 1997).

In some areas the existing regimes appear reasonably stable, with most occupants of communal land experiencing de facto security of tenure (Turner 1999; Adams et al. 2000). On the other hand, these systems are also under increasingly severe strain as a result of overcrowding, weak administration, abuses by traditional leaders, tension over common property resource use, and lack of clarity over the roles and responsibilities of traditional authorities and local government bodies. This can lead to heated debates at the local level about how land rights and administration should be reformed (Claassens 2003). The key problem that tenure reform policy sets out to address is the underlying legal insecurity of land tenure rights, which surfaces most clearly when development projects are planned and implemented (Adams et al. 2000; Kepe 2001).

Tenure reform in South Africa is seen a constitutional imperative. Section 25 (6) of the Bill of Rights in the 1996 Constitution asserts that:

> A person or community whose tenure of land is legally insecure as a result of past racially discriminatory laws or practices is entitled, to the extent provided by an Act of Parliament, either to tenure which is legally secure or to comparable redress.

The South African White Paper on Land Policy (DLA 1997: 57-8) sets out an approach that seeks to give effect to this constitutional right. Land tenure policies must 'move towards rights and away from permits' and aim to build a 'unitary non-racial system of land rights for all South Africans'. It must 'allow people to choose the tenure system which is appropriate to their circumstances' (including both group and individual ownership) but these 'must be consistent with the Constitution's commitment to basic human rights and equality'. In order to secure tenure, 'a rights based approach has been adopted' which must 'recognise and accommodate the de facto vested interests which exist on the ground', including legal rights but also 'interests which have come to exist without formal legal recognition'. Where overlapping and conflicting rights cannot be reconciled within one area, additional land will be required to relieve land shortages, to ensure that strengthening the rights of some does not lead to the eviction of others. In the White Paper individual titling was accepted as one possible option, but the greatest emphasis was placed on a democratic reform of collective systems, within which members will 'have the power to choose the structure which represents them in decisions pertaining to the day to day management of the land and all issues relating to member's access to the land asset' (ibid: 63).

Within the broad category of 'communal tenure', a wide range of situations can be identified. For example, in some areas occupation has been continuous over long periods of time, and people were not subject to forced removals. In other regions, by contrast, a great deal of population relocation occurred, laying the basis for a large number of land restitution claims. In some areas rural land purchased for occupation by black people by the South African Development Trust (SADT) after 1936 was intensively administered by state bureaucrats who monitored and enforced the PTO system (Cross 1992). Some parts of the Eastern Cape were subject to colonial policies aimed at individualising land tenure, but in many of them elements of a 'communal' system persisted or re-emerged over time (Kingwill 1996). Land rights in small-scale irrigation schemes often took the form of a variant of the PTO system but involved additional complexities (Lahiff 2000), and a degree of de facto individualisation is occurring in 'communal areas' adjacent to towns and cities, where informal land markets have emerged (Cross 1992; Royston 2004). This diversity poses huge challenges to policy.

The Land Rights Bill of 1999

Government's initial approach to the question of how to give full legal recognition to the rights of people in 'communal' areas was based on a paradigm of transferring ownership from the state to groups or individuals. However, experience in a number of test cases in 1997 and 1998 revealed inherent difficulties (Claassens 2000: 253-4). One was how to define the 'unit of ownership': should land be transferred to 'tribes', often consisting of hundreds of thousands of people, or to a population under a chief and a designated Tribal Authority, or to smaller units such as wards or villages? Vesting land ownership in a larger group could make it difficult for smaller groups to make meaningful decisions about land within their own localities; on the other hand, vesting rights in members at the local level might deny some rights inherent in the larger group of which they form a part, such as access to shared common property resources. Another lesson was that investigation and consultation with prospective rights holders was resource-intensive and time-consuming. Test cases also showed that the prospect of the transfer of private ownership raised the stakes in tenure disputes and triggered major tensions and conflicts between competing interest groups.

As a result of these difficulties, policy thinking moved towards the creation of 'statutory' rights which would be secure in law but would not entail the transfer of title. A Land Rights Bill (LRB) drafted in 1998/99[2] created a category of protected rights for which the majority of those occupying land in the former 'homelands' would qualify (Claassens 2000: 255). Most 'communal' land is registered as the property of the state. The LRB envisaged clear statutory limitations on the state's rights in respect of this land. It proposed the vesting of occupation, use, benefit and decision making rights in a class of 'protected' rights holders. Critically, the bill provided that the holders of protected rights could not be deprived of land without their consent, except by expropriation, for example when land is required for public purposes, and with compensation. The Minister of Land Affairs would continue to be the nominal owner of the land, but with strictly delimited powers. Protected rights would vest in the individuals who use, occupy or have access to land, but in group systems protected rights would be relative to those shared with other members; individual rights would thus be relative to 'group rules', as decided upon by the majority of members. This in turn would require the definition of the boundaries of the group – a key difficulty, as pointed out above, for the original 'transfer of ownership' paradigm. The solution proposed in the LRB was as follows:

> ... 'boundaries' must be seen as flexible. In other words, the boundary of the group would be determined with reference to who (which group of people) is affected by the particular decision. Thus, if the decision is about a change in grazing practice then the people affected by the change must be consulted, not the entire 'tribe' (Claassens 2000: 255).

Statutory protected rights would secure occupation and use without having to first resolve disputes over the precise nature and extent of these rights. The minimum content of protected rights was set out in the LRB: it included access, occupation, use and benefit. The rights could be bequeathed and,

---

2   I was a member of the team that drafted the Land Rights Bill. This has no doubt influenced my assessment of the Communal Land Rights Act.

potentially, transacted and mortgaged. Beyond its basic minimum content, the LRB enabled a process of group decision making with regard to augmenting the content of protected rights, in particular in respect of the ability to transact and develop land. This might result, for example, in a decision allowing internal sales of the right to homestead plots to 'community' members in a particular area, but limitations on transactions with outsiders.

The LRB proposed that people had the right to choose which local institution would manage and administer land rights on their behalf. Agreed group rules would have to provide 'bottom line' protections for members, consistent with constitutional principles of democracy, equality and due process, and rights holders and local institutions would be supported by a Land Rights Officer based in each district. Where rights are overlapping and contested due to forced removals and evictions in the past, confirmation of rights would only take place after a rights enquiry, with government providing incentives to stakeholders to negotiate acceptable solutions, mainly in the form of additional land to relieve overcrowding.

The draft LRB never saw the light of day. In June 1999 a new Minister of Agriculture and Land Affairs took office[3], and the LRB was set aside. In her view the approach adopted was too complex and would be too costly to implement. She was in favour of a law that transferred title of state land to 'tribes' (or 'traditional communities'), allowed traditional leaders to administer land, and did not require high levels of institutional support to rights holders. Following several false starts, a Communal Lands Rights Bill was drafted between 2001 and 2003 and eventually enacted in early 2004 (for a detailed account of this process see Cousins and Claassens 2004). Three years on, implementation has yet to begin, in part because of inadequate departmental capacity, in part because of a pending constitutional challenge to the Act.

The Communal Land Rights Act of 2004

The Communal Land Rights Act (CLRA) extends private ownership of land to rural 'communities'. Within areas of 'communally owned' land it establishes a register of 'new order rights' vested in individuals. It also provides for a land administration committee to exert ownership powers on behalf of the 'community' it represents, and allows 'tribal councils' to act as such committees (RSA 2004).

Transfer of ownership

The CLRA transfers title of communal land from the state to a 'community', which must register its rules before it can be recognised as a 'juristic personality' legally capable of owning land. Individual members of this community

---

are issued with a Deed of Communal Land Right, which can be upgraded to a freehold title if the community agrees. The Minister must make a determination on whether or not 'old order rights' (i.e. communal land rights derived from past laws and practices, including 'customary law and usage') should be confirmed and converted into 'new order rights', and must determine the nature and extent of such rights. New order rights can be registered in the name of a 'community' or a person, but where title is transferred to a 'community' the individual new order rights are not equivalent to (individual) title. The minimum content of new order rights is not set out in the Act.

Before transfer of ownership can occur the boundaries of 'community' land must be surveyed and registered. Also a rights enquiry must take place, to investigate the nature and extent of existing rights and interests in land (including competing and conflicting rights), options for securing such rights, measures to ensure gender equality, and spatial planning and land use issues. The Minister will then determine the location and extent of the land to be transferred, and whether or not the whole of an area or some portion of it should be transferred to the 'community'. A part of the land may be subdivided and transferred to individuals, and portions may be reserved to the state.

The CLRA requires that community rules are drawn up before any transfer of land, to regulate the administration and use of communal land. The Act does not specify the process whereby such rules are to be drawn up and agreed, nor its timing (e.g. whether or not the drawing up of such rules precedes the establishment of a land administration committee).

Definition of 'community' & the vesting of rights

The CLRA vests ownership in the 'community', defined as 'a group of people whose rights to land are derived from shared rules determining access to land held in common by such group'. Senior government officials have stated in parliament that they view the population of areas under the jurisdiction of tribal authorities, headed by chiefs, as the relevant 'communities'.[4] Land administration committees represent the 'community' and take decisions on its behalf. Tribal authority boundaries are often contentious, many having been demarcated during the implementation of the Bantu Authorities Act early in the apartheid era.

Gender equality

The CLRA contains a general provision that a woman is entitled to the same tenure rights as a man, and no laws, rules or practices may discriminate on the grounds of gender. It provides for the Minister to confer a 'new order right' on a woman, even where 'old order rights' such as Permission to Occupy certifi-

---

4   Dr Sipho Sibanda of the Department of Land Affairs, addressing a meeting of the Portfolio Committee on Agriculture and Land Affairs, House of Assembly, 26 January 2004.

cates (PTOs) were vested only in men. New order rights are deemed to be held jointly by all spouses in a marriage, and must be registered in all their names. Adult female members of households who use land, but who are not spouses, are not provided for. The CLRA also requires at least that one third of the membership of a land administration committee be female.

Constitution of land administration bodies

In the CLRA, a 'community' which applies for title must establish a land administration committee, which 'represents a community owning communal land', and has the powers and duties conferred on it by the CLRA and by the rules of such a 'community'. It must allocate land rights, maintain records of rights and transactions, assist in dispute resolution, and liaise with local government bodies in relation to planning and development and other land administration functions.

Where they exist, traditional councils established under the Traditional Leadership and Governance Framework Act (TLGFA) of 2003 'may' exercise the powers and functions of such land administration committees.[5] There are competing interpretations of this provision. In one view, it allows for choice on the part of rights holders as to which local body will perform land administration functions, but another view holds that the word 'may' is permissive only, enabling a traditional council to exercise the powers of a land administration committee, rather than creating a choice for rights holders. The Act does not explicitly provide for choice, for example by setting out procedures and oversight mechanisms, which suggests that the latter interpretation is correct.

Determination of group boundaries

The CLRA provides for the Minister to make a determination of 'community' boundaries, on the basis of the land rights enquiry. Transfer of title involves demarcating and surveying the boundaries of the 'community' that will become the legal owner of communal land, as well as of internal boundaries in terms of a 'communal general plan'. As described above, one interpretation of the Act is that 'communities' will coincide with the population currently under tribal authorities, when these are reconstituted as 'traditional councils'. These areas typically have populations of between 10,000 and 20,000, and tribal authorities and the chiefs that head them have jurisdiction over a great many wards and villages, under the authority of sub-chiefs, headmen, or sub-headmen. They are thus aggregates of a large number of smaller 'communities'. The fact that many groups and individuals now fall under the jurisdiction of

---

5   Section 21 (2) of the CLRA states that 'If a community has a recognised traditional council, the powers and duties of the land administration committee of such community may be exercised and performed by such council'. The TLGFA allows existing Tribal Authorities to be deemed traditional councils if they 'transform' themselves within one year, after which time 40 per cent of members must be elected and 30 per cent must be women.

chiefs and tribal authorities that they had had no previous connection to, and whose authority they now contest, is not acknowledged.

Decision making in relation to land

The CLRA establishes land administration committees to make key decisions and exert ownership powers on behalf of the 'community'. It does not require land administration committees to consult with the 'community' members it represents in relation to major decisions such as disposal of land or of rights in such land. The only requirement in such a case is ratification of a decision by a provincial Land Rights Board. The CLRA does not set out procedures for decision making (e.g. in relation to the adoption of 'community' rules or the holding of a land rights enquiry), but states that rights enquiries must be open and transparent, and that decisions must be informed and democratic.

Debating the Communal Land Rights Act

The key policy decisions embodied in the CLRA are to transfer private ownership to 'communities', after a rights enquiry and detailed Ministerial determinations. Deeds of Communal Land Right, the form in which the 'new order rights' of community members are to be registered, are secondary rights of occupation and use, subordinate to group ownership. Land administration committees will have powers akin to those of owners. This approach has been widely criticised and was debated at length in parliamentary consultations before the law was enacted, with the powers of traditional councils over land being one of the most controversial issues (Cousins and Claassens 2004; Murray 2004; Cousins 2005).

Both the draft law and presentations to parliament by senior officials made it clear that 'communities' would be defined as those people living within Tribal Authority boundaries, that traditional councils would be recognised as land administration committees, and that rights holders would have no effective choice in this matter. These provisions were greeted with dismay by community groups and NGOs, which saw this as undermining fundamental democratic rights. Some observers suggested that the last-minute inclusion of this provision in the draft law of 2003, just days before parliamentary consultations were to begin, was the result of a back-room political deal with the traditional leader lobby in the run-up to a national election (Govender 2004; Murray 2004). In response to the overwhelming rejection of these provisions by the majority of parliamentary submissions, the draft law was substantially amended before its approval in 2004, and the Act, as outlined above, is now somewhat ambiguous about whether or not rights holders have choice in relation to how a land administration committee is to be constituted (see above). This aspect remains highly controversial.

In April 2006 four rural groupings, self-identified as 'communities', initiated a constitutional challenge to the Act, with the assistance of the Legal Resources Centre and associated lawyers. The question of whether or not traditional councils will act as land administration committees wherever they exist is one of the key issues in the challenge. In all four cases a history of interference with the land rights of groups and individuals by chiefs informs residents' anxiety that implementation of the CLRA will result in control over land being vested in traditional councils ('transformed' tribal authorities) at the expense of the rights of current land holders. In two of the four cases the jurisdiction of tribal authorities over subordinate groups ('communities') is deeply contested.

Legal papers also assert that the CLRA is unconstitutional because the nature and content of 'new order rights' are not clearly defined, and the Minister of Land Affairs is given wide and sweeping powers to determine these rights on a discretionary basis. It is argued that no clear criteria to guide the Minister's decisions are provided by the Act, and few opportunities to participate in making these crucial decisions, or to challenge them, are created. A critical omission is the lack of consultation with rights holders on whether or not they desire a transfer of title.

Some critiques of the CLRA (Claassens 2005; Cousins 2005) suggest that the Act entrenches particular versions of 'customary' land tenure that resulted from colonial and apartheid policies, and that this will have the effect of undermining rather than securing land rights. In many pre-colonial tenure systems, it is argued, land rights were derived in the first instance from accepted membership of a group. Decisions in relation to residential and arable land (including the transfer of rights to others through inheritance, bequeathing, lending, sharecropping or sale) were made primarily at household level. Security of rights derived from a relative balance of power between authority structures and rights holders. The CLRA shifts the balance of power away from individuals and households towards the group and its authority structures, on the one hand, and towards the Minister (as advised by officials), on the other. Ownership at the level of the traditional council/chieftaincy will 'trump' the rights that exist at lower levels, such as household and individual rights to residential and arable land.

A second argument is that the transfer of ownership of communal land from the state to 'communities', with the requirement that outer boundaries be surveyed and registered, conflicts with the nested and overlapping character of land rights in 'communal areas'. As a result, implementation of the CLRA is likely to exacerbate existing tensions and disputes over boundaries (including disputes with sub-groups placed under the jurisdiction of chiefs under apartheid), and generate new tensions in areas which are currently relatively stable (Cousins 2005).

In relation to gender equality, it has been suggested that the CLRA undermines the tenure rights of female household members who occupy and use land other than as wives, such as mothers and divorced or unmarried adult sisters. In addition, it is unclear what land rights can be claimed by women who are divorcees at the time that a determination is made by the Minister, since they will no longer be married and thus cannot be deemed to be the joint holder of an 'old order right' (Claassens 2005).

Underlying these debates over the CLRA (and the Traditional Leadership and Governance Framework Act) are competing views of the relationship between custom and democracy. Some emphasise tensions between the values, practices and political identities associated with 'customary systems' and liberal democracy (Comaroff and Comaroff 2006), but others see them as potentially reconcilable (Nhlapo 1995). Government defends the approach adopted in the CLRA as consistent with both the nature of customary land tenure and democratic rights (Sibanda 2004). Some critics see the CLRA and the TLGFA as a complete betrayal of democracy, and assert that attempts to reconcile custom and democratic rights are inherently contradictory (Ntsebeza 2004).

South African debates echo those in the wider African context (see further below). On one hand, recent years have seen a marked emphasis in both advocacy and state policy on recognition of 'customary' law and institutions, together with the idea of devolving responsibility for land management to local institutions. This is in large part a reaction to the evident failures of individual land titling in countries such as Kenya. On the other hand, this policy stance has been criticised for 'positing a panacea' (Daley and Hobley 2005: 34) that fails to adequately acknowledge socio-economic differentiation and the realities of local politics and power relations, within which 'the democratic substance of village governments ... is often unclear' (Daley 2005b). Disquiet over the manipulation of ideas about the 'customary' by powerful men informs Whitehead and Tsikata's (2003: 103) view that there are 'too many hostages to fortune in the language of the customary at a national level for it to spearhead democratic reforms and resistance to centralised and elite-serving state power'.

In relation to South African tenure reform, I suggest that an alternative approach to the CLRA is both necessary and feasible, and that this alternative is not individual titling. Policy must take cognisance of the complexities and realities of current regimes of claims, rights and their governance, i.e. how 'actually-existing' tenure systems operate in practice. It must then aim to build upon those characteristics that provide an appropriate basis for securing land rights and democratising land administration, and at the same time address problematic features of current systems such as gender inequality. The next section attempts to identify the relevant characteristics, through a review of some of the literature on land tenure in South Africa (and, where relevant, elsewhere in Africa) from the pre-colonial era to the present.

Analysing 'communal' land tenure in South Africa: underlying principles, continuity & change

'Western-legal' regimes of private property are historically specific and the concepts and terms associated with them must be used with caution. Administrators and anthropologists in the early colonial period recognised that legal concepts and language derived from European systems of law would not be appropriate in African (and other) contexts, but did not always agree on which concepts to use in their place (Bohannan 1963; Gluckman 1965). According to Biebuyck (1963: 52) 'common general formulae like ... ultimate or sovereign rights, rights of allocation or of control, or rigid oppositions between ownership, possession, use and usufruct... have often obscured understanding of the scope and nature of rights and claims relating to the land'.

Okoth-Ogendo (1989) does not rely on European legal doctrine in his persuasive analysis of the nature of property rights in Africa. In his view a 'right' signifies a power that society allocates to its members to execute a range of functions in respect of any given subject matter. Where that power amounts to exclusive control one can talk of 'ownership' of 'private property', but it is not essential that power and exclusivity of control coincide in this manner. Access to this power (i.e. a 'right') and its control are distinct, and there are diverse social and cultural rules and vocabularies for defining access and control.

In Africa, according to Okoth-Ogendo, land rights tend to be attached to membership of some unit of production; are specific to a resource management or production function; and are maintained through active participation in the processes of production and reproduction at particular levels of social organisation. Control of such access is attached to 'sovereignty' (in its non-proprietary sense) and vested in political authority over different levels of social organisation and units of production. Control occurs primarily for the purposes of guaranteeing access to land for production purposes. In these land tenure regimes there is no coincidence of access and control, and property does not involve the vesting of the full complement of power over land that is possible (i.e. private property). Variations in power (i.e. rights) derive from social relations, not the market. Control is exercised through members of the units of production; control is not simply the product of 'political superordination' (ibid: 11).

I make use of Okoth-Ogendo's conceptual framework in tracing patterns of continuity and change in land tenure regimes in South Africa from the pre-colonial era through to the present.[6] I concur broadly with his view that 'indigenous norms and structures' in relation to property have demonstrated great resilience in the face of colonial and post-colonial policies of 'subversion,

---

6 The main focus in this review is the South African literature, but reference is made, where relevant, to materials from the wider African context.

expropriation and suppression' (Okoth-Ogendo 2002: 10). Building on this insight, I argue that some key underlying principles and characteristics can often be observed in land tenure regimes over time. These are briefly described here, and numbered for ease of reference in the discussion that follows, that provides concrete illustrations.

1. Land and resource rights are directly embedded in a range of social relationships and units, including households and kinship networks; the relevant social identities are often multiple, overlapping and therefore 'nested' or layered in character (e.g. individual rights within households, households within kinship networks, kinship networks within wider 'communities').

2. Rights are derived primarily from accepted membership of a social unit, and can be acquired via birth, affiliation or allegiance to a group and its political authority, or transactions of various kinds (including gifts, loans, and purchases).

3. Land and resource rights include both strong individual and family rights to residential and arable land and access to a range of common property resources such as grazing, forests, and water. They are thus both 'communal' and 'individual' in character.

4. Access to land (through defined rights) is distinct from control of land (through systems of authority and administration). Control is concerned with guaranteeing access and enforcing rights, regulating the use of common property resources, overseeing mechanisms for redistributing access, and resolving disputes over claims to land. It is often located within a hierarchy of nested systems of authority, with many functions located at local or 'lower' levels.

5. Social, political and resource boundaries, while often relatively stable, are also flexible and negotiable to an important extent; this flows in part from the nested character of social identities, rights and authority structures.

I am aware of the dangers of 'abstracting institutions from ... specific historical circumstances ....' (Kuper 1997: 74) and of Moore's (1998: 39) critique of Etienne le Roy's attempt to define and model African land relations, which she suggests is essentialist and reductionist and 'at quite a distance from the multiple, shifting, permutating, recombining practices of rural Africa'. Nevertheless, my review of the literature suggests that the general principles listed above can often be discerned, embodied within a range of contextually specific land tenure regimes, both in the past and today. The extent to which, and ways in which, these principles are found in 'actually-existing' land tenure regimes are variable, given complex histories of state interventions and diverse, adaptive responses to these interventions. In specific cases some of these characteristics may be absent altogether. Where these characteristics are present, however, property regimes remain distinct from 'Western-legal' forms of private property, which is why they present such a challenge to tenure reform policy.

The pre-colonial era

Anthropologists undertaking fieldwork in the early to mid-twentieth century attempted to identify the general characteristics of African land tenure in the pre-colonial era. Biebuyck (1963: 52-64) provides a useful summary: land was plentiful and exploitation of resources was generally extensive; land was essential for livelihoods but had little exchange value; land was 'vested in groups' (chiefdoms, villages, lineages or other social groupings) represented by their chiefs, elders and/or councils. There was 'a close relationship between features of social and political organisation and principles of land tenure' (ibid: 52) (principle 1).

All members of a group had rights of access to land, derived from membership in the group, and in some cases from allegiance to a political authority such as a chief (principle 2). Rights in land could also be obtained through marriage, migration, friendship and formal transfer. The exercise of any right was always limited by obligations and counterbalanced by others' rights and privileges. Individual security was great, provided the necessary respect for the ethical code of the group was maintained. Effective use and appropriation were generally required for the maintenance of individual and family rights in a particular piece of land. Often a number of individuals, households or larger social units exercised rights and claims in the same piece of land. Land tenure was everywhere both 'communal' and 'individual' (ibid: 54-55) or what Bennett (2004: 381) terms a 'system of complementary interests held simultaneously' (principle 3).

There is some ambiguity in the literature on the source of individual rights in land. Thus Gluckman (1965: 78) asserts that the underlying principle of African land tenure (in common with most 'tribal societies') is that rights to land 'are an incident of political and social status. By virtue of membership in the nation or tribe, every citizen was entitled to claim some land, from the king or chief, or from such political unit as exists in the absence of chiefly authority'. Colson (1963) describes the case of the Valley Tonga of present-day Zambia, where before 1900 people lived in neighbourhoods under the ritual leadership of a sikatonga. Individual cultivators had rights over land they brought into cultivation and 'no authority within the community had the right to allocate land' (ibid: 141). Men and women were 'equally eligible' to receive lineage land (ibid: 142). Colson (1971: 197) argues that land rights in pre-colonial central Africa could not be bought nor ceded 'any more than the citizenship upon which it rested'.

For Biebuyck (1963: 55), writing from an Africa-wide perspective, land allocation was not necessarily undertaken by the representatives of the landholding groups; the primary role of chiefs and elders was often to maintain peace between the land-using units, to defend the integrity of the territory, or to ensure its fertility (principle 4). Other ethnographers, in contrast, state that individual land rights derived in the first instance from an allocation by a traditional authority. In Swaziland, for example, according to Kuper (1961: 44), 'the land and the people are interlocked, and the political bond between rulers and subjects is based largely on the power that the rulers wield over the soil on which the people live', and 'as representative of the nation, the king allots land to his people' (ibid: 45).[7]

Although the anthropological literature often uses the term 'individual rights' in describing how people held residential and arable land, it emphasises that land was controlled by family units, which were often large 'extended' households of descent groups, and that along with control came a host of social obligations (principle 1). Sansom (1974: 159-62) emphasises that in most societies in the southern African region family assets were demarcated as 'house property' and 'men's property'. These assets 'were encumbered': the rights of wife and children were maintained against male authority by the possibility of appeals to kin, and rights in grain and other produce gave each wife a 'measure of power and control' (Schapera, 1955: 202). According to Hunter (1979: 119) a married woman in Pondoland selected her own fields for cultivation, provided she did not encroach on someone else's; they were not allotted to her. Once she turned over the soil, she had an exclusive right to cultivate that field, no matter how long she left it in fallow. There was no limit to the number or size of the fields she could cultivate.

A key feature of pre-colonial African tenure systems was the right of access to and use of shared resources such as grazing, water and a variety of other natural resources (e.g. grass for thatching, trees for building, fences and fuel wood, wild fruits and vegetables, clay and sand). Regulation of resource use in the common interest occurred to a greater or lesser extent, and was particularly evident in relation to grazing. A great deal of variation was evident in relation to the boundaries of the areas within which rights to resource use were shared (principle 5), and thus also in relation to the location of administrative authority with regulatory responsibilities (Sansom 1974).

Many ethnographic studies describe land administration functions, along with other aspects of authority (judicial, military, religious) as practised at different levels of authority, nested or layered within one another (principle 4). Schapera (1955: 89), for example, describes how in Tswana tribes the regulation of common property resources often took place at higher levels of authority, but the acquisition of rights to residential and arable land was highly decentralised. In the first instance, a man would ask his father for a space to build his dwellings, and for fields to plough; if not available, he might try to acquire some land from a relative or friend; if that did not succeed he

---

7   cf. Reader 1966, for a Zululand case. It may be significant that in both the Zulu and Swazi cases state power became highly centralised in the period immediately before colonial subjugation; this may have resulted in a shift in conceptions of the origins of land rights.

would apply to the headman for some ward land held in reserve; and only if none was available would the headman take the applicant to the chief for an allocation (ibid: 204).

Sansom (1974) reviews a large number of cases (Tswana, Sotho, Pedi, Zulu, Mpondo, Lovedu, Venda) and suggests that 'a similar apparatus for the delegation of authority to administer rights in land is found in all Southern Bantu tribes' (1974: 145). He follows Gluckman (1965) in describing the nested nature of land administration in terms of a series of estates. The anthropological literature on political authority describes both the revered status of leaders and a number of checks on their power, notably through the threat of desertion by followers (Mamdani 1996: 42-6; for the Tswana case see Schapera, 1955: 62-3; for the amaPondo see Hunter, 1979: 393). The difficulties of exerting centralised political control over commoners are stressed by Kuper (1997: 74-5):

> In pre-conquest south-east Africa the political units ... were typically made up of diverse populations, yoked together by a leader. There were no tribal, homogeneous chiefdoms, and no stable political communities until some were deliberately established by colonial rulers. At any one time, the allegiance and autonomy of various major chiefs was open to question.... The social and political boundaries of the chief's domain were always contentious. There was a constant leakage of commoner households from central control ... amongst the Xhosa the most effective check on chiefly authority was 'gradual emigration'.

The colonial period

The imposition of colonial rule impacted upon how land was held and used. According to Biebuyck (1963: 56) the early colonial period was characterised by increasing scarcity of land due to increased population, agricultural development, the development of new markets and a heightened demand for good quality land. Governments passed laws on land, disputes came before the courts, and large-scale resettlement of people took place. There was a range of responses to these new circumstances. New ideologies of inheritance and economic co-operation came into being. Sales of land became widespread in some areas, but elsewhere were spurned; in some places rights became highly individualised, in others they remained under the control of groups or political authorities. A general tendency in areas where land was vested in 'villages' was for inheritance rights to fields to be exercised more strongly by individuals and families than before, and where it was held by kinship groupings, the size and genealogical depth of these groups tended to shrink (ibid: 59). Nevertheless, in general land relations remained socially embedded (principle 1). Biebuyck (1963: 60) notes that:

> ... in many situations the growth of a feeling of insecurity and of hostility towards outsiders, as the outcome of increased land scarcity and greater demand for land, have resulted in stressing the concepts of inalienability, of group ownership and of ritual sanction in land tenure.

In South Africa, the government of the Cape Colony attempted to provide individual titles in some of the 'native reserves'. The Native Locations and Commonage Act of 1879 allowed the Governor to divide land in the Ciskei into individual 'quitrent' titles with areas reserved as communal grazing but in a diluted and discriminatory form – no conversions to freehold were allowed, and a title-holder could not alienate his land without permission. The response was disappointing – there was a widespread failure to take up titles, in part because of reluctance to pay the costs of survey and titling, in part, according to the Surveyor-General, a 'preference for tribal or common tenure' (Delius et al. 1997: 10). Another attempt, the Glen Grey Act of 1894, was portrayed as 'modernising' the conditions of African rural existence but was designed principally to facilitate the supply of migrant workers to the mining industry. Married men were entitled to only one arable plot and security of tenure was not very strong. As with quitrent, the new system experienced problems: boundaries of cultivated lands were not observed, the distinction between arable and commonage land became blurred, and inherited titles were often not registered.

In Natal, by contrast, individualisation of land rights was not pursued. Pursuing a policy of indirect rule, the British provided a central role for chiefs in local administration. Customary law was recognised where it was deemed to be 'not repugnant to the general principles of humanity' (cited in Delius et al. 1997: 19). Many of the despotic powers enjoyed by Zulu chiefs under Shaka were enshrined in law.

In the Transvaal, a relatively weak Boer state and determined resistance by Africans meant that for much of the nineteenth century 'competing systems and conceptions of land rights co-existed in varying degrees of tension and conflict' (Delius et al. 1997: 24). There were debates about establishing reserves for African settlement, but none were designated until after 1881. Before then, to secure their independent land rights many Africans had no choice but to purchase farms. Since only white burghers could buy land, many communities requested missionaries to purchase farms on their behalf, using money from cattle sales or migrant wages. After 1881 Africans were allowed to acquire land, as long as it was registered in the name of the Superintendent of Natives. Internally the tenure systems continued to operate as versions of 'communal', 'customary' or 'traditional' tenure – although many land purchasing groups were socially heterogeneous and not necessarily 'tribal' in character (Small and Winkler 1992).

According to Sansom (1974: 168-69) the general trend in southern Africa was towards 'adaptation' of customary tenure to meet the new conditions of land shortage resulting from both population increase and the restrictions of Africans to the reserves. He cites Gluckman's (1961) view that the basic principle that every male member of the tribe has a right to land to support his family was generally upheld by chiefs (principle 2), who were then forced by scarcity progressively to commandeer and re-allocate first unused land, then fallowed land, and then to restrict each family to a defined area. Sansom also cites evidence of bribery of chiefs in relation to land (ibid: 169).

Chanock (1991: 64) questions the accuracy of models of customary land tenure developed in the early colonial period, and suggests that:

> The development of the concept of a leading customary role for the chiefs with regard to ownership and allocation of land was fundamental to the evolution of the paradigm of customary tenure.... the chiefs were seen as the holders of land with rights of administration and allocation. Rights in land were seen as flowing downward. Whatever they were, they were derived from the political authority, rather than residing in the peasantry.

This essentially feudal model suited colonial powers seeking to acquire land for settlers and urban settlements and became part of the apparatus of indirect rule. As a consequence, both individual ownership and sales of land were anathema, because these would 'tend to disrupt the native polity'.[8] A model based on chiefs' control over land helped to underpin a system of local political control (ibid: 69).

In addition, there was 'spirited opposition to individuation' from within African society itself (ibid: 66). This was partly because the ambitions of settlers and corporations to increase their land holdings and to limit those of Africans aroused the resentment and anxiety of peoples already displaced and fearing further loss of their land. Communalism was 'a way of certifying African control of occupation, use, and allocation of land, rather than a description of rights exercised. Individualism was a code word for sale to Europeans' (ibid: 66).

Chanock recommends stepping back from attempts at systematisation, and from 'ideologies of traditional communalism' (ibid: 70). Instead, questions should be asked about specific conflicts of interest over land during the colonial period: just who was pressing for a greater individualisation of rights? What sort of rights did they have in mind? Who was resisting this pressure, and why?

A cultivator might say 'mine' when title was challenged, or if it was advantageous to sell or mortgage, may think in terms of 'ours' – in terms of nuclear family – when asserting a right of inheritance against a larger group of kin, or 'ours' in terms of a lineage – if the claimant was outside the lineage (as a spouse might be) (ibid: 72-3).

A detailed account of the changing character of 'communal tenure' over time is found in Beinart's (1982) study of Pondoland. In the mid-nineteenth century relationships between chiefs and their people were structured mainly by the social relations governing the circulation of cattle, in the form of loans and bridewealth payments, through which followings were built and homesteads extended. According to Beinart (1982: 18):

---

8   Meek (1946) cited in Chanock 1991: 64.

Chiefs certainly did not exercise their power primarily by controlling access to specific pieces of land. Once a group had been accepted by the chief and had an area of settlement pointed out, the distribution of land for cultivation was largely left to individual homestead heads.... Chiefs did, however, exercise more direct control over communal resources such as the major forests.

Pondoland was annexed by the Cape in 1894, the area was divided into districts under the control of colonial magistrates, and hut taxes were introduced. Districts were divided into locations under government appointed headmen. Most chiefs became headmen but their geographical jurisdiction was limited to one location even if it had previously been much larger; commoners were also elevated to chieftaincies. These appointments and the associated delimitation of boundaries generated major disputes, and became part of a struggle between the colonial state and the paramount chief for the support of headmen. This, together with their intermediate position between the state and the people, allowed headmen to build local power bases for themselves, and undermined the system of paying tribute or 'customary dues' to chiefs, which declined. Wage labour became vitally important, and advances of cattle by traders against future migrant income altered the balance of power within large, composite homesteads. Younger migrant men gained more independent access to wives and could begin to establish their own homesteads. Homestead heads began to play a less central role in the allocation of land, which was in any case seen by the colonial state as a function of headmen (ibid: 97).

In the early decades of the twentieth century chiefs and headmen resisted any attempts to dispossess Mpondo of their land or to radically alter the system of communal tenure. A minority of wealthier cultivators who wanted to grow cash crops and extend their arable lands may have found communal tenure a constraint, but the majority of the rural population supported communal tenure because it was 'their ultimate guarantee of access to both arable plots and grazing' (ibid: 126). Furthermore, the allocation of land through chiefs and headmen enabled ordinary people to 'exercise some control over land' through influencing local political processes, and communal tenure 'was symbolised by the powers of the chieftaincy'. For Beinart this apparent convergence should not obscure the fact that significant changes in the tenure system had occurred and that 'there were different shadings of interest at work' (ibid: 126), explaining persistent tensions between chiefs, headmen, the administration and commoners. This account echoes Chanock's (1991: 70) emphasis on interest groups and power relations as the key to understanding both continuities and changes in land tenure through the colonial transition.

These interests were deeply gendered, as Beinart's account makes clear. Walker (2002) emphasises shifts in the character of women's land rights, in the context of pressures towards individualised interpretations of custom:

> ... the interpretation of 'customary' law by colonial administrators and magistrates served to strengthen, not weaken, patriarchal controls over women

and to freeze a level of subordination to male kin (father, husband, brother-in-law, son) that was unknown in precolonial societies... this project involved not simply the imposition of eurocentric views and prejudices on the part of colonisers, but also the collusion of male patriarchs within African society, who were anxious to shore up their diminishing control over female reproductive and productive power (Walker 2002: 11).

In sum, indigenous social formations in southern African societies were deeply affected by the transition to colonial rule and the incorporation of local agrarian economies into wider political and economic relations. These resulted in a number of (sometimes contradictory) changes in and adaptations of pre-colonial tenure regimes: (a) a greater stress on individual and family rights and decision making in relation to land; (b) a defensive stress on the group-based nature of land rights; (c) redefinitions of women's land rights as 'secondary' and subordinate to those of husbands and men; (d) chiefs and headmen becoming the symbol of resistance to colonial rule and loss of land; (e) chiefs and headmen being used by the state as instruments of indirect rule and as a result acquiring greater powers over land than they had previously enjoyed; (f) the erosion of mechanisms that constrained the power of traditional leaders and kept them responsive to rights holders, these being replaced by a requirement for 'upward accountability' to the state, creating opportunities for abuse of power and corruption.

Despite the clear evidence of change, continuities are also observable. The principles identified above are much in evidence in descriptions of a variety of specific land tenure regimes in the colonial period, with individual and family rights to land remaining defined and limited by social relations and collective identities to varying degrees, even where they were asserted more strongly than before in response to changing conditions. Land rights continued to be derived in the first instance from accepted membership of a group, with outsiders able to join the group through a variety of mechanisms. Production systems continued to include shared grazing areas and household use of other common property resources. In relation to principle 4 (the clear distinction between access and control) it is clear that policies of indirect rule, and the 'decentralised despotism' they gave rise to (Mamdani 1996) led to tighter control over land allocation by chiefs and headmen than had been the case in many tenure systems in the pre-colonial era – nevertheless, many decisions over land continued to be made at the lower levels of the hierarchy of traditional authority.

The Era of Segregation & Apartheid

The 1913 Land Act was intended to lay the basis for a 'segregationist social order' in the newly established Union of South Africa. It did not create the reserve system so much as entrench the existing locations and overall distribution of land. The Act was a holding measure while the Beaumont Commission developed recommendations for a permanent land dispensation. The scheduled 'native areas' covered seven per cent of the land area of the country, but in practice Africans occupied a much larger area. There were long delays in the making of policy, and the impasse created a need to allow African land purchases outside the scheduled areas, which was possible if the Governor General gave his approval. Land so acquired was held in trust by the Minister of Native Affairs, and had to be effected on a 'tribal' basis rather than as a purchase by a 'community' or a partnership. Some groups, however, managed to purchase land as companies (Delius et al. 1997).

The 1936 Land and Trust Act added another six per cent of the country to the area in which Africans would be allowed land rights. A body called the South African Native Trust[9] was established, in which all crown land set aside for 'native occupation' would vest. The Act also allowed regulations to 'prescribe the conditions on which natives may hire, purchase or occupy land held by the Trust', and to control soil erosion. Regulations were passed that drastically reduced tenure security. Land holders' rights to transfer or bequeath land were limited, the size of allotments was set, and women's land rights were severely circumscribed. As Delius et al. (1997: 38) comment, 'access to land depended upon the whims of white officials and strict observation of a host of regulations', and there was 'a reduction in the scope for flexibility and diversity in land holdings which had characterised "customary" systems'. Resentment of this pattern of intensified state intervention in land tenure helped provoke major rural revolts (as in Sekhukhuneland and Pondoland) from the 1940s to the early 1960s (Chaskalson 1987). Trust land was also used by the state to accommodate the victims of forced removals or farm evictions from the 1950s onwards.

Large numbers of farms purchased and long-settled by Africans became known as 'black spots'. Located mostly in the Transvaal and Natal, they were targeted for forced removals when apartheid policies were implemented after 1950. Often operating systems of communal tenure within their boundaries, these areas also accommodated large numbers of evictees from farms, usually as tenants of the land owners in the (black) areas they were moved to, partly due to the continuing strength of the African land ethic. The high population densities that resulted often led to severe strains on the tenure system.

A drive towards uniform approaches and increased levels of state interference was evident in the Native Administration Act of 1927 (Delius et al. 1997). Africans were to be governed in a distinct domain legitimated by 'custom' and chiefly rule, but under strict control from above. The Governor General, as 'supreme chief of all natives in the provinces of Natal, Transvaal and the Orange Free State' could recognise or appoint anyone as a chief or headman and define the boundaries of any tribe or location.

The Bantu Authorities Act of 1951, along with betterment planning and

9   Later renamed the South African Development Trust (SADT)

authoritarian regulation of land rights under Trust tenure, was a key factor in the rural rebellions of the 1950s (Mbeki 1964). It involved the establishment of tribal authorities, a version of 'traditional rule' that was highly authoritarian, 'stripped of many of the elements of popular representation and accountability which had existed within pre-colonial political systems and which had to some extent survived within... the reserves' (Delius et al. 1997: 39). Many chiefs used their new-found powers and reduced accountability to allocate better quality land to themselves and their supporters, and to demand higher payments for allocations (Mbeki 1964; Mamdani 1996; Ntsebeza 2003).

Proclamation R.188 of 1969, issued under the powers vested in the State President (formerly the Governor General) under the Native Administration Act and the 1936 Land Act, was intended to regulate further the operation of land tenure in black areas. Two forms of tenure were recognised – quitrent for surveyed land and 'Permission to Occupy' (PTO) certificates for unsurveyed land. Severe limitations on the content of the rights of holders were laid down, for example, one man-one lot; restrictions on plot size; a rigid system of male primogeniture to govern inheritance; and non-recognition of female land rights. Officials were given extensive powers to appropriate land and to cancel quitrent titles and PTOs. Chiefs and headmen undertook the task of allocation, agricultural officers surveyed the boundaries of sites and fields, and magistrates issued the PTOs. Registers of permit holders were kept at the magistrate's offices.

In the Bantustan era (1948-90) large areas of land occupied by blacks (including, in the Transvaal in particular, a large number of purchased farms) were transferred to the 'self-governing territories' and many communities were placed under the jurisdiction of government-recognised chiefs and Tribal Authorities. The governments of the Bantustans passed a host of laws to further regulate land tenure.

In the colonial and apartheid eras the retention of 'communal' land tenure was intended to underpin cheap labour policies and cost-effective control of rural populations from above. But the system also widened access to relatively independent, land-based livelihoods and helped rural communities to resist exploitation and state control, and was often actively defended by them (Beinart 1982; Delius et al. 1997). The effect was to provide elements of both continuity and change in land tenure systems, to varying degrees in different areas, depending on the outcomes of local political struggles and how, and how much, state policies were implemented.

The contemporary period

Most contemporary South African case-studies of 'communal tenure' echo earlier ethnographic descriptions in characterising land tenure in the former reserves as being simultaneously 'communal' and 'individual' in nature (principle 3).[10] This literature also contains contrasting interpretations of the origin of land rights and the meaning of 'land allocation': some authors portray rights as deriving primarily from allocations of plots by an authority structure (Ntsebeza 1999: 75, 101; Ntsebeza 2005: 219-20; Oomen 2005: 157-8), while others see the origin of rights in accepted membership of a 'community', and portray 'allocation' as an essentially administrative procedure to ensure that land is distributed fairly and to avoid boundary disputes (Alcock and Hornby 2004: 13). Fay (2005: 189-90) describes land access in Hobeni in the Eastern Cape as occurring largely through inheritance or sub-division of existing plots, without any need to consult with the headman or sub-headman (principle 4). Small and Winkler (1992: 6) describe land allocation amongst the Bafarutse ba Braklaagte as being undertaken by an elder representing the clan on the kgotla (council of elders) within large areas set aside for extended family groups or clans (*kgoros*).

Rights to residential and arable plots are usually portrayed as being held by households with married men at their head (Cross and Friedman 1997; Turner 1999; Alcock and Hornby 2004). In some contexts single women with children to support are also allocated land (Meer 1997; Thorp 1997; Sithole 2004; Fay 2005). The principle that families who need land to establish an independent base for their livelihoods must be allocated plots is still widely upheld. The pre-1994 system of issuing Permission to Occupy (PTO) certificates is still in place in some areas and provinces but not in others. Whether or not officials still survey and demarcate plots, as they used to do in the apartheid period, is also highly variable (Macintosh et al. 1998). The lack of clarity over how land should be administered at present can itself gives rise to tensions and disputes over land rights (MacIntosh et al. 1998; Turner 1999; Lahiff and Aphane 2000).

The idea that communal land cannot be bought or sold is still strongly articulated by many residents (Alcock and Hornby 2004: 17), but in some areas, such as Pondoland, it is evident that sales do in fact take place (Kepe, personal communication). Sale of buildings or other permanent improvements such as fruit trees is usually seen as acceptable, but allocation of the land itself must then follow a procedure similar to that followed when outsiders apply for land (Turner 1999: 13). However, in some areas chiefs and headmen sell land to outsiders without such procedures being applied (Ntsebeza 1999: 74-5; Oomen 2005: 158, 173).

In Ekuthuleni, a former mission station farm in KwaZulu-Natal, landholders have the right to allocate, lend and bequeath their land, and to sell houses, hence, in effect, the land they occupy (Hornby 2000). Relatives who need land

10   For KwaZulu-Natal, see Alcock and Hornby 2004, Cross 1994, Ferguson and Sithole 2004, Hornby 2000, Liversage 1993, Sithole 2004 and Walker 1997; for Eastern Cape, see de Wet 1996, Fay 2005, Kingwill 1996, Kepe 1999 and 2001, McAllister 1986, Ntsebeza 1999, and Turner 1999; for Limpopo see Claassens 2001; Lahiff 2000, Lahiff and Aphane 2000, and Oomen 2000, 2005; for North West, see Small and Winkler 1992; for Mpumalanga, see Levin and Mkhabela 1997 and Small and Winkler 1992.

(including single mothers, widows and elderly women) are generally allocated plots, and in practice neither allocations nor sales to outsiders currently occur. Vacant land is the responsibility of the local headman or nduna to allocate in consultation with an ibandla (group of neighbours). There is currently a lack of agreement over some aspects of the tenure system (e.g. whether or not loans are permanent, and whether or not payment to the nduna is required), over precisely what a land allocation means, and over how disputes should be resolved. This has led to anxiety over tenure security, deriving from 'unclear adaptations of rules and procedures', themselves an indication of 'processes of change in response to internal and external pressures' (Ziqube et al. 2001: 6).

In some parts of the country the apartheid-era relocation of large numbers of people, together with attempts to consolidate 'homeland' boundaries and the placement of all rural residents under the jurisdiction of a tribal author-ity, led to the creation of patchworks of farms occupied by groups of diverse origin and identity. Registered titles are sometimes held by different 'owners', and some farms are subject to competing restitution claims. Two detailed case-studies from Limpopo Province illustrate the complexities and the ten-sions that can result – Dikgale (Lahiff and Aphane 2000), and Rakgwadi (Small 1997; Claassens 2001). These illustrate a more general point: simplistic notions of homogenous 'communities', with clearly defined social and territo-rial boundaries and under the accepted authority of traditional leaders, are inappropriate in many communal areas in South Africa.

Awareness of post-1994 constitutional rights to gender equality has led to recognition in some areas that widows, unmarried women and divorcees with children to support are entitled to land in their own right (Turner 1999; Alcock and Hornby 2004; Sithole 2004), but the extent of these new practices appears to be uneven (Claassens and Ngubane 2003). In parts of the Eastern Cape it applies only to residential land (Turner 1999). In Limpopo province it has been reported that women are particularly vulnerable to accusations of witchcraft, which constitutes grounds for loss of land rights (Lahiff and Aphane 2000: 26). Because of these problems, some women in communal areas are in favour of individual title as a way to secure their independent land rights (Claassens 2003).

Contemporary studies reveal that rights of access to common property resources are still important for rural livelihoods in many areas (Shackleton et al. 2000). Rights to land usually include rights to use or collect natural resources from the commons (principle 3). In some cases rights and duties are subject to well-defined community rules and management regimes, enforced by local authorities such as traditional leaders or elected committees (Cous-ins 1996; McAllister 2001). In others these management regimes have broken down and 'open access' prevails (Turner 1999). The area within which com-munity members may use or collect common property resources usually varies by the resource in question (principles 4 and 5). For example, often grazing is restricted to the boundaries of a village, or of a group of villages under a head-man (sometimes called 'wards' or 'administrative areas', or isigodi in Kwazulu-Natal). Primary rights to use resources such as forest patches or woodlots may be held by specific villages, or wards, or may be held by members of the wider 'community' (e.g. the 'tribe'). In most cases these boundaries are flexible and negotiable, rather than being exclusive (Alcock and Hornby 2004). They can also be the focus of conflicts (Cousins 1996; Turner 1999).

Many case-studies show that land administration is spatially and institutionally nested (principle 4). Despite attempts by colonial and apartheid regimes to centralise decision making in the hands of an 'upwardly account-able' traditional leadership, in many areas allocations of residential and arable land to newcomers are still undertaken at the local level and involve prospec-tive neighbours as key decision makers, usually under the oversight of either a traditional or an elected leadership (Turner 1999; Alcock and Hornby 2004; Fay 2005; Ntsebeza 2005). The relevant social and administrative unit is vari-ously termed a neighbourhood (e.g. the isithebe in Pondoland), a sub-ward (umhlati in isiZulu-speaking areas), a sub-village, or a village. In some places traditional leadership is no longer seen as legitimate and elected committees play these roles (Turner 1999).

Fay (2005) describes the situation in Hobeni in the Eastern Cape as one in which land access is governed at the level of the neighbourhood, with varia-tions in tenure practices related to their kinship composition. These neigh-bourhoods are nested within a number of larger structures but primary deci-sion making rests with 'those who inhabit and use the land: neighbourhoods organised under sub-headmen' – and is characterised by 'downward account-ability and flexibility' (ibid: 199).

Land allocation to an outsider often requires payment by the applicant of a fee of some kind, seen as 'chief's dues' in some places, or an indication of acceptance of the authority of traditional structures (khonza in isiZulu-speaking areas), or simply as an administrative fee (Alcock and Hornby 2004; Kepe personal communication). However, in many places payments for land rights are made to chiefs or headmen without any oversight by neighbours or the wider community (Ntsebeza 1999; Oomen 2005) who often perceive this as corruption (Claassens 2003).

The contemporary literature contains many examples of underlying com-monalities and continuities in land tenure regimes. These studies also show, however, that social and political values, identities and relationships are under stress as a result of ongoing processes of change, giving rise to tension and conflicts over the precise definition of both collective identities and individ-ual rights (Kepe 1999; Ntsebeza 1999; Hornby 2000; Claassens 2001; Oomen 2005). 'Community members' are increasingly of heterogeneous social origin, given high levels of mobility, and acquisition of rights via birth is only one of several routes to such membership. Although not documented much in the available literature, anecdotal evidence suggests that purchase is an increasingly common mechanism for acquiring land rights, either from individual residents or from traditional leaders.

Commonality & continuity

The five 'underlying principles' identified here might have a degree of validity as descriptions of key elements of 'communal' tenure regimes, but this is a different matter to explaining why, in some instances, to different degrees, and in different ways, they have persisted over time and are shared across a range of variable conditions and circumstances. Explanation is always more challenging than description, and I do not attempt to address this issue in a systematic manner here, suggesting only some possible lines of enquiry. Commonalities and continuities may arise as a result of a combination of these factors:

a) similar state policies in different times and places that aimed at preserving 'customary' regimes of land tenure and governance, such as policies to create and maintain labour reserves for migrant labour, or to save costs in maintaining order through systems of 'indirect rule' via chiefs;

b) the practical advantages of 'communal' tenure to Africans, who across the region were losing or had lost land to settlers and saw this form of tenure as a way to collectively defend their rights to productive resources (cf. Beinart 1982);

c) the significance of common property resources and rights within production systems based on dryland cropping, animal traction and communal grazing, or on shifting cultivation, as well as the importance of continued access to other natural resources from the commons;

d) underlying commonalities in 'culture' and 'values', or perhaps what Guyer (2004: 6) calls 'plausible conventions and institutions', those 'persistent elements and relationships by which people individually and collectively create economies'.

Wider African debates

What does recent writing on land tenure in Africa more broadly have to say on these issues? One key theme is change and conflict, leading to scepticism about 'idealised' models of communal tenure (Chimhowu and Woodhouse 2006: 348). Berry's (1993) influential view that property rights are flexible and involve ongoing social and political processes of negotiation as the key to understanding is being challenged. Peters (2002; 2004), for example, takes issue with dominant images of African land tenure as 'relatively open, negotiable and adaptive customary systems', and stresses instead 'processes of exclusion, deepening social divisions and class formation'. She suggests that 'commodification, structural adjustment, market liberalisation and globalisation' tend to 'limit or end negotiation and flexibility for certain social groups or categories' (Peters 2004: 270).

Competition and conflict over land are increasing in Africa, Peters argues, because of the confluence of a number of intersecting processes: the need of many rural families to produce more from their land even though inputs are declining; civil servants and others in employment seeking to produce food and cash crops from family land; the state and environmental groups trying to extend the area under conservation; and the intensification of the exploitation of resources such as minerals, wildlife, water and trees (ibid: 286). These realities require analysts to go beyond formulations of land being 'socially embedded' in order to raise questions about 'the type of social and political relations in which land is situated, particularly with reference to relations of inequality – of class, ethnicity, gender and age' (ibid: 278). Peters sees a key 'socio-cultural dynamic of differentiation' emerging within social units such as the family, lineage, village, 'tribe' or 'ethnically defined group', which can be understood as 'a process of narrowing in the definition of belonging', with 'group boundaries [becoming] more exclusively defined' (ibid: 302).

Other scholars have drawn attention to the increasing prevalence of land being acquired through a variety of market transactions, including purchase, rental and sharecropping (Lund 2001; Andre 2003; Mathieu et al. 2003; Sjaastad 2003; Woodhouse 2003; Daley 2005a, 2005b; Chimhowu and Woodhouse 2006). This brings with it 'an increasing individualisation of control of land and in some instances its alienation from any form of customary authority, amounting to effective privatisation of land' (Chimhowu and Woodhouse 2005: 352). In most cases, however, market-based access 'remains encumbered by customary tenure', and hence transactions in these 'vernacular' land markets have no form of statutory protection (ibid: 392). Scarcity of land due to population growth is only one driver of this process; others include the growth of markets for agricultural commodities (e.g. horticultural products for urban markets), the impact of new technologies for water management, tree cropping or crop transport, growth in non-farm and wage income, population migration, and urbanisation and the emergence of land markets in 'customary' areas around towns and cities (ibid: 353-6). Three main categories of buyers are identified – 'new big men' with jobs and influence, migrants without claims to customary rights, and those with kinship ties in areas where land is scarce, who purchase or rent from senior male relatives. Key sellers are 'senior men' and especially tribal chiefs (ibid: 359). For Chimhowu and Woodhouse, land policies need to consider the 'key question' of how 'regulation and reform of such markets relates to their impact on the poor' (ibid: 366).

Some analysts describe the emergence of informal institutional innovations in the recording of signed documents to legitimise increasingly widespread transactions in land, in an attempt to reduce the ambiguity and uncertainty associated with the rights so acquired (Mathieu 2001; Andre 2003; Lavigne-Delville 2003; Mathieu et al. 2003.) They can involve local officials (who witness these transactions in the name of the government department they represent, but according to 'unofficial rules') as well as private individuals with local legitimacy (Lavigne-Delville 2003: 102). These records are often not sufficient, however, to prevent their being contested by others with prior claims based on kinship or custom (Mathieu et al. 2003: 123; Chimhowu and Woodhouse 2005: 400), and 'idioms of tradition' together with 'the perseverance of local politics and the logic of inclusion' preclude easy assumptions as to the exclusionary outcomes of such processes (Benjaminsen and Lund 2003: 9).

The picture that emerges from these studies is not one of steady evolutionary change towards individualised forms of property and the disappearance of 'customary' identities and claims to land. Mathieu et al. (2003: 126-7) suggest that where land becomes scarce and has increasing economic value, 'there is a social demand for more individualised, precise and formalised land ownership rights', but that 'this change is not so simple, nor is it linear or automatic'. The process is 'totally embedded in social relationships' and hence 'contradictory, complex and ambiguous', since past meanings of land 'retain their significance in the local social reality'. Chimhowu and Woodhouse (2005: 401) acknowledge that 'the transition from the "gifts" expected as tokens of acknowledgement of customary authority and of anticipated reciprocity, to payments more closely related to exchange values of the land, is not always easy to define'. Lund (2001: 157-9) points out that formalisation of individual and private titles, as in Kenya, has not necessarily produced greater certainty and security of land rights because of a lack of social legitimacy, and that processes of 'informal formalisation' probably depend on a degree of uncertainty remaining as to the status of such transactions at the 'margins of the law as well as of customs'.

More generally, processes of change often generate resistance, contestation and the reassertion of 'customary' claims to land. As Peters (2004: 302) suggests, (citing Woodhouse et al. 2000: 2) they are inevitably 'uneven and contradictory' in character. 'Moreover, boundaries, physical and legal, do not automatically ensure exclusion where (some of) the excluded reject the legitimacy of the exclusion' (Peters 2004: 303). Alongside change is continuity in the nature of land rights, argued for and actively reproduced because of its advantages for many within the rural population, including, in some contexts, women (Odgaaard 2003: 83). Flexibility and negotiability, which in many places have given way to differentiation and exclusion, 'remain an important asset to small-scale producers across the continent' (Peters 2004: 305-6).

This brief excursion into the wider literature suggests that contemporary processes of social, economic and political change can produce fundamental shifts in the nature of land rights and associated systems of authority, so that the distinctive features discussed above may no longer be present as 'underlying principles'. However, there is also evidence that the social and political embeddedness of land relations remains key to understanding how land tenure systems work in practice, and that in many cases land rights are still shared rather than exclusive, are based on accepted group membership, involve access to the commons, and are nested or layered in character – in short, that these principles have not been completely eclipsed in contemporary Africa, and assist in understanding the nature of current processes of change.

Alternative approaches to tenure reform

What are the implications of this analysis for policy? In the South African context, debates around the Communal Land Rights Act demonstrate how problematic attempts to recognise 'customary' land rights can be. In a larger context where private property dominates and security of tenure is equated with exclusive ownership, but chiefs continue to be a significant political interest group, transferring private ownership to 'traditional communities' ruled by traditional councils, and without effective mechanisms for downward accountability, threatens rather than secures land rights. One reason, as Claassens and I have argued (Cousins and Claassens 2004), is that this approach entrenches a version of 'custom' that emerged during the colonial era, and continues to lead to abuses of power.

In my view, the underlying principles identified above have proved remarkably resilient in the South African context, informing context-specific practices that evolve over time. Is there a way, then, to secure these distinctive forms of land rights without replicating problematic versions of 'custom', and in a manner that promotes democratic decision making? Can policy both secure rights on the ground, and also allow rights-holders to adapt or alter their tenure system through deliberate choices over time in response to changing circumstances? Relevant here are the tenure reform principles set out in the South African White Paper on Land Policy (DLA 1997). These require that the law be brought in line with de facto realities, but that these realities also be transformed to bring them in line with constitutional principles of democracy and equality, and thus to include freedom of choice in relation to both land rights and the institutions that will administer those rights.

The way beyond the 'customs versus rights' polarity, I suggest, is to vest land rights in individuals rather than in groups or institutions, and to make socially legitimate existing occupation and use, or de facto 'rights', the primary basis for legal recognition. These claims may or may not be justified by reference to 'custom'. Rights holders would be entitled to define collectively the precise content of their rights, and choose, by majority vote, the representatives who will administer their land rights (e.g. by keeping records, enforcing rules and mediating disputes). Accountability of these representatives would be downwards to group members, not upwards to the state. Gender equality would be a requirement before legal recognition of rights could occur.

A key question is the nature of those individual rights. I am not suggesting a form of individual titling, which has been so problematic in Africa, but rather a form of statutory right that is legally secure but also qualified by the rights of others within a range of nested social units, from the family through user groups to villages and other larger 'communities' with shared rights to a range of common property resources. Women's rights within the family as well as other units need to be explicitly recognised.

Another central issue is the boundaries of the relevant social units within which land rights are held, and should therefore be the key decision making units. Again, existing practice that is socially legitimate could provide the basis for decisions by groups of rights-holders as to their social and territorial boundaries, and allow legal recognition of grounded institutional realities, within a framework that requires the democratisation of decision making. A key requirement, however, would be recognition of the relatively flexible nature of those boundaries, depending on the resources and decisions in question, and given the nested or layered character of rights to shared resources. There would thus need to be acknowledgment of the multiple 'communities' within which land rights are held.

This approach does not require attempts at codification of what are likely to be dynamic and changing practices, but does allow the key features of property regimes that are distinct from 'Western-legal' regimes to be secured in law. Moore's (1998) and Berry's (1990) suggestions that policy must aim to strengthen institutional spaces for the mediation of competing claims to land are critically important, but so are the views of Lavigne-Delville (1999), Peters (2004) and Woodhouse (2003), who emphasise that unequal power relations within local institutional contexts have to be addressed. What is 'socially legitimate' is always subject to contestation. This means that the political embeddedness of land rights must be explicitly acknowledged. Democratising land administration will require providing support to rights-holders within local institutional processes, and a degree of central government oversight (Woodhouse 2003). In addition to clarifying the nature of the rights at stake, this approach could provide 'a framework for their further evolution' (Sawadogo and Stamm 2000, cited by Daley and Hobley 2005: 35).

Conclusion

Land tenure reform remains a key policy issue in Africa, given the large proportion of the population that relies on land and natural resources for their livelihoods. It is not enough to recognise the socially and politically embedded character of land rights, or the unequal outcomes of contemporary forms of 'enclosure'. Privatisation and complete individualisation of land are uneven and contested, and in many places the nature and content of land rights remain quite distinct from 'Western-legal' forms of property. In these situations, individual titling is not a feasible solution. If one adopts a 'rights without illusions' perspective (Hunt 1991), legal recognition of these distinctive forms of land rights can form part of a broader strategy to secure rights through political struggle, and must involve external support for rights holders within local institutional and political processes.

The alternative to individual titling is not a simple ratification of current systems of 'customary' land rights, which often privilege both traditional and non-traditional 'big men' (and men in general) – but vesting rights in individuals who share rights with others within a variety of nested social units, the territorial boundaries of which vary with the resource or decision at issue, and are thus flexible. The alternative approach also requires that decisions concerning these shared and relative rights are subject to the democratic principle of downward accountability to a majority of rights-holders. In turn this implies a key role for the central state in overseeing local governance. This takes us beyond the 'custom vs rights' polarity, in a manner that accords with the perspectives of many of those affected, like the rural groupings challenging the constitutionality of South Africa's Communal Land Rights Act.

References

Adams, M., B. Cousins and S. Manona. 2000. 'Land tenure and economic development in rural South Africa: constraints and opportunities', in B. Cousins (ed.), *At the Crossroads: Land and Agrarian Reform in South Africa into the 21st Century*. Cape Town: Programme for Land and Agrarian Studies, University of the Western Cape and National Land Committee), pp. 111-28.

Alcock, R. and D. Hornby. 2004. 'Traditional Land Matters: A Look into Land Administration in Tribal Areas in KwaZulu-Natal' (Pietermaritzburg, Legal Entity Assessment Project).

Andre, Catherine. 2003. 'Custom, Contract and Cadastres in North-West Rwanda', in T.A. Benjaminsen and C. Lund (eds), *Securing Land Rights in Africa*. London and Portland, OR: Frank Cass, pp. 153-72.

Beinart, W. 1982. *The Political Economy of Pondoland, 1860-1930*. Johannesburg: Ravan Press.

Beinart, W. and C. Bundy. 1987. *Hidden Struggles in Rural South Africa. Politics and Popular Movements in the Transkei and Eastern Cape, 1890-1930*. Johannesburg: Ravan Press.

Benjaminsen, T.A. and C. Lund (eds). 2003. *Securing Land Rights in Africa*. London and Portland, OR: Frank Cass.

— 2001. *Politics, Property and Production in the West African Sahel*. Uppsala: Nordiska Afrikainstitutet.

Bennett, T.W. 2004. *Customary Law in South Africa*. Cape Town: Juta.

— 2002. 'Debating the Land Question in Africa', *Comparative Studies in Society and History* 44, 4, pp. 638-68.

— 1993. *No condition is permanent: The social dynamics of agrarian change in sub-Saharan Africa*. Madison, WI: University of Wisconsin Press.

— 1990. 'Land Tenure and Agricultural Performance in Africa', Conference on Rural Land Tenure, Credit, Agricultural Investment, and Farm Productivity, Nairobi, 4-8 June.

Biebuyck, D. 1963. 'Introduction', in D. Biebuyck (ed.), *African Agrarian Systems*. London:

Oxford University Press, pp. 1-64.

Bohannon, P. 1963. '"Land", "Tenure", and Land Tenure', in D. Biebuyck (ed.), *African Agrarian Systems*. London: Oxford University Press, pp. 101-15.

Chanock, M. 1991. 'Paradigms, Policies and Property: A Review of the Customary Law of Land Tenure', in K. Mann and R. Roberts (eds) *Law in Colonial Africa*. Portsmouth: Heinemann Educational Books, pp. 61-84.

Chaskalson M. 1987. 'Rural resistance in the 1940s and 1950s', *Africa Perspectives*, New Series 5 and 6, pp. 47-59.

Chimhowu, A. and P. Woodhouse. 2006. 'Customary vs Private Property Rights? Dynamics and Trajectories of Vernacular Land Markets in Sub-Saharan Africa', *Journal of Agrarian Change* 6, 3, pp. 346-71.

Claassens, A. 2005. 'The Communal Land Rights Act and women: Does the Act remedy or entrench discrimination and the distortion of the customary?' Occasional Paper 28, Cape Town, Programme for Land and Agrarian Studies, University of the Western Cape.

— 2003. 'Community views on the Communal Land Rights Bill'. Research Report No. 15, Cape Town, Programme for Land and Agrarian Studies, University of the Western Cape.

— 2001. '"It is not easy to challenge a chief": Lessons from Rakgwadi'. Research Report No. 9, Cape Town, Programme for Land and Agrarian Studies, University of the Western Cape.

— 2000. 'South African proposals for tenure reform: the Draft Land Rights Bill', in C. Toulmin and J. Quan (eds), *Evolving Land Rights, Policy and Tenure in Africa*. London: International Institute for Environment and Development and Natural Resources Institute, pp. 247-66.

Claassens, A. and S. Ngubane. 2003. 'Rural women, land rights and the Communal Land Rights Bill'. Paper presented at a conference on Women and the Law, Cape Town, Women's Legal Centre.

Colson, E., 1971. 'The impact of the colonial period on the definition of land rights', in V. Turner (ed.), *The Impact of Colonialism*. Cambridge: Cambridge University Press, pp. 193-215.

— 1963. 'Land Rights and Land Use among the Valley Tonga of the Rhodesian Federation: the Background to the Kariba Resettlement Programme', in D. Biebuyck (ed.), *African Agrarian Systems*. London: Oxford University Press, pp. 137-56.

Comaroff, J. and J. Comaroff. 2006. 'Reflections on Liberalism, Policulturalism and ID-ology: citizenship and difference in South Africa', in S.L. Robins (ed.), *The Limits of Liberation after Apartheid: Citizenship, Governance and Culture*. Oxford: James Currey, pp. 33-56.

Cousins, B. 2005. 'Tenure Reform in South Africa: Titling versus Social Embeddedness', *Forum for Development Studies* 2, 2005, pp. 415-42.

— 1997. 'How Do Rights Become Real? Formal and Informal Institutions in South Africa's Land Reform', *IDS Bulletin* 28, 4, pp. 59-68.

— 1996. 'Livestock production and common property struggles in South Africa's agrarian reform', *Journal of Peasant Studies* 23, 166-208.

Cousins, B. and A. Claassens. 2004. 'Communal land rights, democracy and traditional leaders in post-apartheid South Africa', in M. Saruchera (ed.), *Securing Land and Resource Rights in Africa: Pan-African Perspectives*. Cape Town: Programme for Land and Agrarian Studies, University of the Western Cape, pp. 139-54.

Cross, C. 1994. 'Shack Tenure in Durban', in D. Hindson and J. McCarthy (eds), *Here to Stay, Informal Settlements in KwaZulu-Natal*. Durban: Indicator Press, pp. 170-90.

— 1992. 'An Alternate Legality: the Property Rights Question in Relation to South Africa Land Reform', *South African Journal of Human Rights* 8, 3, pp. 305-33.

Cross, C. and M. Friedman. 1997. 'Women and tenure: marginality and the left-hand power', in S. Meer (ed.), *Women, land and authority: perspectives from South Africa*. Cape Town: David Philip, pp. 17-34.

Daley, E. 2005a. 'Land and Social Change in a Tanzanian Village 1: Kinyanambo, 1920s – 1990', *Journal of Agrarian Change* 5, 3, pp. 363-404.

— 2005b. 'Land and Social Change in a Tanzanian Village 2: Kinyanambo in the 1990s', *Journal of Agrarian Change* 5, 4, pp. 526-72.

Daley, E. and M. Hoble. 2005. 'Land: Changing Contexts, Changing Relationships, Changing Rights'. Paper commissioned by Department for International Development.

Delius, P.K.R. and M. Chaskalson. 1997. 'A historical investigation of underlying rights to land registered as state owned'. Report commissioned by the Tenure Reform Core Group, Pretoria, Department of Land Affairs.

Department of Land Affairs (DLA). 1997. White Paper on South African Land Policy (Pretoria, Department of Land Affairs).

Fay, D. 2005. 'Kinship and Access to Land in the Eastern Cape: Implications for Land Reform', *Social Dynamics* 31, 1, pp. 182-207.

Ferguson, C. and M. Sithole. 2004. 'Intersection of Schemes and Customary Land Use Issues'. Paper presented at a workshop on Aligning Development Planning with Communal Tenure Arrangements, Midnet and Legal Entity Assessment Project, Pietermaritzburg.

Gluckman, M. 1965. *The Ideas in Barotse Jurisprudence*. Manchester: Manchester University Press.

Govender, P. 2004. 'Parliament gives rural women a raw deal', *Sunday Times*, 15 February.

Hornby, D. 2000. 'Tenure rights and practices on a state-owned farm: the community of Ekuthuleni', in B. Cousins (ed.), *At the Crossroads, Land and agrarian reform in South Africa into the 21st century*. Cape Town: University of the Western Cape and National Land Committee, pp. 311-17.

Hunter. M. 1979. *Reaction to Conquest*. Cape Town: David Philip.

Kingwill, R. 1996. 'Quitrent Tenure', material prepared for a training course on South African Land Tenure and Policy, Programme for Land and Agrarian Studies (School of Government, University of the Western Cape and Land Tenure Centre, Madison).

Kuper, A. 1997. 'The Academic Frontier. History and Social Anthropology in South Africa', in P. McAllister (ed.), *Culture and the Commonplace: Anthropological Essays in Honour of David Hammond-Tooke*. Johannesburg: Witwatersrand University Press, pp. 69-84.

Lahiff, E. and J. Alphane. 2000. *Communal Land Tenure: A Case Study of Dikgale Tribal Area, Northern Province*. Pietersburg-Polokwane: Nkuzi Development Association.

Lahiff, E. 2000. 'Land Tenure in South Africa's Communal Areas: A Case Study of the Arabie-Olifants Scheme', *African Studies* 59, 1, pp. 45-69.

Lentz, C. 2006. 'Decentralization, the State and Conflicts over Local Boundaries in Northern Ghana', *Development and Change* 57, 4, pp. 901-19.

Lund, C. 2002. 'Negotiating Property Institutions: the Symbiosis of Property and Authority in Africa', in K. Juul and C. Lund (eds), *Negotiating Property in Africa*. Portsmouth: Heinemann, pp. 11-43.

— 2001. 'Questioning Some Assumptions About Land Tenure', in T.A. Benjaminsen and C. Lund (eds), *Politics, Property and Production in the West African Sahel*. Uppsala: Nordiska Afrikainstitutet, pp. 144-62.

MacIntosh, Xaba and Associates. 1998. 'Land administration in the former homelands'. Report commissioned by the Department of Land Affairs.

Mamdani, M. 1996. *Citizen and Subject: Contemporary Africa and the Legacy of late Colonialism*. Princeton, NJ: Princeton University Press.

Mathieu, P., Z. Mahamadou and P. Lucinan. 2003. 'Monetary Land Transactions in Western Burkino Faso: Commoditisation, Papers and Ambiguities', in T.A. Benjaminsen and C. Lund (eds), *Securing Land Rights in Africa*. London and Portland: Frank Cass, pp. 109-28.

Mbeki, G. 1964. *The Peasant's Revolt*. Harmondsworth: Penguin.

Meer, S. (ed.) 1997. *Women, land and authority: perspectives from South Africa*. Cape Town: David Philip.

Moore, S.F. 1998. 'Changing African land tenure: reflections on the incapacities of the state', *European Journal of Development Research* 10, 2, pp. 33-49.

Murray, C. 2004. 'South Africa's troubled royalty: traditional leaders after democracy'. Law and Policy paper No. 3 (Canberra, Federation Press in association with the Centre for International and Public Law, Australian National University).

Nhlapo, T. 1995. 'African customary law in the interim Constitution', in S. Liebenberg (ed.), *The Constitution of South Africa from a Gender Perspective*. Cape Town: Community Law Centre, University of the Western Cape, pp. 157-66.

Ntsebeza, L. 1999. 'Land tenure reform, traditional authorities and rural local government in post-apartheid South Africa'. Research Report No. 3, Cape Town, Programme for Land and Agrarian Studies, University of the Western Cape.

— 2004. 'Democratic Decentralisation and Traditional Authority: Dilemmas of Land Admin-

istration in Rural South Africa', *European Journal of Development Research* 16, 1 pp. 71-89.
— 2003. 'Structures and Struggles of Rural Local Government in South Africa: the Case of Traditional Authorities in the Eastern Cape', PhD thesis, Rhodes University.
Okoth-Ogendo, H.W.O. 2002. 'The tragic African commons: A century of expropriation, suppression and subversion', Occasional Paper No. 24, Cape Town, Programme for Land and Agrarian Studies, University of the Western Cape.
— 1989. 'Some Issues of Theory in the Study of Tenure Relations in African Agriculture', *Africa* 59, 1, pp. 6-17.
Oomen, B. 2005. *Chiefs in South Africa. Law, Power and Culture in the Post-Apartheid Era.* Oxford, Pietermaritzburg, New York: James Currey, University of KwaZulu-Natal Press and Palgrave.
Peires, J.B. 2000. 'Traditional Leaders in Purgatory. Local Government in Tsolo, Qumbu and Port St Johns, 1990-2000', *African Studies* 59, 1, pp. 97-114.
Peters, P. 2004. 'Inequality and Social Conflict Over Land in Africa', *Journal of Agrarian Change*, 4,3, pp. 269-314.
— 2002. 'The Limits of Negotiability: Security, Equity and Class Formation in Africa's Land Systems', in K. Juul and C. Lund (eds), *Negotiating Property in Africa.* Portsmouth: Heinemann, pp. 45-66.
Republic of South Africa. 2004. *The Communal Land Rights Act No. 11 of 2004.* Cape Town: Government Gazette.
Royston, L. 2004. 'Barking dogs and building bridges: a contribution to making sense of Hernando de Soto's ideas in our context'. Paper presented at a workshop on The Perpetual Challenge of Informal Settlements, Wits University, 8-10 November.
Sansom B. 1974. 'Traditional economic systems', in W.D. Hammond-Tooke (ed.), *The Bantu-Speaking Peoples of Southern Africa.* London: Routledge & Kegan Paul, pp. 135-76.
Sawadogo, J-P. and V. Stamm. 2000. 'Local perceptions of indigenous tenure systems: views of peasants, women and dignitaries in a rural province of Burkino Faso', *Journal of Modern African Studies* 38, 2, pp. 279-94.
Schapera, Isaac. 1955. *A Handbook of Tswana Law and Custom.* London: Oxford University Press.
Shipton, P. 1988. 'The Kenyan Land Tenure Reform: Misunderstandings in the Public Creation of Private Property', in R.E. Downs and S.P. Reyna (eds), *Land and Society in Contemporary Africa.* Hanover, NH: University of New England Press, pp. 91-135.
Sibanda, S. 2004. 'Principles underpinning the Communal Land Rights Bill 2001', in M. Roth, V. Nxasana, S. Sibanda and T. Yates (eds), *National Land Tenure Conference: Finding Solutions, Securing Rights.* Durban: LexisNexis Butterworths, pp. 156-84.
Sithole, M. 2004. 'Communal land tenure versus individual housing tenure? Working together in housing provision'. Paper presented at the National Rural Housing Symposium, Johannesburg, 13 May.
Sjaastad, E. 2003. 'Trends in the Emergence of Agricultural Land Markets in Sub-Saharan Africa', *Forum for Development Studies* 30, 1, pp. 5-28.
Thorp, L. 1997. 'Access to land: a rural perspective on tradition and resources' in S. Meer (ed.), *Women, land and authority: perspectives from South Africa.* Cape Town: David Philip, pp. 35-44.
Turner, S. 1999. 'Land rights and land administration in the Herschel and Maluti Districts, Eastern Cape', Occasional Paper No. 10, Cape Town, Programme for Land and Agrarian Studies, University of the Western Cape, a paper presented at a World Bank Regional Workshop on Land Issues in Africa and the Middle East, Kampala, April 29-May.
Woodhouse, P. 2003. 'African Enclosures: A Default Mode of Development', *World Development* 31, 10, pp. 1705-20.
Ziqubu, N., T. Cousins and D. Hornby. 2001. 'Using local practices and records to secure individual tenure rights in common property situations'. Paper presented at the National Land Tenure Conference, Durban, 26-30 November.
Zulu, P. 1996. 'The Political Economy of Rural Livelihoods in KwaZulu-Natal', in M. Lipton, F. Ellis, and M. Lipton (eds), *Land, Labour and Livelihoods in Rural South Africa, Volume Two: KwaZulu-Natal and Northern Province.* Durban: Indicator Press, pp. 239-53.

8

Conflicts & Commercialisation Pressures over Forest Resources in the Post-Fast Track Land Reform Context in Zimbabwe:
A Case of Seke Communal Lands

Shylock Muyengwa

Introduction

Zimbabwe's post-independence land reform programme emphasised distribution of land for social equity to restore the colonially created imbalances (Mamimine 2003; Marimira and Odero 2003). Gonese and Mukora (2003) documented the resettlement models that the Government of Zimbabwe undertook on attainment of Independence in 1980. The main rationale behind the programme was to address:

> ... the three major dimensions of national land resource in the country namely historical inequality in distribution, the optimality of use and long term sustainability (Gonese and Mukora 2003: 174).

Market-based land redistribution represented by willing-buyer, willing-seller land acquisition was from 2000 onwards superseded by the Fast-Track Land Reform programme which involved the accelerated acquisition and demarcation of former white-owned commercial farmland and its allocation to indigenous blacks with minimal infrastructure and services development. The programme resulted in a significant shift in land holding between racial classes and consequently overlapping land and other related resource tenure arrangements in many contexts (Chatora 2003; Rugube et al. 2003).

Tenure is transitional (Bruce and Noronha 1987). In Zimbabwe, the government has managed to eliminate racial discrimination in land distribution but continued with the colonially instituted tenure. Three classes have consequently emerged, namely, state, communal and commercial land systems (Moyo et al. 1991). These de facto land tenure arrangements encompass '... overlapping property relations and multiple actors engaged in struggles over property rights ...' (Bruce and Fortmann 1989: 628). Murombedzi (1991) traces the impact of the colonial regime and how it incapacitated local level organisations as resource management units. The imposition of colonial governance shifted the locus of control of resources from natives to the colonialists.

Colonial state control mechanisms led to the weakening of local level institutions for utilising and managing natural resources. It was postulated that the panacea for resource degradation lay in developing an appropriate institutional framework through which 'clearly defined user groups can regulate resource utilisation and exclude non-users from the benefit of their own common resources' (Murombedzi 1991). The colonial system made irrelevant the local institutions that had worked well to ensure rational utilisation and guarantee equitable access to resources 'atrophied through disuse' (*Ibid*: 47). Colonial legislation and policies frequently faced resistance, prompting colonial regimes to resort to coercive and quasi-military action over the indigenous population. Murombedzi (1991) argues that individualising tenure will not solve the problems created by colonial legislation, especially for the small-scale holders whose livelihoods depend solely on access to the commons.

Thebaud (1995) identifies land tenure as bearing directly on access to and rights over resources. Changes in land use often lead to conflict. For example, Moyo et al. (1991: 11) noted that Zimbabwe's environmental dilemma '... lies in the land tenure system, structural features of the economy and hence the political and economic history'. Land tenure regimes not only result from physical, geographical or economic factors, but also from the user communities' forms of social organisation. It is instructive to note that access to land and related resources can be open where the user groups exploit the commons and at times it is individuals who extract such resources (Thebaud, 1999). Therefore, the natural environment has a social dimension. A tenure shift leads to disruption of the social processes and this might create '... enemies out of the communities for the land and the natural resources ...' (Mariko 1991: 215).

Land tenure regimes are constantly evolving and, depending on the ecological, economic and historical circumstances, different bodies of rights are found and many at times shared among individuals (Thebaud 1995). Land tenure regimes organise access to ground-based resources and determine appropriation mechanisms for the resources, defining who gets to harvest, where, when and how much at any given time. The security of tenure model is based on the assumption that land holding is under the control of an individual. The argument by most policy planners adopting this model is that if security of tenure is enhanced, peasants invest their time, effort and capital for the improvement of their properties or the resources lying on their plots (Fortmann and Bruce 1995). It has, however, been noted that tenure arrangements also encompass social processes, and individualising tenure might not be a solution, especially in contexts where shared norms are disrupted.

Maigga and Diallo (1998) established that investing in a property formerly held under common ownership leads to conflicts over natural resources contained within such jurisdictions. Hoskins (1994) also notes that land use rights can provide an incentive or disincentive for tree management. Therefore, the nature of land holding determines the management outcomes for most of the land-based resources, but there is need for these to balance with the demands of non-holder groups who have previously gained access to these resources. Fast-Track Land Reform led to a transformation of forests into agricultural fields and the loss of fuel wood sources to communal villagers. The new arrangement is indeed exclusionary, and '... remove(s) access to a necessity of life without providing a substitute' (Fortmann and Bruce 1995: 6). The next section reviews policy issues surrounding use of forests and forest resources in Zimbabwe and explores how policy related issues interact with tenure and resource use. This interaction affects relations between different forest resource users in terms of how they organise themselves in order to derive benefits from relevant resource items.

Forest resources management in Zimbabwe

Katerere et al. (1999) contend that forestry policy in Zimbabwe has lacked a single umbrella act – for example, both the Rural District Councils (RDC) Act of 1988 and Natural Resources Act of 1941 supervise the utilisation of forest resources. Separation of land and tree tenure has led to competition between and among land users. Indigenous woodland utilisation policy prohibited the felling of live wood, but it allowed people to harvest branches and collect dead wood. Individuals intending to harvest trees were required to get a permit from the kraal head. However, within the communal context, boundaries between communities are not explicit and some inhabitants encroach into other villages. Furthermore, poorly defined ownership and access rights over forests have led to conflicts; for example the one reported between Machangara and Gombera communities in the late 1990s (Katerere et al. 1999).

It is well demonstrated that land tenure arrangements influence access to and control of forest resources between land holders and non-land holders. However, access and use are mitigated at policy level, through state institutions with the mandate of overseeing use of these resources. The Forest Act (1982) deals with forestry issues and has provisions to set aside state forests and control tree-cutting for mining purposes, as well as for the compulsory afforestation of private land and protection of private forests (Moyo et al. 1991). The Act allows an individual to develop forests on private land and does not limit how he or she may use the trees. Provisions within this Act allow the Forestry Commission to force the owner of the land to afforestate to avert environmental degradation which might lead to erosion and river siltation threatening broader community or national welfare.

The Communal Lands Forest Produce Act (1987) aims to prevent 'outsiders' from extracting timber from communal areas for commercial purposes, and to limit commercial extraction within the communal areas to ensure that the scale of degradation is contained. It also allows communal area inhabitants to exploit the resources for 'own use' but limits commercial extraction

– this provision is, however, ambiguous as 'own use' might mean selling wood to raise income for family upkeep (Katerere et al. 1999). This ambiguity makes it difficult to differentiate between household use and commercial extraction, and the apparent lack of indices for sustainable harvesting is challenging.

There have been several challenges in the management of forest resources and communities have responded in different ways. For example, villagers in Machangara and Gombera villages in Seke District reported that illegal wood-cutting usually took place at night or in the absence of the kraal-head. These villagers sold fuel wood to urban residents. Those apprehended had their tools confiscated and handed over to the headman and subsequently to the police. However, inefficiency was reported to be rampant as most culprits were released within a short period of time, only to continue their illegal harvesting. People argued for increased state participation in the process of monitoring communal forests as a way for government to play a bigger role in financing forestry management (Katerere et al. 1999).

In some areas, ad hoc arrangements between communal villagers and neighbouring commercial farmers allowed the former to access resources within commercial farms. The Forestry Commission allowed for such an arrangement in state-owned forests to minimise conflicts with neighbouring inhabitants. Ad hoc arrangements enabled the Commission to deal with emergent problems like invasion of forests, establishment of settlements in the middle of the demarcated forests and indiscriminate cutting of trees for agricultural purposes. Resource-sharing models allowed the communal people to get firewood from dry trees, collect grass and graze their animals and, in return, help the Commission in protecting the forests. This worked well to minimise conflict between the Commission and the local communities. Such arrangements demonstrate the need to be highly 'in-inclusive' and co-opt all stakeholders so that they derive benefits and participate in the management of forest resources; such lessons could have been carried forward into the post-Fast-Track Land Reform context (Nhira et al. 1998). The following section analyses some of the practices and arrangements adopted in the study area, as well as their limitations in achieving effective natural resource management and minimising conflict over resource access.

Study aim

The presence of good road networks and affluent markets, as well as fuel wood scarcity, increases the potential for resource commercialisation. In such a context, however, there is need to maintain a balance between consumptive and commercial forest resource extraction. The process of maintaining such a balance can be negotiated through institutional mechanisms or may emerge as conflict and competition between different user groups. Fast-Track Land

Reform created challenges and opportunities for communal communities. The literature has pointed to local level institutional weakening due to colonial polices and centrally controlled administration. The strong challenge within the current context is how different groups lacking an institutional framework to control resource use interact and regulate the actions of other users.

This analysis focuses on conflicts emerging between villagers in Seke communal lands and farmers resettled on neighbouring former commercial farms in 2000. It assesses how the shift in tenure and land-use, and increasing population through in-migration in the former commercial farming areas, have increased the demand for fuel wood resources. The study investigated access to and control of forest resources in former commercial areas by communal households by comparing two villages bordering A1 settlements on Dunstan Farm. The specific objectives of the study were:

- to identify uses for forest resources and their sources;
- to analyse rules governing access to forests;
- to assess perceived changes in the wake of resettlement and the community's adjustment mechanisms to these changes.

The study utilised a political economy framework to develop an understanding of human actions as a tool that takes into account broader social and political factors and structural inequalities which have to be made central to develop an understanding of property relations (Cousins 1992).

Study area & methodological issues

The study was carried out at the two villages of Mhindurwa and Mangwende in Seke communal lands. Seke District is in Mashonaland East, has two headmen, Mazhindu and Muswara, and an estimated population of 77,840 (CSO, 2002) whose main economic activities include horticulture and cash crops. It lies within Agro-ecological Regions IIa, IIb and III. The two sites selected lie in Mandedza and Mayambara wards respectively, and are located along Manyame River bordering Dunstan Farm. The study primarily relied on questionnaire interviews, key informant interviews and participant observations. A total of 82 semi-structured interviews were administered. During these interviews, key persons were identified with the help of community members. The participatory observation method involved checking firewood piles at each household and ascertaining harvesting method. Secondary data were collected through desk review while some primary data were also gathered during the 'Firewood Week Campaign' that was run jointly by the Forestry Commission and the Department of Natural Resources from 6 to 10 September 2004. Table 1 below provides a summary of the sample on the basis of age and gender composition.

Village	Age	Gender		Total
		Male	*Female*	
Mhindurwa	below 20	6	5	11
	21-30	11	2	13
	31-40	2	7	9
	41-50	2	4	6
	above 50	10	5	15
Total		*31*	*23*	*54*
Mangwende	below 20	3	1	4
	21-30	9	3	12
	31-40	1	4	5
	41-50	3	1	4
	above 50	2	1	3
Total		*18*	*10*	*28*

Table 1: *Age and gender of respondents*

The questionnaire focused on the following:

- methods and tools used in wood extraction;
- the mode of transportation involved and associated costs;
- location of the resources;
- the rules governing resource use in the given locations;
- resource use arrangements prior to Fast Track Land Reform;
- perceived changes in arrangements for resource use, community adjustment mechanisms to these changes and proposed solutions to any of the challenges they faced.

Findings

Sources of fuel wood

The interviewed villagers relied on fuel wood from Dunstan Farm and within their respective villages. Table 2 below shows the percentage of villagers relying on fuel wood resources in these areas. A greater proportion of villagers (85 per cent) in Mhindurwa relied solely on fuel wood from Dunstan Farm compared to villagers in Mangwende (33.3 per cent). The villages are distantly spaced, hence no cases were reported of villagers encroaching on each other's area. A greater proportion of communal villagers continue to depend on fuel wood resources within former commercial farming areas (Mhindurwa 95 per cent; Mangwende 83.3 per cent). Axes and iron hooks attached on long dry poles used to pull down dry branches ('*ngovo*') were the tools commonly used in collecting fuel wood from Dunstan Farm.

Source of fuel wood	Village of respondents	
	Mhindura (%)	*Mangwende (%)*
Mhindurwa	5	0
Mangwende	0	16.7
Dunstan Farm	85	33.3
Within village sources and Dunstan Farm	10	50
Total	100	100

Table 2: *Sources of fuel wood for communal villagers*

Rules governing use of forest resources at Dunstan Farm

Table 3 shows arrangements for accessing fuel wood at Dunstan Farm prior to the Fast-Track Land Reform. Villagers were allowed to get permits (18.8 per cent), allowed easy access (25 per cent) and other non-prohibitive arrangements (18.7 per cent) to facilitate access to fuel wood. The reported rules include seeking permission from the resettled farmers, prohibition from cutting living trees, and collecting only dry wood. Villagers in Mhindurwa (5 per cent) noted that an emerging rule was one in which they were asked to cut wood for resettled farmers first before being permitted to cut wood for themselves.

Rules that existed prior to 'Fast-Track Land Reform'	Mhindurwa (%)	Mangwende (%)	% of Total
Allowed easy access	15	41.7	25
Given permits	20	16.71	8.8
Not allowed to cut trees	15	16.7	5.6
Trespass laws	5	–	3.1
Other non-prohibitive rules	25	8.3	18.7
No response	20	25.6	18.7
Total	100	100	100

Table 3 *Rules of access prior to Fast-Track Land Reform*

Several rules of access govern the use of forest resources and these have not changed significantly since the Fast-Track Land Reform. Table 4 summarises these rules.

Rules that existed prior to 'Fast-Track Land Reform'	Mhindurwa	Mangwende	% of Total
Completely forbidded	5	16.7	9.4
Ask for permission	10	16.7	12.5
Not allowed to cut trees	15	25	18.8
First cut for resettled farmers	5	–	3.1
Collect dry wood	15	–	9.3
No response	50	41.6	69.9
Total	100	100	100

Table 4: *Rules of access post 'Fast-Track Land Reform*

Current practices in accessing fuel wood in Dunstan Farm were perceived as prohibitive compared to the period before the Fast-Track Land Resettlement. Most of the communal villagers expressed satisfaction with the prior arrangements which were seen as providing for clearly defined ways of collecting fuel wood. Some of the stated ways include getting permits from commercial farmers, collecting dry branches and not cutting living trees. These arrangements were reported to have collapsed with the implementation of the Fast-Track Land Reform as new farmers were allocated pieces of land where communal villagers used to extract fuel wood.

The individualisation of tenure around these areas has led to conflicts between communal villagers and resettled plot owners, as the former persist to look for fuel wood within these areas. Communal farmers feel the resettled farmers impose rules that are highly prohibitive. Some of the reported changes include intimidation and confiscation of tools by the newly resettled farmers. If tools are confiscated, owners have to pay a fee to get them back. In most cases they reported being completely denied access into the former commercial farming areas. While there existed resentment of commercial farmers prior to Fast-Track Land Reform, the current sentiments were characterised by a constant fight between these two groups to exclusively access and use forest resources. Nhira et al. (1998) expressed the need for forest management practices to be highly inclusive and incorporate the needs of different groups so as to minimise conflicts. Lack of an inclusive management practice between communal villagers and resettled farmers only serves to increase conflicts between these groups.

The influx of new inhabitants increased the demand for fuel wood. Communal villagers noted that dry wood remains were getting fewer. This led to increases in distance and time required to gather fuel wood. These shortages have consequently led to changes in harvesting patterns. Communal villagers resorted to cutting trees in order to get fuel wood for brick-making, domestic use and traditional ceremonies. The cutting down of trees on plots allocated to resettled farmers has been reported and this has led to several confrontations, resulting in confiscation of axes and villagers being compelled to pay fines to plot owners. Some youths were reported to be moving into the former commercial farming areas at night using saws to fell trees and axes to threaten plot holders.

However, there are other communal villagers who do not access these resources in such contested ways. In most cases resettled farmers offer to sell wood from their plots to communal villagers. In such instances, trees are felled on land that is purportedly set aside for agricultural purposes. The presence of a fuel wood market and constant demand by communal villagers has led to increasing commercialisation. Conflicting access by other communal villagers has led to a change in access rules. It has become difficult for communal villagers to access fuel wood freely within the resettled and, in most instances, they are forced to buy from resettled farmers.

Sale of fuel wood extends beyond the communal villagers. Some key informants complained about sales to truckers from Chitungwiza and Harare. They estimated that the damage done by the truckers was ten times that caused by communal inhabitants. One informant contended that 'Vave kukoshesa mari kupfuura miti yacho' ('They are now valuing money more than the trees'). The process is facilitated by several factors, including proximity to urban areas and a good transport network. The urban market in Chitungwiza and Harare readily absorbs fuel wood from these areas. On the other hand, communal areas adjacent to former commercial farming areas are resource poor. There are too few well-forested areas in communal areas to meet villagers' energy needs. Demand for fuel wood and the presence of an affluent market creates pressure on existing sources which in turn affects institutional arrangements to regulate access and use by different stakeholders.

Communal villagers felt commercialisation of fuel wood resulted from uncertainty on the part of the resettled farmers. One village elder contented that 'Vanhu ava vanoita sevari kupfuura' ('They behave as if they are passing through'). They felt that most of the farmers were uncertain about land tenure and ownership arrangements, which instead motivated destructive behaviour on their part. The communal villagers felt that resettled farmers seemed unaware of their entitlements since they did not hold title to the allocated land. Such lack of security was, in part, assumed to have led to resettled farmers wanting to maximise their personal gains, through fuel wood selling, and prohibiting free access by communal villagers.

Historically, communal villagers managed to negotiate access through de facto resource sharing arrangements with commercial farmers. They viewed the coming of resettled farmers as introducing new sets of arrangements. These rules are viewed as motivated in part by fuel wood demand mainly from Harare and Chitungwiza. The recurring electricity shortages in these neighbouring urban areas have increased the demand for fuel wood and also created a market value for it. In an attempt to tap all the benefits, the forest resources management practices have shifted from the negotiated access that hitherto existed with evicted commercial farmers, to the outright exclusion of resource users from neighbouring villages.

There were several failures by the Forestry Commission and Department of Natural Resources during the 'Firewood Week Campaign'. Most truckers access these areas during the night and policing failed in most situations due to lack of financial and human resources while the efforts were not committed during appropriate times. The widening socio-environment interface made possible by the Fast-Track Land Reform needed to be followed by some institutional adaptation to meet new challenges and to minimise commercial use. This is supported by Montalembert and Schmithusen (1994) who indicated that tenure transitions have to be followed by institutional reorientation so that they quickly adapt and manage change.

These changes are viewed negatively by some communal villagers and have led to hostility between resettled farmers and communal villagers which is potentially detrimental for forest resources management. Unfortunately, there are no institutions to represent the demands of these villagers and to help organise their claims for fuel wood resources at Dunstan Farm. The literature demonstrates historical institutional weakening on the part of the communal villagers to manage natural resources (Murombedzi 1991; Murphree 1991). For example, communal villagers have not been allowed to organise and assist in the management of forest resources within the commercial farms. Extraction was dictated by commercial farm owners. There is a need to facilitate the development of joint forestry management between the newly resettled and communal villagers.

Those who hold power can make things happen. For example, there are reported cases of *Sabhuku* Mhindurwa mitigating on behalf of his people to get fuel wood for traditional ceremonies. This demonstrates the emergence of a negotiated access which can be tapped into in mapping a resource-sharing arrangement for forests lying in former commercial farming areas. Pre-Fast-Track Land Reform arrangements were an outcome of confrontation to enable inclusion of the marginalised groups. These arrangements are difficult to plan for, but if historical lessons can be carried forward, non-conflicting access and use can be negotiated by local political actors.

Adjustment mechanisms

Humans adapt to manage change. Communal villagers have responded in various ways to cope with these changes. In Mhindurwa, 30 per cent of the respondents relied for fuel wood on field-edge trees demarcating their boundaries, and pruning branches. They reported that there was no land set aside for tree planting. In Mangwende, where comparatively well-forested areas exist, 66.7 per cent of the respondents indicated having a woodlot set aside for domestic use. The *sabhuku* plays a crucial role in regulating use of these trees. None of these communities resorted to planting trees to address fuel wood scarcity and the resultant commercialisation (see also Dewees 1997; Learch and Mearns 1998)

Communities were also self-organising and sourced alternative fuels such as coal and electricity. In Mhindurwa, 50 per cent of the respondents said they had agreed to source electricity, whilst 45 per cent of the respondents had not made such plans and 5 per cent gave no responses. In Mangwende, similar proportions (50 per cent) acknowledged having plans to source electricity while the remainder did not have such plans. Most of the successful electricity installation efforts were reported at individual level. Some of the participants indicated that their plans had reached advanced stages of completion and they were hoping to have electricity installed within the following year (2005). Respective proportions were: Mhindurwa 40 per cent and Mangwende 8.3 per cent. Some of the plans were reported to have gone only as far as the village head meetings and some reported that they had dropped the plans due to non-transparency in the handling of the funds.

Conclusion & recommendations

This analysis presents the perspectives of communal land households in the context of shifts in social organisation for natural resource access and use. It focuses on changes in fuel wood access following the implementation of the Fast-Track Land Reform. Several observations have emerged which are pertinent to natural resource management, including:

- the commercialisation of fuel wood resources;
- conflicts among competing fuel wood resource users;
- perceived fuel wood shortages and changes in rules of access.

Various rules and arrangements for access appear to be motivated by factors like market presence and the interests of different actors benefiting from such resources. A semi-porous institutional arrangement has evolved which is impervious on one side and porous on the other. The impervious side minimises (and protects against) consumptive use (free access) by communal inhabitants while the porous side allows for commercial extraction by both commercial extractors and communal inhabitants.

There have been responses at a formal institutional level to regulate fuel wood access, even though such responses have been limited due to inadequacies in resources for monitoring and control. On the other hand, there have been moves towards negotiated access involving local traditional leaderships. There appears to be a strong need for appropriate bye-laws and other arrangements that could enhance such negotiation processes. Commercialisation of fuel wood resources is indeed a challenge for the communal inhabitants, and an opportunity for the livelihood enhancement of resettled communities.

Lessons

The commercialisation of forest resources in the absence of tradition-based authority and institutions makes it difficult to control the utilisation of these resources in resettlement areas. Tenure over forest resources transcends geographical boundaries and this has not been adequately considered during the land redistribution process. This is vital in preserving shared norms and accumulated learning. In such a state of flux, institutional flexibility and dynamism are required, especially on the part of formal institutions regulating access to resources. There is need to enhance the capacity of both groups to manage resources and in the process overcome colonially created incapacity and support negotiated access to minimise conflicts and the wanton harvesting of forest resources.

References

Bromley D. and M. Cernea. 1989. 'The Management of Common Property Natural Resource: Some Conceptual and Organizational Fallacies'. Discussion Paper, Washington DC, World Bank.

Bruce J.W. and R. Noronha. 1987. 'Land Tenure Issues in the Forestry and Agroforestry Project Contexts', in J.B. Raintree (ed.), *Land, Trees and Tenure*. Madison and Nairobi: Land Tenure Center and International Council for Research in Agroforestry.

Bruce, J.W. and L. Fortmann. 1989. 'Agro-forestry, tenure and incentives', in J.B. Raintree (ed.), *Land, Trees and Tenure*. Madison and Nairobi: Land Tenure Center and International Council for Research in Agroforestry.

Census. 2002.

Chatora, N. 2003. 'Resettlement and beneficiary support settlement and resettlement models in Zimbabwe', in F.T. Gonese and M. Roth (eds), *Delivering Land and Securing Rural Livelihoods: Post Independence Land Reform and Resettlement in Zimbabwe*. Harare and Madison: Centre for Applied Social Sciences and Land Tenure Center, pp. 269-80.

Cousins B. 1992. *The Political Economy Model of Common Property Regimes and the Case of Grazing Management in Zimbabwe*. Harare: Centre for Applied Social Sciences Publications, University of Zimbabwe.

Dewees, P.A. 1997. 'Farmer responses to tree scarcity: the case of wood fuel', in M.J.E. Arnold and P.A. Dewes (eds), *Farms, Trees and Farmers: responses to Agricultural Intensification*. London: Earthscan.

Fortmann, L. and J. Bruce. 1995. *You've got to know who controls the land & trees people use: Gender, Tenure and the Environment*. Harare: Centre for Applied Social Sciences Publications, University of Zimbabwe.

Gonese F.T. and C.M. Mukora. 2003. 'Beneficiary Selection, Infrastructure Provision and Beneficiary Support', in F.T. Gonese and M. Roth (eds), *Delivering Land and Securing Rural Livelihoods: Post Independence Land Reform and Resettlement in Zimbabwe*. Harare and Madison: Centre for Applied Social Sciences and Land Tenure Center, pp. 173-98.

Government of Zimbabwe. 1982. *The Forest Act, 1982*. Harare: Government Printers.

Government of Zimbabwe. 1987. *The Communal Lands Forest Produce Act, 1987.* Harare, Government Printers.

Hoskins, M.W. 1994. *People's participation in forest Tree Management.* EDI Seminar series. Washington DC: The International Bank for Reconstruction and The World Bank.

Katerere, Y., E. Guveya and K. Muir. 1999. 'Community Forest Management: Lessons from Zimbabwe', Issue Paper No. 18, International Institute for Environment and Development Drylands Programme, London.

Learch, G. and R. Mearns. 1998. *Beyond the Wood Fuel Crisis: People, Land and Trees in Africa.* London: Earthscan.

Maigga, I. and A. Diallo. 1998. *Land Tenure Conflicts and their Management in the 5th Region of Mali.* London: International Institute for Environment and Development.

Mamimine, P.W. 2003. 'Administration by Consensus: A quest for client centred institutional structures for land administration in Zimbabwe', in F.T. Gonese and M. Roth (eds), *Delivering Land and Securing Rural Livelihoods: Post Independence Land Reform and Resettlement in Zimbabwe.* Harare and Madison: Centre for Applied Social Sciences and Land Tenure Center, pp. 301-14.

Mariko, A. 1991. 'Reforms, Land Tenure and Restoring Peasants Rights: Some Basic Conditions for Reversing Environmental Degradation in the Sahel'. Paper No. 24, March 1991, 38, London, International Institute for Environment and Development.

Marimira, C. and K. Odero. 2003. 'An analysis of institutional and organizational issues on Fast Track Resettlement: The case of Goromonzi', in F.T. Gonese and M. Roth (eds), *Delivering Land and Securing Rural Livelihoods: Post Independence Land Reform and Resettlement in Zimbabwe.* Harare and Madison: Centre for Applied Social Sciences and Land Tenure Center, pp. 259-68.

Montalembert M.R. and F. Schmithusen. 1994. 'Readings in sustainable forest management', Food and Agricultural Organisation, Policy, Legal and Institutional Aspects of Sustainable Forest Management Forestry Paper 122, Rome.

Moyo, S., P. Robinson, Y. Katerere, S. Stevenson and D. Gumbo. 1991. *Zimbabwe's Environmental Dilemma; balancing resource inequalities.* Harare: ZERO.

Murombedzi, J.C. 1991. *The Need for Appropriate Local Level Common Property Resource Management Institutions in Communal Tenure Regimes.* Harare: Centre for Applied Social Sciences.

Murphree, M. 1991 'Communities as Institutions for Natural Resources Management', Occasional Paper Series, Centre for Applied Social Sciences, Harare.

Nhira, C., S. Baker, P. Gondo and C. Marunda. 1998. *Contesting Inequality in Access to Forests: Policy that Works for Forests and People, Series No.5.* Harare, Centre for Applied Social Sciences and Forestry Commission, London, International Institute for Environment and Development.

Rugube, L., M. Zhou and W. Chambati. 2003. 'Government assisted and market driven land reform: Evaluation of public and private land markets in redistributing land in Zimbabwe', in F.T. Gonese and M. Roth (eds), *Delivering Land and Securing Rural Livelihoods: Post Independence Land Reform and Resettlement in Zimbabwe.* Harare and Madison: Centre for Applied Social Sciences and Land Tenure Center, pp. 115-38.

Thebaud, B. 1995. 'Land Tenure, Environmental Degradation and Desertification in Africa: Some Thoughts Based on the Sahelian Example', Paper No. 57, July, London, International Institute for Environment and Development.

9

Gender Issues Surrounding Water Development & Management in Chishawasha Settlement Area

Chipo Plaxedes Mubaya

Background & introduction

A large proportion (70 per cent) of Zimbabweans live in rural areas and their livelihood is closely linked to access, use and management of natural resources such as water for both subsistence and income generation. Water is increasingly being recognised as a strategic resource that is a hallmark of sustainable development (IUCN 2005). It is essential to human beings and all forms of life and is perceived to be an entry point for poverty alleviation. One of the major challenges faced in rural areas is that women, who are traditionally recognised and accepted as managers and users of water, are absent from the mainstream of decision making processes relating to water management. (Agrawal 1991; Fortmann and Nabane 1992; The World Bank Report 1994; Rocheleau et al. 1996). Most women depend on land water resources to produce food and energy and to earn income, yet they lack legal rights and control over resources and their rights of access are insecure (Rocheleau et al. 1996). The World Bank Report (1994) states that, in relation to access in some customary-based resource systems in Zimbabwe, males hold resources in custody for future generations. Women are not customarily allocated land in their own right. By implication, women only exert usufruct rights, unlike their male counterparts who are allocated land and therefore rights to other resources on the land such as water. Women still have a chance to map their own destiny by being part of the decision making process within the context of community-based natural resources management (CBNRM) (Agrawal 1991).

Women's can increase their opportunities in access to resources such as water. The greater the participation of women in decision making with regard to water allocation and control, the less their vulnerability and the greater their ability to escape poverty.

Prior to operationalising strategies and programmes of sustainable management of water resources, it is necessary to have robust and clear supporting policy and legal instruments (IUCN 2005). This need is even greater where there are elements of social differentiation along lines such as gender. IUCN (2005) contends that it is the recognition of this need for strong policy and supporting legislation in the management of water resources that has seen the emergence of a wide range of national and regional policy and institutional reforms in the SADC region. In Zimbabwe, there has been a fundamental shift in national policy and institutional reforms towards integrated water resources management. These reforms are manifest in the new Water Act (1998) and the Zimbabwe National Water Authority Act (ZINWA) Act (1998) and emphasise economic efficiency, environmental sustainability and social equity (Chikozho 2001).

These acts incorporate the principles of stakeholder participation and decision making and the concept of 'user pays' for urban and large-scale water users. Besides the urban and large-scale water users, the majority of Zimbabweans have primary use rights that guarantee them access to water for drinking, washing, watering livestock and maintaining small gardens, and this does not require any statutes or form of payment (Derman and Gonese 2003).

While the new Water Act is useful in that it seeks to redress the fact that most of the available water in Zimbabwe was being used by a small fraction of the population, i.e. large-scale commercial farmers, it remains disturbing that the Act does not adequately address gender imbalances. The water reform institutions and process recognise a host of fundamental sectors of society, but ignore gender (Derman and Gonese 2003). Among other natural resources such as woodlands and grazing areas, water is considered to be a gendered resource. Water resources are mainly harvested by women and children (Fortmann and Nabane 1992).

This chapter explores gender issues surrounding the management of water resources on the basis of a case-study conducted in Chishawasha settlement area in Zimbabwe. The study investigated gender differentiation in access to, use of and control over water resources. It identified the water sources in question, the policy context for gender entitlements of water resources and the perceptions of the community on the effectiveness of existing institutional arrangements to enhance equitable access, use and management of water resources for both gender groups.

Conceptual framework

Since the early 1980s, policy focussed on preventing women from being marginalised in social and economic development (Doyal 2000). This resulted in programmes aimed at integrating women into economic systems, developments that saw the emergence of the Women in Development (WID) perspective, which was spearheaded by Boserup (1970). This perspective considered women in isolation and was made famous under the broad umbrella of feminism.

This focus on women in development resulted in some improvements in women's lives, but on the whole the status of women did not change significantly. Continuing discrimination against women saw the shift of focus from WID to Gender and Development (GAD) (Agrawal 1991). The GAD perspective is based on the premise that women's problems are societal and deep-rooted in cultural and family values and are best addressed by both gender groups (Cornwall 2005).

The shift of focus from WID to GAD is clearly articulated in the feminist political ecology theory. This theory carries with it the assumption that gender differentiation can be traced to societal division of labour, property rights and power (Nemarundwe 2003). The feminist political ecology approach can be used to analyse gendered access to water resources and the power dynamics that influence decision making processes. It can be adopted to explain a variety of tactics and strategies that women may use to influence resource management structures. Incorporating a feminist analysis can illustrate the ways in which the gender positions of both men and women, vis-à-vis institutions, determine access to land, to other resources and to the wider economy (Rocheleau et al. 1996). This is the conceptual approach that underpinned the study on which this chapter is based.

Methodology

Chishawasha, Ward 15 of Goromonzi District, is located 26 kilometres northeast of Harare in Mashonaland East Province. It covers some 4,857 hectares and is surrounded by Chikurubi, Arcturus, Tafara, Mabvuku and Umwinsidale. The area falls under Natural Regions IIa and IIb, receives an average rainfall of 700mm per annum and has a mean annual temperature of 21°C, making it suitable for both livestock and crop production.

The majority of people in Chishawasha are subsistence farmers whose major livelihood activity is agriculture. Maize is the main cash and subsistence crop. In addition, wild fruits such as the *Uapaca kirkiana* tree, *mazhanje* are gathered when in season. These fruits provide some income to the local community. Some people are employed in the city and in nearby low-density suburbs as domestic workers. Other sources of livelihood include brick moulding and vegetable gardening.

The natural sources of water available are unprotected wells, streams, natural springs and wetlands. Man-made sources are boreholes, dams, and closed and open wells. Chishawasha was selected because of a resource management regime that is quasi-private and communal, unlike in many communal areas. In Zimbabwe, water is subject to a variety of tenurial regimes found in a continuum ranging from intense private property systems to open access where there are no restrictions on off-takes (Derman 1998).

Seven villages make up Chishawasha Settlement Area. The study was con-

Village	No. of Households
Ndoro	109
Murwira	98
Mareke	98
Mandaza	106
Mutimumwe	88
Chikerema	84
Nyamayaro	130
Total	713

Table 1: *Villages in Chishawasha and their household populations*
Source: *Goromonzi Rural District Council (2004), Zimbabwe*

ducted in two of these, Ndoro and Murwira, to gain detail on gender issues in the access, use and management of water resources. Preliminary investigations indicated that the traditional leaders (village heads) were actively involved in development activities in Chishawasha. The village head for Ndoro is a case in point. Besides being village head, he is also in charge of the dip-tank, is the District Security Officer for the ruling party, and is the representative of all village heads. The villages were also selected because activities within them are combined, and some people who fall under Ndoro village reside in Murwira and vice versa. Villagers from both are generally kin, because before they were moved to the present site around the 1930s, they were in one village called Gopera, and even now there is no proper demarcation of the two. On paper they are two but in reality it is one village.

The inquiry was conducted at ward and village levels. A combination of data collection methods was used: unstructured questionnaire interviews conducted with a randomly selected sample of individuals, key informant interviews, Focus Group Discussions (FGD) and Participatory Rural Appraisals (PRA). Participant observation was also done. At the village level, interviews were conducted with the two village heads, the chief's representative and members of the borehole management committee. At ward level, the ward councillor and coordinator were interviewed. A church priest, head of Chishawasha Mission, was also part of the samples. A total of 30 individuals were interviewed. Four FGD and PRA workshops were conducted and participants from the two villages were combined and interviewed at the same time. These were for activities such as resource mapping, transect walks, historical trend analysis and a general discussion guided by the objectives of the study. PRA is viewed as a family of approaches and methods that enable local people to share their knowledge of life and to plan, act and evaluate (Chambers 1997).

Research method	Information collected	Target informants
Resource mapping	Type of water resources in the study area Location of water sources Resource abundance and accessibility	Women, men, the elderly and leaders combined for the two villages
Key informant interviews	Policy issues regarding gendered access, use and control of water Perceptions on differing uses of water by men and women Tenure systems in area Views on gendered conflicts	Elderly men and women from Ndoro and Murwira, village heads, church resentatives, the councillor, traditional and modern institutional representatives
Focus group discussion	Policy issues regarding gendered access, use and control of water Perceptions on differing uses of water by men and women Tenure systems in area Views on gendered conflicts Strategies used to gain access to resources	Elderly men and women, village heads, youth representatives
Transect walks	Conflict areas Identification of water sources Physical count of wells and other water sources	Village heads, elderly men and women
Historical trend analysis	Availability of water resources over time Changes in resource use patterns and availability	Elderly men and women

Table 2: *Summary of methods, information collected and target informants*

For the PRAs an equal number of men and women was selected but restricted to a minimum of eight and a maximum of twelve. During the FGDs, women and men were separated in order to capture the differing perceptions of each group. A summary of methods, the information collected and the target informants is presented in Table 2.

Elderly men (aged from 65 to 70) and women were selected to cater for the

Historical Trend Analysis in water resources availability and not exclusively for gender issues discussion.

Institutions involved in water resources management

The legal framework for water resources management is provided by the Water Act (1998) and the Zimbabwe National Water Authority Act (1998). There has been more emphasis on the Water Act but the two are inter-related. The latter stipulates that all water is vested in the President and that no permit is required to access water for primary use. However, permits are required for exploitation of water resources for commercial purposes, and these are issued by ZINWA under the authority granted to it by the ZINWA Act. Water is managed through Catchment and Sub-catchment Councils in coordination with ZINWA. The Water Act recognises the need for stakeholder participation in the management of national water resources. In this regard, it provides for the involvement of urban and rural local authorities, large-scale commercial farmers, small-scale farmers, mining communities and other stakeholders. Rural communities are supposed to be catered for in terms of representation, by Rural District Councils.

However, the two Acts fall short in ensuring the involvement of institutions at the grass-root level. They do not spell out the roles of traditional leaders such as village heads and spirit mediums, nor are institutions such as borehole maintenance committees and religious institutions provided for.

Several institutions are involved in water resources management In Chishawasha: the District Development Fund (DDF), Agriculture Extension Services (AREX), schools, the Roman Catholic Church, traditional leaders, Village Development Committees (VIDCO) and Ward Development Committees (WADCO). Their roles include:

- drilling and maintaining boreholes;
- digging and protecting wells as well as maintaining cleanliness around them;
- dam construction;
- resolving water-related conflicts.

These institutions were evaluated through a PRA workshop. Each was assigned a score out of ten, and this was used as a basis for ranking them in terms of their importance in water resource management as perceived by the community.

According to these perceptions, the most important institutions are the Ministry of Health, DDF, the Church, Village Development Committees (VIDCOs) and Ward Development Committees (WADCOs). Table 3 summarises the roles that the various institutions have played. It also shows their scoring and ranking by the community. Finally, the table comments on gender considerations and awareness on the part of the different institutions.

Institution	Score	Rank	Comments
DDF	7	2	Provided the two villages with a borehole. Trained members of a borehole management committee so that they can repair defects. Take part in the maintenance of boreholes but to date have not done so for borehole has broken down for about a year and a half. Simply trained members without questioning gender disaggregation although women were among the trainees.
Ministry of Health (Water and Sanitation)	8	1	Provided cement for well-owners to protect them. Provided collector equipment. Monitored the level of cleanliness in use of well, hence encouraged cleanliness. Encouraged digging of wells and construction of toilets. Trained village health workers from each village. However, village workers have not been executing duties of late. Did not require gender disaggregation.
Schools	5	6	Provide water for domestic purposes. Even for funerals – water in large volumes. Do not pay attention to provision of access by gender.
VIDCO/ Kraal heads (the same kraal heads are also VIDCO chairpersons)	6	3	Report to the DDF when borehole is not working. Maintain hygiene at borehole. Mediate in conflict situations. Provided poles and fence for borehole. Do not stipulate gender considerations, rather accept both blindly.
WADCO	6	3	Basically plays the same role played by VIDCO. Members of the VIDCO in this committee. Silent about gender considerations.
Area Board	0	9	Have not played any part in issues to do with access, uses and water management.
Borehole Management Committee	5	6	Maintains cleanliness at borehole area (cutting grass, etc.). Mobilises people to take part. Coincidentally, largely made up of more women than men.
AREX	4	8	Play a very minimal role but once before independence succeeded in stopping people from establishing gardens in water channels. Gender blind.

Table 3: *Institutions in water resources management*
Source: Focus Group Discussions (11 November 2004)

As Table 3 shows, the Ministry of Health and Child Welfare and DDF were ranked first and second respectively. The Church was ranked third, together with VIDCO and WADCO. The case of the Church is interesting in that conflicting perceptions and views about it emerged from the FGD and key informant interviews.

Some members of the community argued that the Church was very important in water issues since it had constructed two large and five small dams, provided dip tank water for the whole area, and constructed bridges and boreholes at Chishawasha Mission and St Ignatius College. Others were of the view that the Church did not have the motive of assisting the local people, but had built the dams for its own use in schools and in livestock projects that they had at that time (Box 1). The dip tank served the same purpose even though they did not deny local people access. It was also argued that the footbridges were intended to ease accessibility for them during heavy rains that generally characterise the area. Further, the St Ignatius College authorities had since barred local men and women from accessing water.

Historically, communities in Chishawasha have been accustomed to receiving donations for school fees and agricultural inputs from the church. This partly explains why they ranked the Church third in water related issues even though its role in that regard remained controversial.

The study found that institutions involved in WRM in Chishawasha area are indifferent to gender considerations. They are silent on gender and do not take into account social and gender differentiation. This is potentially retrogressive in that it may result in sections of the community being marginalised.

One activity that depends heavily on water is vegetable gardening in the wetlands. This is an important source of income and livelihoods for the community, and appropriate water management regimes are necessary for its sustainability. There is a general understanding that garden space is supposed to be allocated by traditional leaders in consultation with AREX officers. In fact traditional leaders are actually expected to undertake the following functions, among other roles:

- regulating resources;
- allocating garden space;
- monitoring activities in wetland cultivation;
- rule enforcement, e.g. no gardens in undesignated areas.

There is also a general understanding that no person should hold more than one garden plot. Villagers should not locate gardens in undesignated areas such as water channels. Activities such as brick moulding should not be undertaken in the wetland areas. Finally, resettlement in the retreating moisture zones is not permitted.

The study found out that traditional and other leaders were not very effective in ensuring compliance with these regulations. Individuals simply allocated themselves garden space without consulting the relevant authorities and nothing was done to deter the offenders. Some villagers own more than one garden plot, and some locate their gardens in undesignated areas. Others engaged in brick moulding in the wetlands and settled in the retreating moisture zones. On whole, there is weak enforcement of the agreed guidelines.

Local water management activities tend to be arbitrary and are in most cases initiated by the communities themselves; there is no coordination among the

---

Box 1: *The case of the dam*

The dam has been controversial for about a decade now. The church was reluctant to carry out any development activities in the area, and relinquished its management of the dam. 'We have to look at economics; we can't keep doing things for people who have to be self-sufficient and we have surrendered the use and management of the dam to them. It has become very expensive to maintain the dam, which needs constant scooping. We do not have that type of money and the villagers are lazy. They take advantage of us and do not make an effort to contribute to the maintenance of the dam,' said the Mission priest in an interview (November 2004). The former councillor, the councillor and other authorities such as kraal-heads however denied the fact that the dam had been surrendered to them. They maintained that it still belonged to the priests and they only used it for livestock watering and that if it had been theirs then they would make extensive use of it. The Ndoro village kraal head said, *'hatiridi nokuti isu hatina mari yekurigadzirisa uyezve nzvimbo inondeyavo.'* ('We do not want to take responsibility of the dam because we do not have the money to maintain it; besides, the land belongs to them').

Source: Interview with key informants (September 2004)

---

local institutions. This situation arises from the fact that WRM legislation disregards informal systems such as those found in communal areas and downplays the resource management potential that these institutions have (Manzungu 2001).

Local institutions have no explicit mandate. In essence, little is known about local institutional arrangements for water resources management in communal areas (Nemarundwe and Kozanayi 2003). The Traditional Leaders' Act (2000), Section III, hardly recognises their role. The Act states that duties of village heads include:

> To ensure the security of schools, clinics, contour ridges, water points, culverts, public fencing and any other public property and, where necessary, to report any contravention of the law to the police.

It is not clear which water points are referred to and what exactly village heads are expected to do.

Generally, in situations where there is no effective institutional framework for monitoring and regulating resource use, and where such institutions are not conscious about gender, the tendency is that powerful members of society, i.e. men, benefit at the expense of the weak, i.e. women.

However, evidence from Chishawasha indicates that this is not always the case. Women are capable of employing strategies and networks to turn such situations to their own advantage. (Box 2)

Although local institutions are silent on gender issues, and have demonstrated weakness in enforcing 'regulations', evidence indicates that women, as much as men and even more so, have adequate access to water resources, as is elaborated below.

Box 2: *The case of multiple gardens (Mrs B. Zenda)*

Mrs. B. Zenda owns four gardens and all of them are on the wetlands close to the homesteads. She acquired the gardens when her late father-in-law, Mr. Michael Zenda, was village head for Murwira village (Mr. J. Mupfumi, current village head for Murwira, took over in 1998 at the death of Mr. Zenda). When she allocated herself garden spaces, her father-in-law did not attempt to stop her or ask her to relinquish some of them and remain with the stipulated number. Participants suggested that no one could stand up to Mrs. Zenda on the issue as people feared to cross paths with her husband, who is a retired army officer and ex-combatant. One villager said in an interview that even the fact that she is a woman did not allow the current village head to question her 'A! Pane angagona kumutanga here? Murume wake musoja uye muexcom. Kana Sabhuku chaiye munhu wemurume anotomutya. Zvimwe ndezvekutarisa.' ('Can anyone stand against her? Her husband is a soldier and liberation war veteran. Even the headman, a man, is afraid of her. Some things are better left out.')

Source: Focus Group Discussion (October 2004)

Gender & community water resources management

Women in Chishawasha have water entitlements and are generally believed to be the owners of water points such as wells. For example, two privately owned protected wells are referred to as *tsime rambuya vaFarai* ('well for Farai's grandmother') and *tsime ramai vaMike* ('well for Mike's mother'). The wells are considered to belong to these women and they play a significant role in the management of them. Women harvest water resources more than men (Table 4), a factor that contributes to their being viewed as the owners of these resources. Men rarely collect water for domestic purposes; they generally access streams that are distant from the households because they are better able than women to travel to them.

Gardens are said to be owned by women, and it is the same women who work in them. Men only work in the gardens when it is really necessary, for instance if the wife is sick or is away. Some women acquire gardens through

Harvesting by men	Harvesting by women
Brick moulding	Domestic uses
Livestock watering	Garden irrigation
Livestock grazing in dambos	Beer brewing
Reeds – mats	Pottery Livestock grazing and watering Brick moulding

Table 4: *Gendered harvesting of water resources*
Source: *Focus Group Discussions (November 2004)*

marriage, or inheritance; others simply allocate themselves garden space.

Some women have 'crossed boundaries' and entered domain that is normally considered to be men's. Brick moulding is generally viewed to be men's domain, but two women were found to be doing it. (Box 3).

With regard to wells, it is again women who access them more as they harvest water from the wells for domestic purposes. Men use wells that they dig in the wetlands for brick moulding purposes.

Box 3: *Mrs. Zenda's case*

Mrs Costa Zenda (23 years old) has been brick moulding alongside her husband since she married three years ago. She said that only one other woman in the area helps her husband; women generally do not do so because their husbands say, *'zvinochembedza vakadzi vedu'* ('It makes our wives age faster'). Mrs Zenda moulds bricks because, *'mumwe nemumwe ane nhamo yake'* ('I have to consider my problems first.') This is an important source of livelihood for her family and they have resorted to brick moulding all year round, even in the wet season. She has to balance this activity with her household chores.

Source: Interview with Mrs. Zenda (5 October 2004)

Management structures such as the borehole management committee are dominated by women. This is partly explained by the fact that Chishawasha is characterised by absentee husbands, creating space for women to be active in decision making. Village heads and other traditional leaders accepted women into the system as the women were more available for these responsibilities.

Women in Ndoro and Murwira villages mobilise themselves when there is need to address issues to do with the community borehole. The borehole management committee has five members, three women and two men. The chairperson is a man; the vice-chairperson, secretary and treasurer are women. The election meeting was dominated by women. Men tend to associate water issues with women and they would rather leave the women to deal with them.

In fact these women had been trained to repair the borehole, regardless of the general perception that such tasks are normally done by men.

Apart from repairing the borehole, the committee ensures that no one breaks the rules around its use:

- drums should not be used to fetch water;
- water for brick moulding should not be fetched from the borehole;
- laundry should not be done at the borehole;
- litter should not be thrown around borehole area;
- the hand pump should not be hit against the ground;
- every borehole user should take part in weeding and cleaning up of the borehole area;
- every borehole user should contribute $5,000 per year for repairs.

These rules were highlighted specifically by elderly women in FGDs, and men indicated that they were not aware of them as in most cases they access water from wells and not from the borehole.

The chairperson usually decides about technical aspects of the borehole, but hardly participates in meetings dealing with other issues. The committee has been effective in maintaining cleanliness of the borehole and enforcing rules other than that concerning financial contributions.

There is generally a high level of social and gender equity regarding access to, use and management of water in Chishawasha Settlement Area. There are few households, if any, that can be said to be at a disadvantage in accessing water resources. A significant number of homesteads and gardens have private water sources in them. The distance travelled by those who do not own water sources is short and this indicates that many people have access to water. On average, people travel less than 100m to fetch water.

It was noted that the Water Act (1998) and the ZINWA Act (1998) did not provide a framework for local institutions to be involved in water manage-ment. It was also noted that there were unwritten rules governing utilisation of water and other resources in Chishawasha. On the whole, the community was aware of these 'rules and regulations'. The exception was that many men were not aware of the borehole rules. But the local institutions did not have the means of enforcing compliance with the social norms.

Some scholars have argued that non-specificity in governance of resources such as water is healthy in that it allows for flexibility in affording access to resources for all sections of society and for solving conflicts (Manzungu 2001). Cases have been documented where institutional arrangements for water resource use are informed by social networks and that social relations deter-mine compliance with existing rules for water resource management. Romwe, in Chivi, is one place where there are no rigid institutional arrangements yet significant success has been registered in management of water (Nemarundwe and Kozanayi 2003).

Contrary to the above, some case-studies have found out that where water is scarce, and there are no local level institutions to enforce compliance with regulations, conflicts in access, use and management of water emerge. A case in point is in Nyanyadzi River Catchment, in Chimanimani (eastern Zimbabwe), where water distribution and allocation are largely decided upon by men (Bolding 1997). There is a clash between formal water users in Nyanyadzi irrigation scheme and the village users – who are mostly female and are not part of the scheme – who believe that water is God-given and should not be formally regulated.

The findings of this study somewhat contradict the existing literature on gender and water resources which assumes that access to and management of water resources is generally skewed towards men. The same literature posits that women are invisible in the realms of water management, allocation and entitlements although they feature significantly in using the resources. Instead, this study found that women are at the centre of control of water resources. Although usually marginalised in access to natural resources, they have on the contrary greater access to and ownership of the sources of water and even hold important management positions. Men feature quite significantly in the harvesting of water resources, but they are almost silent on the subject of responsibilities and rights to the same resources.

Contrary to the notion that social networks and social relations determine compliance with existing unwritten rules for water management, in Chishawasha it was found that violation of these rules was common. But men were not the only violators; women were also able to take advantage of the situation of non-specificity in governance of resources for their own benefit.

Conclusion

This chapter has used the feminist political ecology approach to examine gendered access to, use and management of water resources based on a case-study conducted in Chishawasha Settlement Area. The study found that women are not disadvantaged in terms of access to water resources. They are the major users of this resource and are central to its management. Local institutions are not backed up by national legal statutes. Their role is not made explicitly clear. But the society has developed norms and practices for the exploitation and management of water and related resources. These norms are frequently violated, but this does not turn out to be disadvantageous to women.

The general assumption that men dominate natural resource use and management does not seem to apply in cases where there is abundance of such resources. Similarly the assumption that women tend to lose out in cases where there are no clear rules governing water resources and enforcement mechanisms was not upheld. In fact some women actually took advantage of the situation and acquired garden space beyond the accepted limits.

The major conclusion is that the objective conditions prevailing within a community determine the nature of outcomes with regard to potential conflicts in access to and management of water and other natural resources. In the case of Chishawasha, the prevailing conditions were as follows:

There was abundance of water resources and this reduced the potential for conflict.

Women were the major users of water and men viewed this as a female domain. Similarly they were more involved in market gardening to the extent that both gardens and wells were associated with women, even by name.

A significant proportion of men were employed outside the community.

These conditions made it possible for women to be involved in the management of water resources. One result of women's involvement in management is empowerment, and it is that empowerment that made it possible for some women to come out as 'victors'.

References

Agrawal, B. 1991. 'Engendering the environment debate: Lessons from the Indian subcontinent', Discussion Paper 8, (CASID) Centre for Advanced Study of International Development Distinguished Lecture Series, Michigan, Michigan State University.

Bolding, A.E. 1997. 'Caught in the catchment: Past, present and future of Nyanyadzi water management', in *Towards Reforming the Institutional and Legal Basis of the Water Sector in Zimbabwe*. Harare: Centre for Applied Social Sciences Publications, University of Zimbabwe, pp. 9-18.

Boserup, E. 1970. *Woman's Role in Economic Development*. New York: St. Martin's Press.

Chambers, R. 1997. *Whose Reality Counts: Putting the First Last*. London: Intermediate Technology Publications.

Chikozho, C. 2001. *Towards CBNRM in the water sector: An analysis of legislative changes made under the South African and Zimbabwean water reforms*. Harare, Centre for Applied Social Sciences, University of Zimbabwe and Cape Town, Programme for Land and Agrarian Studies, University of Western Cape.

Cornwall, A. 2005. 'Introduction: Perspectives on gender in Africa,' in A. Cornwall (ed.), *Readings in Gender in Africa*. Oxford: James Currey.

Derman, B. 1998. *Preliminary reflections on a comparative study of the Mazowe and Mupfure catchments in the context of Zimbabwe's new Water Act*. Harare: Centre for Applied Social Sciences Publications, University of Zimbabwe.

Derman. B. and F.T. Gonese. 2003. *Water reform: Its multiple interface with land reform and resettlement*. Harare: Centre for Applied Social Sciences Publications, University of Zimbabwe.

Doyal, L. 2000. A draft framework for designing national health policies with an integrated gender perspective. *www.un.org/womenwatch/daw/csw/draft.htm*. Accessed on 15 March 2007.

Fortmann, L. and N. Nabane. 1992. 'The Fruits of their labour: gender, property and trees in Mhondoro district', Occasional Paper Series – NRM 6/1992, Harare, Centre for Applied Social Sciences Publications, University of Zimbabwe.

IUCN 2005. *Gender mainstreaming in wetlands ecosystems and natural resource management: Bridging the gap: Gender and Conservation in Zimbabwean Projects*. Harare: IUCN.

Manzungu, E. 2001. 'A lost opportunity of the water reform debate in the Fourth Parliament of Zimbabwe', *Zambezia* 28, 1, pp. 97-120.

Nemarundwe, N. 2003. 'Negotiating Resource Access: Institutional Arrangement for Woodlands and Water Use in Southern Zimbabwe', PhD thesis, University of Uppsala.

_____ and W. Kozanayi 2003. *Institutional arrangements for water resources use: A case study from southern Zimbabwe*. Harare: Institute of Environment, University of Zimbabwe.

Rocheleau , D., B. Thomas-Slayter and E. Wangari 1996. *Feminist Political Ecology: Global Issues and Local experiences*. London: Routledge.

SARDC 2002. *Defining and Mainstreaming Environmental Sustainability in Water Resources Management in Southern Africa*. Harare: SARDC.

The World Bank Report 1994. *Making Development Sustainable: The World Bank Group and the Environment*. Washington: The World Bank.

Traditional Leaders Act. 2000. Harare: Government Printers.

Water Act. 1998. Harare, Government of Zimbabwe Printers.

Zhuwao, C. 1990. *An Investigation of Vashawasha 'Kurova Guva' Ceremony and the Catholic Teaching of the Life After Death*, BA (Hons) dissertation, University of Zimbabwe.

Zimbabwe National Water Authority Act. 1998. Harare, Government Printers.

10

Participatory Development of Community-based Management Plans for Livestock Feed Resources in Semi-arid Areas of Zimbabwe:
Experiences from Lower Guruve District

Bright Garikayi Mombeshora, Frank Chinembiri & Tim Lynam

Introduction

For many years there has been awareness and concern in Zimbabwe about the use and management of natural resources by the government and various individuals, researchers, and extension agencies. There have been concerns about the poor management and the resulting degradation and depletion of natural resources such as soils, forests and rangelands in rural areas. Various programmes and recommendations to conserve and improve management have been suggested and implemented. Examples include programmes and projects by the Native Land Husbandry Act (1951), the grazing schemes, and Communal Area Management Programme for Indigenous Resources (Campfire) and the International Centre for Research in Agro-Forestry (ICRAF). However, success in improving resources management has been limited, particularly in the communal areas. In most areas soils are still eroding, forage productivity is still declining, and vegetation and faunal diversity is still being reduced (Mache and Chivizhe 1992; Land Tenure Commission 1994).

Varied suggestions have been made about how to overcome these problems. Technologies were often formulated by scientists, and brought to the community for adoption; the community played little or no role in their development. During the colonial period, and even after independence, technologies from the commercial faming sector and were assumed to be equally applicable in the communal and small scale sectors. The technology development process has tended to address specific problems, thereby ignoring broader and more complex social and economic environments.

During the last few decades, new approaches and methods have been emerging that seek to link biophysical factors with the socio-economic reality in developing and assessing technologies. There has been a growing experience with the 'participatory approach' in agricultural research and extension (Scoones and Cousins 1988; Clarke 1991; Hagman and Chuma 1994). However, 'participation' itself can be interpreted differently by different people. Sustainability of the technologies implemented using this approach has been limited. The question for the project presented in this chapter was how the participatory approach could be used to provide sustainability in the activities. Empowering the local community to develop local technologies was an option. The community was fully responsible for all decisions on the technologies to be tested or implemented and how they were to be implemented; the research team only facilitated the processes of change. Local knowledge and perceptions were accepted as valid sources of information and decisions were made by the community at all phases of the project. This approach was considered appropriate after reviewing recommendations and principles suggested by several scientists (Murphree 1991; Mache and Chivizhe 1992; Murombedzi 1992; Land Tenure Commission 1994) when working in communal resource management. These are summarised as:

- The resources must be recognised as finite;
- The resource managers must be the owners and beneficiaries;
- There should be a close and proportional link between production and benefits;
- The benefits must be tangible and immediate;
- The community must clearly understand the goals and objectives and the tasks required to attain them;
- There should be local autonomy in decisions on how products and benefits of the scheme will be disposed;
- The management objectives must be made by members of the community, and not imposed on them from outside by government, donors or other institutions;
- The user group must be small enough to be cohesive and to lower transaction costs, but not too small that it becomes exclusive and wholly self-serving;
- The leadership must be accountable, transparent and broadly representative of the community it serves;
- The boundaries of the management units should be distinctive and exclusive.

This chapter gives brief reviews of two projects (the Native Land Husbandry Act and the grazing schemes) as examples of attempts to improve communal area natural resources management. It highlights the methodologies used and the success achieved. It then describes the Mahuwe project, to highlight the participatory development of management plans; further, it presents experiences of the project team derived from working with the community. The chapter ends with some recommendations on future needs for research and development in natural resources management.

Land Husbandry Act

The Native Land Husbandry Act (1951) tried to enforce destocking of livestock, among other cropping and conservation rules, in order to conserve grazing and browse resources. Destocking aimed mainly at conserving the grazing lands by limiting the numbers of cattle within the 'carrying capacity' of each area in the communal lands. The carrying capacity was the maximum number of livestock units, calculated by scientists, which could be kept in a grazing area without depleting the grazing and browse resources. Every household owning cattle was required to register them and the cattle numbers were checked when the cattle went for dipping, which was compulsory. By limiting the number of animals per farmer, the role and importance of cattle to the farmers as a major option for investment and their value for various other socio-cultural uses were marginalised. Communal area farmers did not see any tangible benefits from these laws and they resisted the policy. It was so unpopular that it fuelled a tide of nationalism and never achieved its objectives. It was eventually abandoned.

Grazing schemes

The Department of Agricultural Technical and Extension Services (AGRITEX), now the Department of Agricultural Research and Extension (AREX), introduced grazing schemes before the 1980s in the communal areas as an option for managing livestock and the graze and browse resources. The grazing schemes involved demarcating an area as grazing, fencing it off and subdividing the fenced area into paddocks. All livestock would be kept in one paddock for a short time and would be rotated through the others at regular intervals. This 'high density short duration rotational grazing system' had been shown at the research stations to promote fast grass re-growth and higher livestock units per given area. It was a viable option for pasture management and was already being used on commercial farms in the country. The grazing schemes were considered logical in that they improved the use of pastures and increased the stocking rate. Cliffe (1986) noted high popularity of the schemes among the communal farmers across the country, not necessarily for their effects on the pastures, but because fenced-off areas solved the problem of acute shortage of labour for herding. A survey by the Farming Systems Research Unit (FSRU) in 1994 in three provinces – Manicaland, Matebeleland North, and Masvingo – showed that most of the established grazing schemes were operational during the rainy season only. Severe water shortages during the dry season caused farmers to abandon rotational grazing. Donors provided most of the fencing and farmers provided the labour for building the paddocks. In the majority of the schemes, there were no properly defined institutions for maintenance and management. They were designed for areas with clearly defined boundaries which could be managed easily. This was not the case in communal areas, where grazing lands were owned and accessed communally.

Both of these initiatives took a 'technocratic command and control approach' to natural resources management. In line with findings of formal science, recommendations were disseminated and regulations made and enforced. The state played a key role in this, making decisions through interaction with those in the research community and implementing them through different ministries and departments. In the case of pushing through recommendations, AGRITEX played a key role, while in the case of policing implementation it was the Department of Natural Resources that mattered. In some instances, NGOs played an important part. In other instance – the grazing schemes, Campfire and ICRAF – the initiative involved elements of the participatory approach and was promoted by agents of the state and actors in civil society. In all these situations, the decisions were essentially made by the implementing agencies.

The Mahuwe Project

The project, 'Participatory Development of Community-based Management Plans for Livestock Feed Resources', was started in January 2000 and scheduled to end in 2003. The project was funded by the UK Department for International Development (DfID). It sought to develop and promote strategies for the allocation and management of on-farm and locally available resources and knowledge, together with research knowledge, in order to optimise livestock production and livestock contribution to the crop/livestock farming system of the communities in Ward 7 (Mahuwe), in Guruve District, Mashonaland Central Province.

Mahuwe is located in the semi-arid Zambezi valley and is part of the Mid-Zambezi Valley Development project that was established in 1987. It is a resettlement area with land demarcated for various uses – homesteads, grazing, arable, business centres, etc. Government officials planned, classified, demarcated and allocated land without participation of the local community members. The community was not happy with the land types allocated, especially for homesteads and arable fields. From the time the resettlements were established, Mahuwe experienced a rapid increase in population, through both natural growth and in-migration. The new residents, whether children from within or immigrants, were regarded as squatters by the Ward Development Committee (WADCO), Village Development Committees (VIDCOs), the Lower Guruve District Council and the legally resettled farmers. They faced constant threats of eviction by the local leadership and the District Council. There were problems of limited access to grazing areas due to illegal and haphazard settlements in grazing areas, and crop destructions by stray animals.

Mahuwe is in Agro-ecological Region V and the main agricultural activities are mixed crop (mainly cotton) and livestock production. It has a population of about 1,500 households, an area of 21,390 hectares in 11 villages under the leadership of 11 *Sabhukus* (leaders), VIDCOs and a WADCO.

Objectives

The specific objectives of the project were to:

- Identify community objectives for the use of common pool vegetation resources.
- Identify and implement management plans with a high probability of achieving community resource use objectives.
- Identify or establish local organisations and institutions capable of successfully implementing and enforcing the vegetation resource management plans developed by the community.

Approach & methodology

The general approach used was partnership research in which local communities were included as key partners and local knowledge and understanding were accepted as valid sources of information. The project used a variety of tools and techniques, singly or in combination, to achieve specific objectives and outputs according to their suitability (See Table 1).

The approach involved key sets of activities:

- Problem diagnoses or formulations which included needs analysis and formulation of objectives.
- Learning and understanding the system which involves identifying best options and activities to be implemented.
- Action, which was the activities undertaken to achieve the objectives.
- Monitoring and evaluation of all observations and system performance with regard to the achievement of the objectives.

A mechanism for linking the research team and the community was established. Drawing on local leaders, a community based co-ordinating committee (CC) was formed, each village selecting two local informants, or village representatives (VR), and a communication team (CT) member.

At the beginning, several participatory rural appraisal (PRA) exercises were done to obtain a broad understanding of the structure and vegetation resources available and to identify key problems in general. A focussed workshop was held with VRs, CT, and CC to identify the community objectives to be used as a guide for vegetation resource management. These were defined and agreed upon. They were presented first to the village leaders during formal meetings and then to the rest of the community in each village to seek approval. They were unanimously approved and provided a community-approved guide for the rest of the project implementation activities.

All the activities were carried out by the farmers themselves either as a whole community or by the VRs and facilitated by the research team. Permission was granted by the Guruve Rural District Council for the exercise to be conducted.

Main objective	Tools/Processes
Project introduction into the area	Meetings with members of the community, community leaders and Guruve Rural District Council
Collection of basic information about the area	PRA, Government service and development agencies, NGOs, Rural District Council, formal questionnaire surveys, key informants among different stakeholders, maps and diagrams, relevant literature/journals, Government Central Statistical Office
Identifying community objectives for vegetation resources	PRA, meetings with the community and community representatives, workshops
Mechanism for community participation	Village representatives, communication team, coordinating committee, formal and informal meetings, workshops, practical field exercises
Communicating and disseminating of information	Meetings with community representatives and the whole community, drama, pamphlets and posters, school children, field days
Information, analyses and decision making	Mapping, diagrams, ranking/scoring, simulation modelling, spider-grams, videos
Monitoring and evaluation	Sample herd monitoring, animal condition scoring (ILCA 5-point scale), vegetation monitoring

Table 1: *Summary of the tools and methods that were used at different phases of the project implementation to achieve objectives and outputs of the projects*

Outputs/Outcomes

Land use plan

The major output was the development of a new land use plan and various related spin-offs. The land use plan became the basis of all the other resource management plans developed subsequently. After the first few weeks, during which farmers defined and prioritised their objectives for the management of the natural resources and the problems towards achieving these objectives, the community made it clear that it was necessary to first address the underlying tensions concerning access to land. The community considered the re-planning of the land use in the ward and establishing the institutions as a necessary precondition for any future activities.

The then illegal settlers were accepted as members of the community and were allocated arable and residential plots. Boundaries of each village and for village members were clearly defined and confirmed with local leaders.

Grazing management plans

The community developed and implemented management systems in four identified grazing clusters. The systems were selected, from a wide range of options, after the community considered:

- the expected effectiveness of each option in increasing feed availability;
- the expected difficulty in implementation;
- the likely impacts of each option on the community.

Grazing clusters were the specific areas that animals from one or more villages shared as grazing land. These areas represented distinct management practices currently in place and the new management options that were going to be tested and evaluated (Table 2). The grazing management plans were designed according to cluster characteristics in Ward 7. Responsibility for enforcing agreed management practices was through committees chosen by these clusters. The grazing systems implemented were simple, and non-prescriptive. In addition to resource management, the grazing plans also addressed existing problems of access to grazing areas, new land use structures and new power shifts for local leadership.

Local institutions

Mahuwe ward residents had priority areas that they wanted resolved as a precondition to the development of grazing area management systems. Community objectives were stated as:

- Stopping illegal and haphazard land allocations.
- Establishing legitimate leadership; in Mahuwe ward, many people were trying to establish themselves as leaders by creating a local following through illegal land allocations.
- Stopping the acceptance of new settlers from outside Ward 7; some people built homes and cleared fields in the area without the community knowing who had given them permission to settle.
- Producing a new laws and regulations use plan for ward seven showing the land to be used for different purposes such as fields, homesteads, business areas, and grazing areas.

The community agreed on new institutions and bye-laws to achieve these objectives with approval by the Guruve Rural District Council. The major issues addressed by the new institutions included mechanisms for the allocation of new land, at both Ward and *Sabhuku* (village) levels, resolution of conflicts (boundaries, stray animals), cutting of trees for firewood, and livestock and grazing area management. These institutions aimed at making the leadership accountable, transparent and broadly representative of the communities they served.

Name of cluster	Current management system	Proposed new management system
Chirunya	Vast grazing area; animals released to grazing area and come back alone at end of day during the rain season. Draught animals on release are tether-grazed or sent to grazing areas.	Introduce drop-off lines beyond which all animals must be released.
Goredema	No specified grazing area; animals grazed around homesteads, on the mountains, along roads and rivers, shared grazing with those in Kutsikwesora (Hambe area).	Stop grazing around homesteads; instead grow crops around homesteads; herd all animals and pen them at night and release them into designated areas only (mountains and the Hambe-Musakanda areas).
Chombe	Plenty of grazing around homesteads and in grazing areas in Rukoche, Bwazi and Sangojena; veld fires are a major cause of grazing shortages in the dry season.	Rotate grazing areas and keep animals away from homesteads.
Fume	No specified grazing area; animals grazed around homesteads, on the mountains, along roads and rivers, shared grazing with those in Kutsikwesora (Hambe area).	Stop grazing around homesteads; grow crops around homesteads; herd all animals and pen them at night, release them into designated areas only (mountains and the Hambe-Musakanda area).

Table 2: *The grazing management systems, current and proposed, for the different grazing clusters identified in Mahuwe*

Databases

The community developed databases of information on various aspects of the ward such as the names of all residents, sizes of land, types and numbers of live-stock, maps showing ward and village boundaries, demarcations of land types, and locations of residential stands. The databases were intended to increase knowledge of the area as well as assist policy makers and local leadership in planning and decision making regarding management of natural resources.

Field Guide Manual on planning & implementing land use changes

Experiences during the land use planning motivated the project to produce and publish a field guide to planning and implementing land use changes with rural communities. It consists of step-by step instructions on how to develop a community-based land use plan, and attempts to provide enough detail for users with no previous experience of land use planning, and be simple enough to be used by local communities and other stakeholders. It is based on the principle that the planning process must be understood and owned by the community through participation in planning.

Discussion & analysis

The research team emphasised that that the community itself was responsible for identifying any problems and solutions. Community members were expected to participate fully and the research team would only facilitate the process. The community accepted the approach. Commitment and participation in all the project processes by the community was, without doubt, very high. The formulation and agreement on common community objectives made an important contribution to the subsequent commitment and participation. It is considered by some scientists (Toulmin and Scoones 2001) that immediate benefits and incentives are essential if farmers are to participate in development projects. The potential for obtaining legal land ownership status and security of tenure for the 'squatters', the stopping of land claims from those outside the ward, and establishment of legitimate leadership were some of the incentives for participation. It was evident after a number of meetings that the community's priority concerns were not the same as those the project had identified. The people were concerned with the haphazard allocation of land by illegitimate leaders to new immigrants in grazing areas, and security of tenure.

The research plans evolved as the project progressed, and as community objectives were made clear. Subsequently, the project incorporated the development of a land use plan (as demanded by the community) as its priority activity. During project implementation, continuous adjustments to activities and goals were being made in order to address changes that affected Mahuwe during this period. Important changes were the government policy shift in which rural leadership was transferred from VIDCOs to *Sabhukus*, the new land use plan, and land ownership caused by the project itself. The land use plan resulted in changes in access to, and sizes of, grazing areas, animal grazing patterns and management units. The continuous adoption of internal and external changes by the project is what has been termed an 'adaptive management' approach and has been successfully used elsewhere in similar initiatives (Hagman et al. 2003; Lal et al. 2003).

All project decisions were approved by the community through a series of feedback meetings, which helped in developing a feeling of ownership. Tools such as PRA, maps and diagrams, workshops and feedback meetings were not just for information gathering by the researchers; they were also important in enhancing interaction and self-awareness among the community members and within the research team. The project empowered the local community by training individuals and leaders in the use of tools to diagnose, seek alternatives, and test and evaluate innovations, which was a major aim and output of the project. It remains to be seen whether those who obtained these skills continue to use them for community benefit in the future. One problem though was the high turnover of VRs, which implied continuous training and incomplete acquisition of skills packages.

The 'adaptive management' approach enabled the project to address issues that were considered highly critical by the community but were not core activities, namely land use re-planning and the legitimising of local leadership institutions. National policy shifts in the rural institutions of leadership and authority were made during the planning process and the project was able to respond and adapt its activities.

From an environmental perspective, the land use planning resulted in the conversion of grazing lands into arable land thereby reducing access to other outputs as well as habitats for wildlife. Chinembiri (2002) estimated that about 2,000 hectares were to be cleared for new fields but only 450 hectares of previous fields were reassigned for grazing. These negative effects were due to be countered by a new and enlightened awareness of environmental issues among community members (bye-laws had been formulated regarding cutting of trees for poles and firewood, the selling of firewood, burning and use of resources at village level).

From a project management perspective, the participatory approach requires considerable time and skills to develop a partnership between the community and the researchers as well as gain a detailed understanding of the underlying issues and to subsequently develop community consensus on the objectives and solutions. This was the case with the Mahuwe project and it led to increased time pressure towards the end of the project. An application to extend the project time frame was rejected by the donors. Accepting the objectives and priorities as defined by the community, which may conflict with original project objectives, requires courage and flexibility. These appear difficult to reconcile with traditional donor supported initiatives that always have pre-defined objectives and strict time limits.

It was easy to illustrate new concepts and techniques to the community members using locally relevant examples. However, there can be no recipe for the tools and methods to use. Each project has to find the methods and tools that satisfy its objectives and outputs, hence the need to combine high technology systems like computer simulation and GPS with simple farmer-usable techniques in the development of land use planning and vegetation and land use maps.

In conclusion, the outputs were achieved because of the development and operation of a meaningful partnership and dialogue between the community and the research team. Also important were the development of a sound understanding of the system, facilitating the development of a community vision and accepting local priorities, working with local people at all stages, and close coupling of planning and implementation phases and effective communication.

Lessons

Communication. Timely and regular dissemination of information, and the promotion of frank debates and discussion are essential to the operation of a project.

Knowledge of community objectives and priorities. Projects should understand and respect the priorities and objectives of the community, and be able to adapt objectives and activities to those of the community.

Indigenous knowledge and local leadership. Local leadership and local knowledge must be recognised and utilised.

Participation of local residents. Local residents should be the decision makers and should participate in all activities concerning their livelihoods.

Project flexibility. Project objectives and activities must be flexible in response to emerging community objectives.

The future

For the successful conservation and management of grazing lands in communal areas, local community concerns about immediate tangible benefits must be integrated with the long-term concerns about the environment at different levels – community, national, regional and global. This can be accomplished by building on indigenous knowledge and traditions (Saxena et al. 2003) and by involving the local community and stakeholders in decision making (Conroy et al. 2002).

The philosophy and perceptions among research and development workers must change to accommodate new voices and promote a different type of science, based more on local understanding of key issues and problems. This is relevant to Zimbabwe, particularly in light of the recent land reform, which has opened up new settlement types, a larger number of farmers with different goals and priorities regarding natural resources, and new institutions for managing the resources. Participants in natural resources research must recognise this change.

Our experience in the mid-Zambezi Valley resettlement area demonstrated the importance of the consultative approach. Even when the central government intends to enact laws for natural resources management and use, it should consult at the lowest level to ensure acceptability and relevance of interventions to those targeted. Instead of simply rehabilitating degraded areas and protecting existing resources, research and development should also seriously consider incorporating commercial production for income generation when developing interventions. This would improve the economic livelihoods of those involved as well as increasing stakeholder commitment to protecting the resources.

A holistic approach to natural resources management and use is recommended because of the complexity with respect to values, socio-economic environments, multiple uses of natural resources (firewood, building poles, browse, fruits, thatch grass, artefacts, habitat for wild animals, etc.), and the spatial and temporal distribution that exists within and across communities.

The process of facilitating negotiation among the stakeholders to obtain agreement on solutions and activities needs to be developed. The tools and techniques to be used by local communities must not be 'standardised' or 'prescriptive' but must be developed and adapted for specific situations. The issue of continuity and sustainability in development efforts remains a big challenge and more effort must be directed towards the general empowerment of the communities to adapt, on their own, to any situation that may arise in future.

Acknowledgements

The U.K. Department for International Development (DfID) is gratefully acknowledged for supporting the research.

References

AGRITEX. 1998. *Learning Together through Participatory Extension: A guide to an Approach Developed in Zimbabwe*. Harare: Department of Agricultural and Extension Services.

Chinembiri, F. M. 2002. 'Impact of the land use plan Mahuwe ward, Guruve District', unpublished report. Harare: Institute of Environmental Studies, University of Zimbabwe.

Clarke, J. 1991. 'Forestry as a component of participatory rural development: lessons and challenges drawn from the Zimbabwean experience', paper presented at a conference on African Agroforestry, Nelspruit, 19-22 August.

Cliffe, L. 1986. 'Policy Options for Agrarian Reform in Zimbabwe: A Technical Appraisal'.

Conroy, C., A. Mishra and A. Rai. 2002. 'Learning from self-initiated community forest management in Orissa India', *Forest Policy and Economics* 4, pp. 227-37.

Hagman J., E. Chuma, K. Murwira, M. Connolly and P. Ficarelli. 2003. 'Success factors in integrated natural resources management R & D: Lessons from practice', in B.M. Campbell and J. A. Sayer (eds), *Integrated Natural Resources Management: Linking Productivity, the Environment and Development*. Wallingford: CABI Publishing, pp. 37-64.

Hagman, J. and Chuma, E. 1994. *Transformation of Agricultural Extension and Research in Zimbabwe towards Farmer Participation: Approach and Strategy Based on Experiences from Masvingo Province. Masvingo, Zimbabwe, Conservation Tillage Project*. Agritex/GTZ.

Lal, P., H. Lim-Applegate and M. Scoccimarro. 2003. 'The adaptive decision making process as a tool for integrated natural resources management: Focus, attitudes and approach', in B.M. Campbell and J. A. Sayer (eds), *Integrated Natural Resources Management: Linking Productivity, the Environment and Development*. Wallingford: CABI Publishing, pp. 65-86.

Land Tenure Commission. 1994. Report of the Commission of Inquiry into Appropriate Agricultural Land Tenure Regimes, *Volume 2*. Harare: Government Printers.

Mache, B and J.B. Chivizhe. 1992. Institutional dynamics in communal grazing regimes in Zimbabwe: The Agritex Experience', in B. Cousins (ed.), *Institutional Dynamics in Communal Grazing Regimes in Southern Africa*. Harare: Centre for Applied Social Sciences, University of Zimbabwe.

Murphree, M.W. 1991. 'Communities as institutions for resource management', Occasional Paper NRM. Centre for Applied Social Sciences, University of Zimbabwe.

Saxena, K G., K.K. Rao, R.K. Maikhuri and R.L. Semwal. 2003. 'Integrated Natural Resource Management: Approaches and Lessons from the Himalaya', in B.M. Campbell and J.A. Sayer (eds), *Integrated Natural Resources Management: Linking Productivity, the Environment and Development*. Wallingford: CABI Publishing, pp. 211-25.

Scoones, I. and B. Cousins. 1988. 'A participatory model of agricultural research and extension: the case of vleis, trees and grazing schemes in the dry south of Zimbabwe', *Zambezia* XVI, pp. 45-65.

Toulmin, C and I. Scoones. 2001. 'Ways forward? Technical choices, intervention strategies and policy option', in Scoones (ed.), *Dynamics and Diversity: Soil Fertility and Livelihoods in Africa*. London: Earthscan, pp. 176-208.

11

Local Environmental Action Planning:
Making it Work

Jeanette Manjengwa

Introduction

Despite huge efforts and large amounts of international aid money, little progress has been made in reducing poverty, and the world's environment is regarded as still too fragile (Kothari and Minogue 2002). The situation remains of the struggle of rural people to find acceptable livelihoods within a deteriorating resource base. There is evidence that poor people are getting poorer, and the environment continues to be degraded, thereby threatening future livelihoods of those often too poor to invest in it (Murphree 1996).

Many donor projects are based on the assumption that the efforts that the donor initiates will take on a momentum of their own. Unfortunately, the development landscape is littered with the remains of projects that have died when donor funding ended (Turner and Hulme 1997). Such projects were intended to foster a process of self-sustaining development, but in reality, they provided little more than a temporary infusion of assets, personnel and services (Morss et al. 1985). Although aid money has helped in some cases, it has failed in general to seriously reduce destitution. The world of the local-level natural resource managers, who are often eking out a living from a degraded natural resource base, remains divorced from the international arena of endless debate and discussion on community-based natural resource management and sustainable development.

People-centred conservation currently enjoys international popularity as an environmental philosophy that seeks to link conservation concerns with local needs and governance (Murphree 1996). Effective environmental management driven by local initiative and participation should provide the key to reducing rural poverty, as well as conserving the natural resource base (Woodhouse et al. 2000). The active involvement of local people in the process is therefore perceived as being a prerequisite for sustainable development.

However, the record of community-based natural resource management is highly mixed. While there are outstanding cases of success, more often the picture is one of qualified achievement or, even, abysmal failure. Sometimes community-based natural resource management has been misconstrued and applied to the wrong contexts. Imposition of community-based natural resource management on rural communities, poor extension work and local factionalism are also blamed for poor performance.

This chapter looks at two interventions, namely District Environmental Action Planning (DEAP) and local level scenario planning, iterative assessment and adaptive management that both aim to empower local level natural resource users to better manage their natural resources for their own livelihood benefits, whilst conserving the environment. Although the two initiatives have similar overall aims, they have different approaches, methodologies, time frames, geographical location, scale and implementing agencies. Rather than attempt a comparative analysis, the chapter aims to throw light on the more general problem of why interventions that claim to link conservation with development are failing not only to empower local people, but to improve livelihoods and enhance the natural resource base.

The DEAP programme was implemented in the 1990s by the Ministry of Environment and Tourism, through its Department of Natural Resources (DNR),[1] with financial assistance from the United Nations Development Programme (UNDP) and technical support from the International Union for the Conservation of Nature (IUCN). It is described in official documents as a community-based participatory planning approach that aims to integrate environmental concerns with development planning (Mukahanana et al. 1996; Chenje et al. 1998; DNR 1999), and to assist communities to assess their human and environmental well-being and develop capacity for strategic planning and taking action at the community level (DNR 1999). Despite the participatory methodology used, the programme had little impact and did not result in ownership by the local people, nor result in any substantial improvement of either human or environmental well-being (Manjengwa 2004, 2007). The chapter investigates what went wrong with the DEAP programme, particularly the paradox of too much participation, which rendered it both socially and financially unsustainable, and too little participation in that a participatory approach was applied to only part of the process and local people were not in control.

Local level scenario planning, iterative assessment and adaptive management is currently being implemented by the Centre for Applied Social Sciences (CASS), University of Zimbabwe, with financial assistance from the International Development Research Centre (IDRC). The main objective of this initiative is to enhance the ability of local level natural resource managers to collectively manage and benefit from their natural resources through the development and refinement of the research and managerial methodology of scenario analysis. It takes the methodology of scenario modelling and makes

---

1   Under the Environmental Management Act (Chapter 20:27), DNR was transformed into the Environmental Management Agency.

it a people-centred set of collective experiments, iteratively reflecting their aspirations, their assessments and their adaptations over time. The concept was developed by Marshall Murphree, and draws on his long experience with the Communal Areas Management Programme for Indigenous Resources (Campfire) and holistic analysis of community based natural resource management. The concept has been documented in a number of papers (including Murphree 2001, 2004).

The local level scenario planning initiative is currently being piloted with communities in the Great Limpopo Trans-frontier Conservation Area (GLTFCA) in Zimbabwe, Mozambique and South Africa. It aims to improve the understanding of GLTFCA planners of the needs and aspirations of the resident populations and ensure their consideration in overall planning and implementation. The process involves action research in which interdisciplinary teams of scholars participate in local planning and assessment, but only in an invited and facilitative manner. This initiative aims to refine a methodology that places professional and local civil science into a new relationship, in which the former is less intrusive and the latter less marginal.

The chapter then looks at how this new approach to local planning has the potential to address some of the shortcomings of development initiatives that were highlighted by the implementation of DEAP, namely ensuring that the process is truly participatory, locally owned, and grounded at local level. Presentation of the two initiatives is followed by a discourse on the appropriateness and effectiveness of participatory approaches, as this issue emerges as an important factor in bestowing ownership for local level natural resource management initiatives.

The chapter draws on research carried out on DEAP by the author (Manjengwa 2004, 2007), and the local level scenario planning proposal developed and refined by Marshall Murphree and the CASS team (CASS 2006).

District Environmental Action Planning (DEAP)

The DEAP process

The concept of DEAP arose out of the larger global environmental and developmental agenda of the World Conservation Strategy and Agenda 21, but was adapted to the Zimbabwean situation. The rhetoric of DEAP is rooted in people-centred, bottom-up, participatory approaches and building capacity at local level, which aims to empower people to use and manage their own natural resources efficiently. The original methodology is spelt out clearly as a series of steps in two booklets produced by IUCN: 'Assessing Rural Sustainability – 40 Steps' and 'Planning for Rural Sustainability – 39 Steps'. The IUCN was developing a methodology for the assessment of well-being and piloting a participatory approach as part of a wider international project. During implementation the steps were condensed by the DNR into the following six main stages that became known as the DEAP Process:

- District environmental profile
- Pre-field visit
- Assessment stage
- Action planning
- Implementation of action plan
- Monitoring and evaluation.

According to the IUCN booklets, the first two steps were the collection and organisation of external technical data. This was to provide background information on the ecosystem and people of the district, and was supposed to have been communicated to the villagers so that they could use it and integrate it with their own information. However, these steps were not carried out by the DEAP teams. Instead, a series of District Environmental Profiles were produced at a later date by consultants hired by the Ministry of Environment and Tourism, in a procedure that was completely unconnected to the rest of the DEAP process and was described by a former DNR officer as a 'sort of afterthought'. The profiles provided district databases including details of physical geography, population, administrative structures, economic activities, settlements and services, investment opportunities, potential for sustainable resource use and ongoing programmes and activities.

Although the profiles provided a lot of information, very little of it was relevant to the compilation of village assessments and action planning. The scale of information was not compatible with the level of action planning. The profiles contained information about the whole district, whereas DEAP was implemented in villages in only one or two wards. Detailed information for individual wards was not available in the profiles. To all intents and purposes, the profiles did not become an integral component of the DEAP process, were never integrated into development planning, and were not endorsed by the communities.

In its assessment and action planning stages, DEAP makes use of a variety of participatory rural appraisal tools: ice-breakers such as the square game and the river code where communities start to visualise problems and hurdles; metaphors to understand the interdependence between ecosystem and human well-being, such as the egg of sustainability where the yolk represents people and the white the ecosystem; the barometer of sustainability which shows that neither the environment nor the people can be improved without the other; the pyramid of action which shows that projects based on community actions with little or no external assistance are more sustainable; participatory mapping and transect walk; investment and cause-and-effect analysis; institutional audits; ranking of priorities; and criteria for effective action planning.

Implementation of the action plans was determined by the amount of donor funds available. Although DEAP is primarily a planning and capacity-building process, during its implementation projects became a major focus. In all pilot districts only a fraction of the projects and activities identified in the action planning process have been implemented, with only a few villages in one or two wards of each district benefiting. In some cases, projects were started, but not completed due to lack of funds. Unfortunately, DEAP seed money was limited and uptake by other donors, except for a few isolated cases, never really got off the ground. Various reports were produced by the DNR and the DEAP teams documenting DEAP's activities, projects and achievements in the pilot districts (see for example DNR 1995; 1999). However, research in the villages illustrates discrepancies between what the documents say about DEAP and the reality. An example is provided by the Hwange ostrich project, which illustrates how the rhetoric can be completely out of touch with reality on the ground. During a field visit to the project site at Nhlovu Village, Lukunguni Vlei, Hwange District, the members of the ostrich project committee said that there were no birds left as project members had eaten the surviving ones. No birds had been sold commercially as they never attained the required weight due to difficulties in acquiring the correct food. Technical back-up was inadequate. The villagers said that the project was a disaster and a waste of time and effort. One villager declared that 'the ostrich project was just like throwing money into the Zambezi!' Information that none of the ostriches were left and that the project was a complete failure had not reached district level, let alone national level.

Disillusionment with DEAP

As long as DEAP was perceived as being for projects rather than a planning process, there was bound to be disillusionment as there was too little money provided for project implementation. The process raised a lot of expectations. People expected money but it did not come. The intensity of these expectations can be seen in the example given by another researcher who was carrying out an evaluation for a programme in Mberengwa District where the local people confused it with DEAP. An elderly woman remarked that they know everything about the sustainable egg, but what they wanted now was money to implement the projects.

Implementation of the DEAP process was generally a 'one-off' initiative with no assessment or iteration, punctuated by a number of donor-led programmes. There was negligible monitoring and evaluation, no feasibility studies and very little technical back-up. The DEAP process has no guidelines, methodology, procedural steps or definitions of how environment and sustainability issues arising from its participatory rural appraisal assessments and action planning would be integrated into Rural District Council development plans. Rather than being mainstreamed into development planning, it appears that DEAP was designed to come up with a parallel planning system at the district level. For the most part, the environmental action plans, developed through the DEAP process, were an end in themselves.

Bridging the gap between micro & meso/macro levels

The DEAP programme was implemented with the anticipation of rectifying problems associated with traditional top-down technocratic planning, which had so far failed to work in Zimbabwe (Chenje et al. 1998; Hulme and Murphree 2001). However, it too failed to bridge the gap between micro and macro levels. Although Platteau and Abraham (2002) assert that the participatory or decentralised approach can be an effective channel of development for communities if they receive genuine delegation of powers and responsibilities, this assumption of devolution rather than decentralisation is often not the case in practice. In Zimbabwe, devolution to community level has not yet been fully realised. With DEAP, the required institutional arrangements at sub-district level, such as the Community Strategy Teams, were not firmly enough established enough to ground such a programme at local level. There was no mechanism for upward transmission of plans. Despite the rhetoric of being bottom-up, and including participatory rural appraisal exercises with local people, the approach used in DEAP was top-down, and ownership was perceived as being at national level, or with the international agencies. The DNR is regarded as the authority on what environmental measures need to be taken, with people in rural areas being told how to manage natural resources (Keeley and Scoones 2000).

Local-level scenario planning, iterative assessment & adaptive management

Evolution of the concept

Unlike the DEAP initiative, the local level scenario planning, iterative assessment and adaptive management initiative was devised by national scholar-practitioners. CASS has been involved in national and regional programmes for the decentralisation of natural resource management to local levels for over 20 years using participatory methodologies. In the inaugural stage of such programmes as Campfire, CASS played a participatory research role, advising programme implementers and communities and using this experience for analysis. In recent years, it has assumed a more holistic analytic role, placing community-based natural resource management within larger development and livelihood contexts (see for example Hulme and Murphree 2001).

Local level scenario planning, iterative assessment and adaptive management proposal has had a long gestation. Arising from CASS's association with

Campfire and other southern African community-based natural resource management initiatives has been an awareness that communities frequently seek to visualise their futures and that modest forms of local scenario projections have been used in extension work. But the notion of taking scenario modelling and linking it to local planning, self-assessment and adaptive management in a structured and iterative way was first put forward by CASS at a seminar at the University of California, Berkeley (Murphree 2001). This formed the basis for the project proposal that was reviewed and revised a number of times during which it acquired a geographical location within the Great Limpopo Trans-frontier Conservation Area (GLTFCA). Nearly half of this three-country, 100,000 km² area is communal land and a very high proportion (80 per cent) of the people are living below the poverty datum line.

Methodology

Variants of the approach can be found in some community-based natural resource management programmes, but what has usually been lacking is the explicit freedom to experiment and carry this planning forward in systematised assessment and adaptation.

The methodology has five sequential components:

Scenario modelling, in which communities collectively construct their preferred vision of the future in their localities for specified time frames, based inter alia on their projected needs, both material and cultural, resources, modes of production, institutions and extra-local relationships. Scenario modelling must include not only 'visioning' and aspirations, but also a consideration of constraints and alternatives – 'negotiating the future' starts here – and it must include an agenda for action. At this point scenario modelling becomes scenario planning, which must include considerations of cost and the assignment of responsibilities.

Implementation of projected activities, i.e. experimentation with the plan.

Self-assessment. The experiences of implementation are treated as experimental probes. Criteria and means of assessment are collectively agreed, and expectations are compared with performance on the ground. Through periodic reviews, the attainment of goals is assessed. If progress is not satisfactory, the reasons are examined: is it a failure of design or implementation? the fault of internal actors or external actors? what needs to be changed, and how? A revised action plan for the next period is thus negotiated.

Adaptation, in which experience is turned into learning, and learning is used to correct errors, negotiate agreements, change expectations and revise action plans.

Iteration. The steps outlined above constitute a cycle. It is assumed that the cycle will take one year for completion, although there is no intrinsic reason why it should not be more or less. Adaptive management infers iteration and a long time frame is required.

It is envisaged that iterative scenario modelling will become institutionalised, in whatever modified forms experience dictates, in communities of the

GLTFCA over the next few years.

A fundamental aspect of the methodology is that local perspectives, assessments and decisions should drive the entire process. It reflects the insight of Emery Roe: 'The obvious challenge is to come up with varieties of inside-out planning for ecosystem management, where local leaders and residents are themselves the experts and where the planning process is itself initiated and guided from within the local ecosystem' (Roe 1998:130). Thus the participation of communities must be voluntary, and the visioning, planning, implementation, evaluation and adaptation must reflect a sense of localised authority and responsibility. During implementation, it is crucial to avoid a situation where resident 'participation' is in fact a manipulative local response to access project funding rather than collaboration in a larger enterprise enhancing local developmental efforts – a syndrome which has led to failure in so many conservation and development projects.

The initiative anticipates potential disjunctions in perspectives and interests which represent both the challenges to, and opportunities afforded by, the methodology. Experience suggests that technical inputs are more likely to be accepted when they are seen as invited contributions to local planning rather than external impositions. Provided that 'ownership' of the process is perceived to be local, technical inputs would be welcomed. The key to all these processes is effective, 'light-touch' facilitation in the planning and evaluation exercises, which introduces project perspectives and larger-scale GLTFCA concerns and objectives without violating local senses of ownership.

This initiative seeks to turn the relationship between professional 'externals' and local 'internals' on its head. Initiation and implementation stems from and is the responsibility of the local; professional involvement becomes invited rather than imposed, directed rather than directive, facilitative rather than manipulative. It should represent professional science in the service of local civic science. Funding from IDRC provides an opportunity to initiate this approach in a number of pilot sites in the GLTFCA, and facilitate the process for another four years, after which it is expected that the planning process will have a momentum of its own.

Time scale

Durable local natural resource management regimes require a sense of long time frames and planning and implementation which marches to a local agenda. However, there are usually mismatches between short-term practice and management and long-term ecological processes. Sustainability is a concept inherently related to temporal scale and the relationships between the present and the future. Temporal scale also features in debates on inter-generational equity.

Natural resources planning is generally carried out in short time frames at both national and local levels. In their survey of case-studies in Africa, Bernstein and Woodhouse (2000: 207) conclude that 'Indigenous communal institutions do not appear to act on matters of (long-term) resource management as distinct from (current) allocation...' Imposed planning and implementation does little better, following the two- to five-year time horizons of donor-funded projects. As a result research data on process is weak and synoptic, having to infer process by 'back-casting' or predictive speculation. Scholarship is defective in dealing with significant time scales, and offers little to those who might use it in negotiating their futures. At local levels, dealing with significant time scales is also defective today, since communities rarely have the entitlements necessary for them to experiment. Scenario modelling and planning provides the fulcrum for scale-sensitive research and action methodology that gives emphasis to the future and to sustainability.

Problems with participation

Not enough participation

Theoretically, participatory approaches are expected to confer local ownership. The ultimate aim of participation is achieved by allowing people to take control of decision making in research and planning development, thereby promoting the sustainability of development projects (Stadler 1999). Research on DEAP found that despite the participatory methodology used, the process did not result in ownership by the local people; a participatory approach was applied to only part of the process. Consequently, DEAP cannot be considered a truly participatory process. Local people were not in control. The methodology was devised by an international team; the schedule was organised, and the finances controlled, from above. The local people played a passive role waiting for events to be organised for them. Although they identified their priority activities, major decisions were taken at higher levels. They had to fit within the broader resource allocation and political commitments of the Government of Zimbabwe, and the DEAP process was considered to be technocratic planning, rather than genuine participation and empowerment (Keeley and Scoones 2000).

This lack of ownership is not unique to DEAP. Even in the Campfire programme, where people's participation in wildlife is promoted, communities often do not see themselves as the joint owners of the wildlife, but regard it as belonging to the government or Rural District Council (RDC) (Murombedzi 1999; Sibanda 2001). Sometimes participatory approaches can be window-dressing to make the initiative more acceptable to development agencies whilst concealing strong vertical control (Mosse 2002). Decisions are made at a higher level with little reference to the locally produced knowledge (Cooke and Kothari 2001). Participatory planning and their local knowledge can be easily manipulated by external interests and outsider analysis of problems and so-called 'local choices' shaped by the development agendas of government officers, scientists, foreign researchers, donor advisors and agencies (Mosse 2002). Often, programmes described as participatory do not deliver functional participation and claims made about the use of participatory approaches tend to be exaggerated (Vivian and Maseko 1994). PlanAfric (2000) assert that although the rhetoric of participatory planning approaches may exist in virtually all rural development programmes, its application in practice is limited. These types of contradictions characterise virtually all participatory interventions, but are easily concealed (Mosse 2002). Participation remains a way of talking about rather than doing things (Cooke and Kothari 2001).

In the case of the local level scenario planning, iterative assessment and adaptive management initiative, after an awareness-raising workshop introducing the concept and inviting discussions that lead to modifications and refinement, interested communities will invite facilitation. This is expected to secure commitment and ownership by the community. Although local people were not involved in the initial development of the concept, the methodology is experimental and provides opportunities for revisions and adaptation during implementation. This point of adaptive management and the experimental nature of the approach was emphasised by CASS in discussions during the proposal review process with IDRC. An important challenge will be to develop a methodological culture of respect for different perspectives, local agendas, and rigour in evaluation and adaptability in implementation.

Too much participation

The participatory approach used in DEAP, with its tools such as the Egg of Sustainability, actually contributed to the disillusionment felt by local participants. The participatory rural appraisal exercises raised false expectations that were not fulfilled. The research found that what local people wanted was development projects on the ground.

In participatory approaches, good logistics, such as venue, equipment, materials, accommodation, food, finance and allowances, are important (Chambers 2002). However, these are expensive and from a practical point of view, both time and good logistics imply significant costs and place new demands on resources (Mosse 2001). The DEAP experience has shown that these requirements have made the process heavily reliant on donor funding. More money was spent on facilitating the process, on overheads, administration and substantial allowances, than on actual improvements on the ground. Gathering people together and facilitating participatory processes is an expensive activity.

Even if participatory approaches increase economic and managerial efficiency by reducing administrative and management costs due to the proximity of local participants, as suggested by Mohamed-Katerere (2001), this does not exclude costs involved for the facilitation of the participatory approach. Implementation of the participatory approach in DEAP within a top-down system predisposed it to be expensive because the system necessitated travel and subsistence allowances for so many government officials to go to the field to train local people how to participate. Some NGO practitioners who have criticised DEAP for being too expensive a process claim that their organisations do participatory rural appraisal at no extra expense. However, an ex-DNR officer refuted this, saying that it is not participatory rural appraisal that they do, rather simple consultative interviews.

The cost of participatory approaches is is often overlooked. There have been calls to recognise both the costs and benefits of participation for individuals (Mayoux 1995). However, these have not been followed up and the need for an analysis of the resources needed for participatory approaches in order that they can be low-cost and high-benefit, has been identified as an area for further work (Cleaver 1999). The importance of keeping recurrent costs and external resources to a minimum in order to encourage self-reliance has long been recognised (See for example Gow and Van Sant 1985).

When donors introduce the conditionality of participatory approaches, expenses are incurred that can usually only be provided by donors themselves. Options for breaking this dependency cycle include national governments budgeting for the application of a participatory approach, or reducing the time and personnel for participatory rural appraisal. In Zimbabwe, examination of other options was precipitated by the withdrawal of bilateral and some multilateral donors because of the political situation. For DEAP, cost-cutting options include reducing the number of facilitators and the length of the action planning sessions. The dilemma of how to make DEAP sustainable, or even how to make it useful, hangs on how much quality of information and detail can be sacrificed to reducing the length and thereby the cost of the participatory approach. In an attempt to address this dilemma, the local level scenario planning, iterative assessment and adaptive management methodology uses local facilitators from the community. The role of professional facilitators is gradually reduced and eventually dispensed with. Furthermore, there is no prescribed suite of participatory rural appraisal tools.

Is participation necessary?

Development projects have been criticised for having too much participation and too little impact on rural livelihoods (Cooke and Kothari 2001; Mosse 2002). Unless participation is truly functional and interactive, and the relevant institutional and legal frameworks are in place, local communities cannot be empowered to plan for and manage their natural resources. Even when development initiatives contain stages that are highly participatory, as with DEAP, it is unlikely that ownership will be ensconced at local level, and so the participatory rural appraisal exercise will be an expensive luxury.

There was no indication from the research that the projects identified through the DEAP process were any better than, or different from, those identified using other methods. A general criticism was that the environmental action plans that emerged from it were merely long lists of demands for basic infrastructure and services, sometimes with the inclusion of environmental issues, rather than imaginative plans emanating from the community, for natural resource management (Keeley and Scoones 2000; Ministry of Environment and Tourism 2000). This research indicates that even with the use of participatory rural appraisal in environmental action planning, local people pragmatically tailored their needs to what they thought the donor could offer. Similarly, with local level scenario planning, iterative assessment and adaptive management it is anticipated that the first stages of discussions will result in a wish-list of immediate needs. While this would be instructive, it is not scenario planning, which seeks to focus attention on desired future conditions, and this is where facilitative intervention would be useful. The community itself should drive the agenda of the exercise and should reflect the entire spectrum of local aspirations.

It has been suggested that in some cases participatory approaches might not be necessary as outsiders may be better able to initiate development changes because of their skills, experience and relative impartiality (Vivian and Maseko 1994). Participatory methodologies and community-based natural resource management does not always protect all groups or improve the situation of the most disadvantaged people (Tendler 1982; Cleaver 1999; Hulme and Woodhouse 2000). Villages are highly stratified, and elites often make decisions that are not in the interest of the community as a whole (Ribot 2002). Mosse (2002) suggests that the link between participatory processes and efficient implementation, although widely validated, may be absent in practice. Vivian and Maseko (1994) found that 'participatory' or community-based infrastructure projects are usually disappointing in terms of completion rates, quality of structure and maintenance. On the other hand, they found that beneficial impacts of the least participatory projects, those such as dam and borehole construction, where input from the community was not sought either in terms of planning or labour, were more impressive.

McGee (2002) found that even among its proponents, opinions diverge on the extent to which participation is appropriate or convenient. It appears that the importance of participatory approaches may be over-exaggerated in some situations and their appropriateness has been questioned (Guijt and Cornwall 1995; Stadler 1999; Cooke and Kothari 2001; Mafuta 2001). In the case of DEAP, more emphasis was placed on the assessment of human and ecosystem well-being and the selection of priority projects, than on actual sound implementation of these projects or integration into development plans. Thorough feasibility studies were rarely carried out and the project committee groups did not have adequate management skills or back-up technical services. Although participatory development is being promoted in terms of Africa's development to enable the poor to achieve some measure of economic and political influence, until these trends are measured and assessed, their true overall impact remains unknown (Oakley and Clegg 1999).

Conclusion

DEAP was not entrenched at the local level, and a participatory approach was applied to only part of the process; although communities identified their priority activities, major decisions were taken at higher levels. Furthermore, the process did not allow for a merger of local and technical scientific knowledge. It is crucial to avoid such shortcomings where the participation is merely window-dressing to conceal strong vertical control.

Local level scenario planning, iterative assessment and adaptive management, implies more than just scenario visioning and planning; it links the implementation of the plans, self-assessment and adaptive management in an iterative process. The expectation is that through such a truly participatory initiative the planning process will be taken up by local communities and institutionalised at local level. If the methodology maintains the essential characteristic of successive evaluative iteration, it will be a powerful tool.

The failure of DEAP was due to flaws in design as well as weaknesses in implementation. The adaptive nature and experimental design of the local level scenario planning initiative goes a long way towards anticipating and rectifying some of the shortcomings experienced by other local level interventions. However, implementation is just beginning and the concept has still to be tested and validated.

References

Bernstein, H. and P. Woodhouse. 2000. 'Whose environments? Whose livelihoods?', in P. Woodhouse, H. Bernstein and D. Hulme (eds), *The Social Dynamics of Wetlands in Drylands*. Oxford: James Currey, p. 207.

CASS. 2006. 'Local level scenario planning, iterative assessment and adaptive management project', project proposal document, Centre for Applied Social Sciences, University of Zimbabwe, June.

Chambers, R. 2002. *Participatory Workshops: Sourcebook of 21 sets of ideas and activities*. London: Earthscan.

Chenje M., L. Sola and D. Paleczny (eds). 1998. *The State of Zimbabwe's Environment 1998 Report*. Ministry of Environment and Tourism, Harare: Government of Zimbabwe.

Cleaver, F. 1999. 'Paradoxes of Participation: Questioning Participatory Approaches to Development', *Journal of International Development* 11, pp. 597-612.

Cooke, B. and U. Kothari (eds). 2001. *Participation: The New Tyranny*. London and New York: Zed Books.

DNR, 1999. 'DEAP Programme: Overview and Achievements Summary'. Harare: DNR, Ministry of Environment and Tourism, May.

— 1995. 'Review of DEAP process', á report compiled for the Department of Natural Resources, November 1995, by a group from DNR, IUCN-ROSA and IUCN. Harare: Ministry of Environment and Tourism.

Gow, D.D. and J. Van Sant. 1985. 'Decentralisation and participation: Concepts in need of implementation strategies', in E.R. Morss and. D.D. Gow (eds), *Implementing Rural Development Projects: Lessons from Aid and World Bank Experiences*. Boulder, CO, and London: Westview Press.

Guijt, I. and A. Cornwall. 1995. 'Editorial: Critical Reflections on the Practice of PRA', PLA Notes, No. 24, Special Edition. Harare: Sustainable Development Programme. London: International Institute for Environment and Development (IIED), pp. 2-7.

Hulme, D. and M. Murphree (eds). 2001. *African Wildlife and Livelihoods: The Promise and Performance of Community Conservation*. Oxford: James Currey.

Hulme, D. and P. Woodhouse. 2000. 'Governance and the Environment: Politics and Policy', in P. Woodhouse, H. Bernstein and D. Hulme (eds), *African Enclosures? The Social Dynamics of Wetlands in Drylands*. James Currey, EAEP, David Philip.

Keeley, J. and I. Scoones. 2000. *Environmental Policy-making in Zimbabwe: Discourses, Science and Politics*. Institute for Development Studies, Sussex.

Kothari, U. and M. Minogue. 2002. 'Critical Perspectives on Development: An Introduction', in U. Kothari and M. Minogue (eds), *Development Theory and Practice: Critical Perspectives*. New York: Guilford Press.

Mafuta, C. 2001. 'Biodiversity in Forests in Southern Africa', paper presented at the Sixth Southern Africa Biodiversity Forum, Pretoria, November.

Manjengwa, J. 2004, 'Local environmental action planning in Zimbabwe: An analysis of its contribution to sustainable development', PhD. thesis, Institute for Development Policy and Management, University of Manchester.

Manjengwa, J. M. 2007. 'Problems Reconciling Sustainable Development Rhetoric with Reality in Zimbabwe', *Journal of Southern African Studies*, Vol. 33, Issue 2, June.

Mayoux, L. 1995. 'Beyond naivety: Women, gender inequality and participatory development', *Development and Change* 26, pp. 235-58.

McGee, R. 2002. 'Participating in Development', in U. Kothari and M. Minogue (eds), *Development Theory and Practice: Critical Perspectives*. New York: Guilford Press.

Ministry of Environment and Tourism. 2000. 'District Environmental Action Planning Programme: Terminal Evaluation', by R. Mbetu, unpublished document, Ministry of Environment and Tourism, Harare, April.

Mohamed-Katerere, J. 2001. 'Participatory Natural Resource Management in the Communal Lands of Zimbabwe: What Role for Customary Law?', *African Studies Quarterly*, 5, p. 3.

Morss, E.R., D.D. Gow, and C.W. Nordlinger. 1985. 'Sustaining Project Benefits', in E.R. Morss and D.D. Gow (eds), *Implementing Rural Development Projects: Lessons from AID and World Bank Experiences*. Boulder, CO, and London: Westview Press.

Mosse, D. 2002. 'Linking Policy to Livelihood Changes through Projects', The Western India Rainfed Farming Project Seminar and Discussion, July, 2002, Performance Assessment Resource Centre (PARC), Document No. 8.1.

— 2001. 'People's Knowledge, Participation and Patronage: Operations and Representations in Rural Development', in B. Cooke and U. Kothari (eds), *Participation: The New Tyranny*. London and New York: Zed Books.

Mukahanana, M., A. Hoole, M. Munemo, E. Mhaka and S. Chimbuya. 1996. *Zimbabwe: National Conservation Strategy*. Harare: IUCN.

Murombedzi, J. 1999. 'Policy Arena: Devolution and Stewardship in Zimbabwe's Campfire Programme', *Journal of International Development* 11, pp. 287-93.

Murphree, M.W. 2004. 'Negotiating the future: Local level Scenario Modelling, Iterative Assessment and Adaptive Management', paper prepared for the WWF SARPO Concept workshop on Self-Administered Performance Protocols, Johannesburg, 4-6 August.

— 2001. 'Experiments with the future', A seminar on an interdisciplinary, longitudinal and interactive methodology to explore environmental and institutional sustainability in the human use of nature, Berkeley, UCB Botanic Garden, 20 October.

— 1996. 'Ex Africa Semper Aliquid Novi?: Considerations in Linking African Environmental Scholarship, Policy and Practice', in N. Christoffersen, B. Campbell and J. Du Toit (eds), 'Communities and Sustainable Use', proceedings of the Pan-African Symposium on the Sustainable Use of Natural Resources and Community Participation. Harare: IUCN-ROSA, June.

Oakley, P. and I. Clegg. 1999. 'Promoting Participatory Development as a Strategy of Poverty Alleviation in Sub-Saharan Africa: A Review of Some Current Practice', *Journal of Social Development in Africa* 14, 1, pp. 31-52.

PlanAfric. 2000. 'Local Strategic Planning and Sustainable Rural Livelihoods: Rural District Planning in Zimbabwe: A Case Study', *Environmental Planning Issues* No. 23, December, London, IIED.

Platteau, J.P. and A. Abraham. 2002. 'Participatory Development in the Presence of Endogenous Community Imperfections', *Journal of Development Studies* 39, 2, pp. 104-36.

Ribot, J. C. 2002. 'Rebellion, Representation and Enfranchisement in the Forest Villages of Makacoulibantang, Eastern Senegal', paper submitted to the IASCP Ninth Biennial Conference, Victoria Falls, June.

Roe, E. 1998. *Taking Complexity Seriously: Policy Analysis, Triangulation and Sustainable Development.* Boston: Kluwer Academic Publishers, 130.

Sibanda, B. M. 2001. *Wildlife and Communities at the Cross-roads: Is Zimbabwe's Campfire the Way Forward?* Harare: SAPES Books.

Stadler, J. 1999. 'Development, Research and Participation: Towards a Critique of Participatory Rural Appraisal Methods', *Development Southern Africa* 12, p. 6.

Tendler, J. 1982. 'Turning Private Voluntary Organisations into Development Agencies: Questions for Evaluation', AID Programme Evaluation Discussion Paper No. 12, Washington DC: USAID.

Turner, M. and D. Hulme. 1997. *Governance, Administration and Development: Making the State Work.* Hampshire and New York: Palgrave.

Vivian, J. and G. Maseko. 1994. 'NGOs, Participation and Rural Development: Testing the Assumptions with Evidence from Zimbabwe', Discussion Paper DP49, Geneva, United Nations Research Institute for Social Development (UNIRSD).

Woodhouse, P., H. Bernstein and D. Hulme. 2000. 'Africa's "Wetlands in Drylands": From Commons to Enclosures?' in P. Woodhouse, H. Bernstein and D. Hulme (eds), *African Enclosures? The Social Dynamics of Wetlands in Drylands.* London: James Currey.

12

Trying to Make Sense of it All:
Dealing with the Complexities of Community-Based Natural Resource Management

Michael A. Jones

It comforts us to reduce and simplify, and avoid the complexities and contradictions, and the open ended vagueness, of living beings in process. Though nothing seems to stand still long enough to manipulate, we persist in our endeavours because we see the social as material – because we have been successful in dealing with matter. Yet the social is something other. Kaplan (2002)

Introduction

After some twelve years of experience with communal natural resource management in southern Africa, Murphree (2000) found that the robust devolution necessary for effective local management regimes had not been achieved. Paraphrasing G. K. Chesterton, Murphree suggests that like Christianity, CBNRM 'has not been tried and found wanting, it has been found difficult and not tried'. A number of other authors have questioned the efficacy of CBNRM as a strategy for addressing the problems of rural poverty and biodiversity conservation. In a response to earlier critiques of community approaches to conservation that emanated from conservation biologists, Hutton et al. (2006) ask whether there is a movement 'Back to the Barriers?' where biodiversity is conventionally conserved inside state protected areas. After conducting an extensive review of programmatic interventions aimed at poverty alleviation and biodiversity conservation, Agrawal and Redford (2006) ask whether such interventions are not just 'Shooting in the Dark?' Blaikie (2006), who examined CBNRM projects in Malawi and Botswana, reports growing evidence of disappointing outcomes despite the popularity of CBNRM among international funding institutions and asks, 'Is Small Really Beautiful?' In contrast to the findings of these papers and Murphree's earlier questioning of CBNRM (Murphree, 2000); Rihoy et al. (2007), investigating recent changes at Mahenye in Zimbabwe, ask whether their findings illustrate 'Evolution and resilience in the face of adversity or another case of CBNRM in crisis?'

Is there really a crisis in CBNRM? Has it failed as a conservation and development strategy or are there deeper and more powerful changes occurring which indicate that it might be a sound strategy, despite the short-term failures and disappointments that have occurred? Murphree (2004) suggests that the outcome of CBNRM has been positive in addressing rural poverty and biodiversity conservation in southern Africa, when certain conditions are met. Furthermore, he points to the institutional and organisational changes that have occurred at the local level as a result of these communal approaches and the potential of such approaches to contribute to the evolution of governance in Africa.

One of the difficulties with CBNRM stems from people's tendency to treat social planning problems with traditional linear analytical approaches, a fact that was recognised by Rittel and Webber (1973) but which seems to have escaped the attention of scholars and practitioners concerned with community conservation. Both Agrawal and Redford (2006) and Blaikie (2006) recognise that community conservation is a complex matter but neither paper uses the models and paradigms that are emerging from complexity science to enhance understanding of complex environmental problems or to suggest how solutions to these problems might be found. In contrast Ruitenbeek and Cartier (2001) used a complex systems framework to assess the utility of Adaptive Co-Management (ACM) as a strategy for forest conservation that improved human wellbeing and ecosystem sustainability. Their approach led Ruitenbeek and Cartier (2001) to suggest that the institutional changes (North 1990) required for communal approaches to conservation will emerge in response to the failure of attempts of either privatisation or government control to address the tragedy of the commons (Hardin 1969).

Ruitenbeek and Cartier (2001) recommend that policy should protect the conditions of emergence of ACM and contribute to the conscious[1] awareness of agents in an ACM system. This chapter uses some of the paradigms of complexity science to examine a small selection of recent CBNRM literature[2] in an attempt to raise a broader understanding of communal approaches to natural resource management. A complex systems perspective suggests four propositions about the nature of CBNRM as a conservation and development strategy:

- CBNRM is a process that attempts to modify social-ecological systems.
- Social-ecological systems are subject to complex problems for which there are no definitive or objective solutions, which in turn creates more problems.
- CBNRM may therefore be more difficult than Murphree (2000) suggested and it is certainly more difficult than the log-frame approach commonly required by donors would suggest.
- Crisis and change are essential for the sustainable development of CBNRM as a conservation and development strategy.

[1] Consciousness is also an emergent property of complex neurological systems (Ruitenbeek and Cartier 2001).

[2] The papers chosen for this analysis were selected for no other reason than the words in their titles, which suggested their content was relevant to the matter of the so-called CBNRM crisis and the future of CBNRM as a conservation and development strategy.

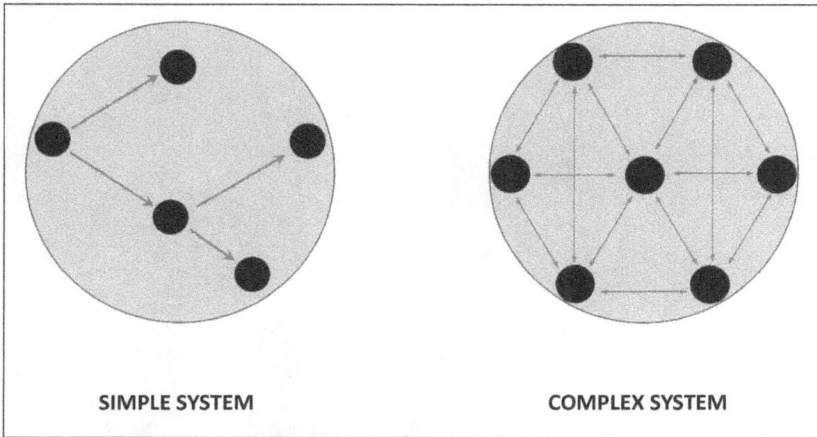

SIMPLE SYSTEM   COMPLEX SYSTEM

Figure 1: Simple and Complex systems showing the interactions between their constituent elements.

Complex systems & CBNRM

The literature on complex systems is extensive[3] and for the uninitiated, may be difficult to understand. Complex systems are perhaps most readily explained by pointing out that the fundamental difference between them and simple systems lies in the nature of the reactions between system elements (Figure 1).

In simple systems elements react in causal chains and solutions to problems can be validly based on models, prediction, control and measurable outcomes. Complex system elements adapt and change over time due to reciprocal interactions between elements in complex causal links. Solutions to problems can only be based on educated guesses, are affected by uncontrollable events, and have unpredictable outcomes that are difficult to measure. Simple systems have 'tame' problems while complex systems give rise to the 'wicked' problems described by Rittel and Webber (1973).

Extending this to the human component of CBNRM (Figure 2) gives some indication of how complex CBNRM can be. This model is representative of CBNRM organisational arrangements where scale is confounded with bureaucratic hierarchy, so it is unlikely that the scale of the management will match the ecological scale at which the resource should be managed for sustainability. Sedentary species will be managed in the same manner as species that range over large areas and water is likely to be managed at the sub-catchment rather than the catchment level. Some of the complexity and problems that arise in CBNRM systems can be reduced by devolving management authority to the household or village level and a better match between organisational

3   Ruitenbeek and Cartier (2001) give a useful overview of some of major complex system research initiatives.

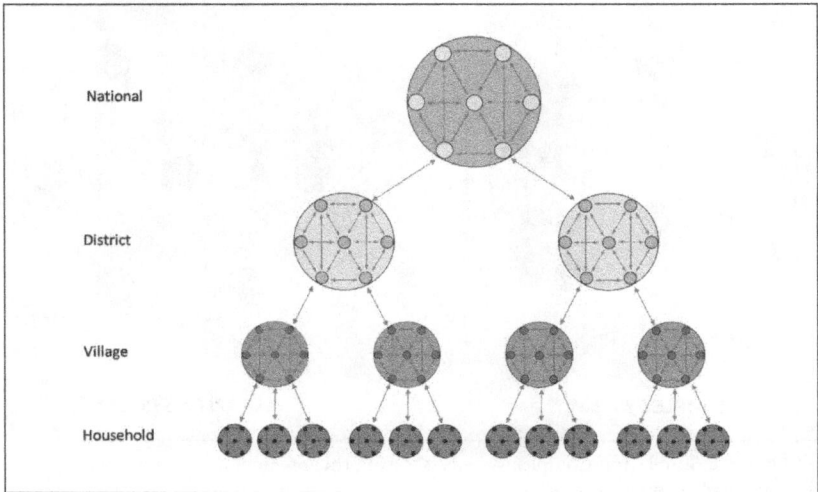

Figure 2: A simple model of complexity in the human component of a CBNRM system

and ecological scales can be achieved by scaling up from the bottom as a way of transcending local jurisdictional boundaries (Murphree 2000). Devolution to avoid some of the problems of complexity and subsequent scaling up would be consistent with Hardin's (1985) maxim to 'never globalize a problem if it can possibly be dealt with locally' and Ostrom's (1990) design principles for common property regimes.

A second concept from complexity science that is relevant to CBNRM is the paradigm of social-ecological systems (SESs), defined by Walker and Salt (2006) as coupled systems of people and nature that behave as complex adaptive systems and exist as hierarchies of linked adaptive cycles at multiple scales known as panarchies (Holling 2001; Gunderson and Holling 2002). A complex adaptive system is defined by Ruitenbeek and Cartier (2001) as a system that contains populations or agents that seek to adapt. Furthermore, social-ecological systems have some key attributes that make them intractable to conventional management approaches (Walker and Salt 2006):

- They have non-linear dynamics with threshold effects.
- They are self-organising and exhibit emergent behaviour.
- The effectiveness of management interventions depends on where a system is in the adaptive cycle and the relationship between the system of interest and systems at scales above and below that level.

In other words, interactions between people and nature at different levels of scale can lead to changes in ecosystem components that are neither predictable nor controllable. The adaptive cycle and panarchy are illustrated in Figures 3 and 4.

The two loops of the adaptive cycle occur sequentially to produce growth and stability on the fore loop, change and variation on the back loop. This

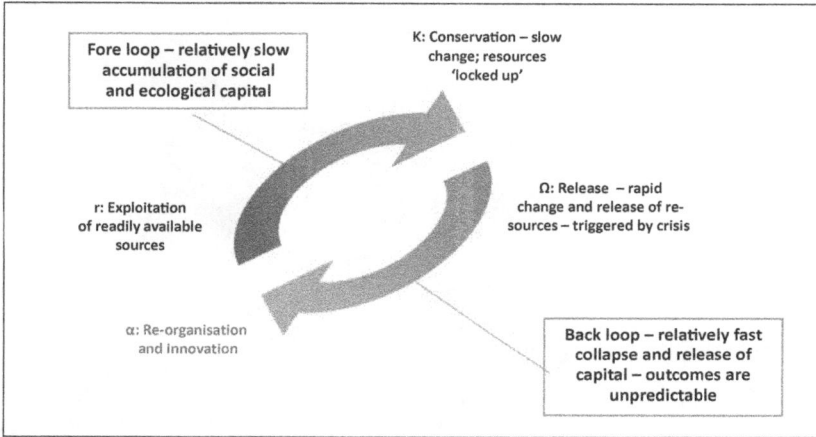

Figure 3: The four-phase adaptive cycle of social-ecological systems (Holling 2001; Walker and Salt 2006)

model is consistent with historical records of human development which occurs in short periods of intermittent and catastrophic change followed by longer periods of growth and development that inevitably sow the seeds of their own destruction (Holling 2001). Democratic societies and smart businesses promote change during the fore loop to prevent the rigidity and crisis that inevitably occurs if unchecked growth is allowed (Holling 2001).

Adaptive cycles at different scales are linked by revolt and remember interactions which constitute the non-linear dynamics of social-ecological systems that have threshold effects and can lead to major changes including the emergence of novel systems. The French revolution is an example of a revolt that created democracy from autocracy, as the resources available to the monarchy were eroded by the activities of the revolutionaries. In rangeland ecology, loss of plant cover (fast variable) can lead to loss of soil nutrients and water (slow variables). If plant cover changes are not repeated frequently, water and nutrient capital stored in the soil enables a 'remember' feedback and the disturbed area recovers. If plant cover loss occurs frequently and is synchronised over a large area, the 'revolt' link precipitates a decline in system productivity as the nutrients and water needed for plant growth have been lost. The productivity of semi-arid rangelands has been reduced and vegetation structure changed on a global scale through this process (Walker and Salt, 2006).

The final point to make with regard to the complex nature of CBNRM is that the planning and policy problems posed by it all fall within the category of Rittel and Webber's (1973) 'wicked' problems that cannot be solved by science because 'they are ill-defined; and rely upon elusive political judgement for resolution'. The first five and the last of Rittel and Webber's (1973) ten characteristics of 'wicked' problems are quoted together with a précised explanation

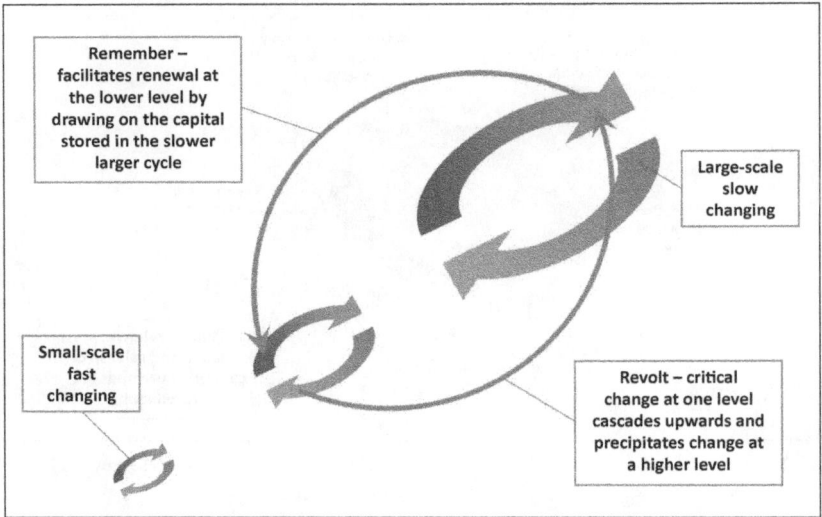

Figure 4: The Panarchy – hierarchies of linked adaptive cycles (Holling, 2001; Walker and Salt 2006)

of the characteristic (Box 1). Characteristics six to nine are omitted because in one way or another they are corollaries of the first five.

Rittel and Webber (1973) conclude their discussion of 'wicked' problems with the following:

> We are thus led to conclude that the problems that planners must deal with are wicked and incorrigible ones, for they defy efforts to delineate their boundaries and to identify their causes, and thus to expose their problematic nature. The planner who works with open systems is caught up in the ambiguity of their causal webs. Moreover, his would-be solutions are confounded by a still further set of dilemmas posed by the growing pluralism of the contemporary publics, whose valuations of his proposals are judged against an array of different and contradicting scales.

Anybody who has been involved in the practical application of CBNRM will recognise the truth of Rittel and Webber's statements. It is clear that reductionist science cannot solve 'wicked' problems so we need the paradigms of complex systems to help us understand CBNRM and suggest alternative practices that are not based on a simple system perspective. The differences between simple, complicated, complex and chaotic systems and their relevance to CBNRM is illustrated in Figure 5, which is based on the sense-making model developed by Snowden (2002) and Kurtz and Snowden (2003) who investigated complexity in business management.

The primary division in this model is between order and un-order. On the ordered side of the matrix, knowledge refers to that which is known to society as opposed to individuals (Kurtz and Snowden 2003). In simple systems

---

Box 1: The first five and the last of Rittel & Webber's (1973) ten
characteristics of 'wicked' problems faced by social planners.
Italics are added to emphasise points that are relevant
to the practice of CBNRM

1. *There is no definitive formulation of a wicked problem*
   Unlike tame problems for which solutions can be defined based on
   existing knowledge, the problem statement for a wicked problem
   depends on who is describing it and their knowledge of the
   potential solutions.

2. *Wicked problems have no stopping rule*
   The process of solving the problem is the same as the process of
   understanding it because there are no ends to the causal chains
   that link interacting open systems.

3. *Solutions to wicked problems are not true-or-false, but good-or-bad*
   There are no objective criteria for determining whether a solution
   is true or false, therefore solutions are judged by individuals
   according to their values and beliefs.

4. *There is no immediate and no ultimate test of a solution to a wicked problem*
   Solutions to tame problems can be tested by those who have control
   over the problem but solutions to wicked problems generate waves
   of consequences some of which may be undesirable and outweigh
   the intended advantages.

5. *Every solution is a one shot operation; because there is no opportunity to
   learn by trial-and-error, every attempt counts significantly*
   Every implemented solution to a "wicked" problem leaves traces
   that cannot be easily undone and have long half-lives. Thus every
   trial counts and attempts to correct for undesired consequences
   will pose another set of wicked problems, which are subject to the
   same dilemmas.

10. *The planner has no right to be wrong*
    Planners aim to improve some characteristic of the world but they
    are liable for the consequences of the actions they generate and the
    effects can matter a great deal to those people who are touched by
    those actions.

---

where cause and effect are known, behaviour can be predicted and solutions
to problems can be achieved through the application of best practice. This is
the space that policy designers and planners typically operate from when they
misdiagnose 'wicked' problems as simple problems (Webber and Rittel 1973).
In complicated systems that are potentially knowable, cause and effect relations are only partly known but given sufficient research they can migrate to
the domain of what is known. Complicated systems are the domain of good
practice and modern scientific management that is becoming more rooted in

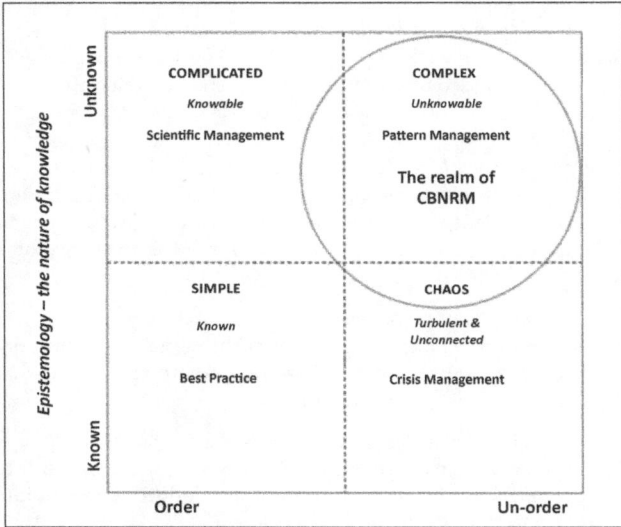

Figure 5: A 'sense-making' model after Snowden (2002) and Kurtz and Snowden (2003) that relates different kinds of system and management approaches to knowledge and order. At present CBNRM lies mostly in complex systems space and the aim of scientific management is to draw it into knowable and eventually known space.

systems thinking with greater focus on the human rather than the mechanical (Snowden and Stanbridge 2004). Entrained thinking, an unwillingness to accept new ideas, and professional hubris can be major issues for knowable systems and lead to the kinds of crisis and political gridlock that gives science a bad name (Holling et al. 2001).

In chaotic systems, there is no perceivable connection between cause and effect. Although chaos is generally viewed as undesirable, it is a useful space that can be actively created to change entrained thinking by challenging the expert's assumptions. Chaos is the space into which all human enterprises are inevitably precipitated (Holling, 2001; Holling and Gunderson 2002) and it is the space from which new order will emerge. As we saw earlier, crisis can be induced at the appropriate point on the fore loop of the adaptive cycle to prevent system rigidity and maintain resilience but it requires strong leadership and innovation to avoid the leakage of essential resources to the point where the system flips into a different and degraded stable state or poverty trap (Holling 2001).

In the unknown and un-ordered domain of complex systems where cause and effect are only known in retrospect, management is achieved by identifying emerging patterns, relating them to past events and making decisions based on perceived future patterns (Kurtz and Snowden 2003). Pattern management is the process that most people (including management experts and policy designers) use to make decisions most of the time (Klein 1998). Entrepreneurs can manage this space well; bureaucracies tend to lack the flexibility do so. Being able to recognise patterns and protect the conditions of emergence of those that seem favourable is the recommended aim of policy for ACM (Ruitenbeek and Cartier, 2001). Adaptive management in its various forms that range from traditional methods of trial and error (Berkes and Folke 2002; Colding, Elmqvist and Olsson 2003), through passive adaptive management to the active adaptive management of formal scientific enquiry (Holling 1978; Walters and Holling 1990) is the mechanism by which people learn and adapt to environmental change.

Humans have a number of characteristics that distinguish human systems from biological or physical systems (Kurtz and Snowden 2003; Snowden and Stanbridge 2004). These include the ability to recognise emerging patterns; to create stability and predictability in their environment; to create and maintain multiple identities; and to modify their environment at all scales from the local to the global. The social-ecological systems of CBNRM are indeed complex and it is little wonder that they are prone to 'wicked' problems. Simple and complicated systems can be regarded as subsets of social-ecological systems that arise from the human ability and tendency to create stability and predictability in the environment. Chaotic systems are a short-lived phase of complex systems that occur periodically during the adaptive cycle to enable the stability and variation needed to maintain system resilience (Holling 2001; Holling and Gunderson 2002).

Applying the lens of complex systems to the CBNRM 'crisis'

Back to the barriers?

The back to the barriers narrative (Hutton et al. 2006) can be summarised as follows:

- Community-based approaches to conservation emerged in the 1970s as a response to the difficulties of maintaining fortress parks in the face of expanding human populations and growing demand for resources.

- Community-based conservation projects began in the 1980s and evolved into various kinds of conservation and sustainable development projects in the 1990s that are now widespread.

- In the early 1990s conservation biologists argued that fortress parks were the only way to maintain biodiversity because maintaining human populations and biodiversity conservation were mutually exclusive goals.

- In the late 1990s donors switched funding support from CBNRM to Trans Boundary Natural Resource Management (TBNRM), direct payments, public private partnerships and mainstreaming.

- Hutton et al. (2006) argue that there is much wrong with fortress conservation, and that the primary problem with CBNRM is that there has not been enough devolution to enable rural communities to manage their resources effectively and improve their livelihoods.

- They conclude that both fortress parks and community-based approaches are needed to conserve biodiversity.

A panarchist's view of this narrative suggests a different perspective (Figure 6). Interaction between park managers and social scientists led to the emergence of a new group of community conservationists, despite the resistance offered by 'old school' conservation biologists. This in turn led to the emergence of two new categories of protected areas, namely, community conserved areas and TBNRM areas (more commonly known as Trans Frontier Conservation Areas), each of which complements the existing state protected area system. Overall the diversity of conservation options has increased and added to the resilience of the global conservation areas system.

Donors continued to do what they generally do, which is fund whatever appears to offer a successful solution to the problem being addressed. Resistance from community conservationists may have created a short-term crisis for those in the CBNRM community who were dependent on funds from certain donors, but how many people lost jobs and how many organisations collapsed as a result?

Shooting in the dark?

Agrawal and Redford (2006) use a reductionist approach to analyse 37 peer reviewed writings about programmatic interventions to address poverty alleviation and biodiversity conservation. Their two main findings were that:

- Projects over-simplified complex situations: thirty-four of the papers 'focus on processes and outcomes in a single case and single time period, and a drastic simplification of the complex concepts of poverty and biodiversity'.

- Science cannot produce simple models of biodiversity conservation and poverty alleviation: 'As a result of these shared features, the mass of scholarly work on the subject does not permit systematic and context-sensitive generalisations about the conditions under which it may be possible to achieve poverty alleviation and biodiversity conservation simultaneously.'

Various parts of their paper show that defining and measuring poverty is a 'wicked' problem of the kind described by Webber and Rittel (1973):

... different dimensions of poverty are not independent of each other, but we do not possess metrics or mechanisms through which to commensurate them.

... although we can say that there are cause and effect linkages among the different dimensions of poverty, we know neither their nature nor their strength across different contexts.

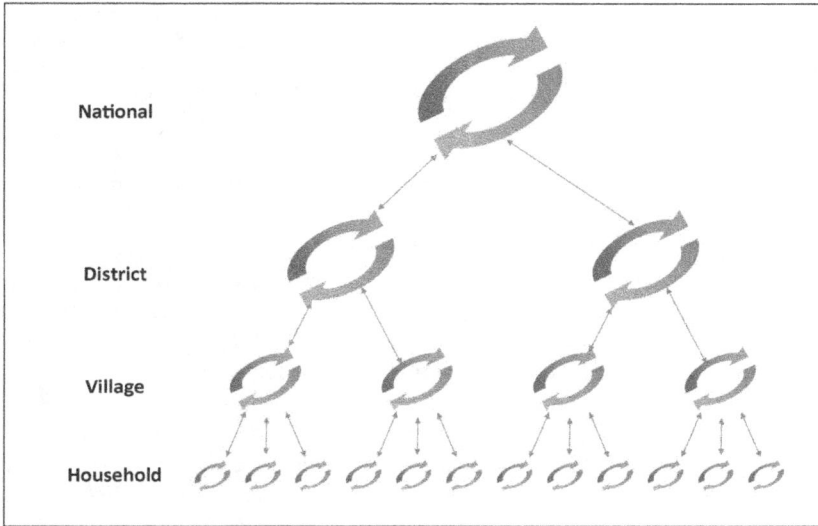

Figure 6: A panarchist's view of the back to the barriers narrative

Even if it is necessary to adopt more complex approaches to poverty reduction that incorporate social, political, economic, and cultural strategies, we do not yet know which of these prongs of a poverty reduction program should receive greater emphasis in a given context.

Defining and measuring biodiversity conservation was found to be equally 'wicked' and so conflated with political issues that it was impossible to find two or three simple measures of biodiversity:

As biodiversity conservation has become a common objective, the term itself has assumed an even broader range of meanings ... the word has been pulled from its roots in the biological sciences, becoming a political term with as many meanings as it has advocates.

In this social and political discussion around biodiversity, what is often at stake is not its conservation but who gets to claim it and use it, the institutional arrangements to regulate its use, and allocation regimes for losses and gains from use.

... in the conceptual and theoretical literature on biodiversity, there is no single measure of the concept – or even two or three measures taken together – that provides a comprehensive or systematic sense of biodiversity at a given scale.

Agrawal and Redford's (2006) findings lead them to what might be called the reductionis'ts dilemma – how can we avoid unintended consequences if we can't predict the outcome of policy? It's symptomatic of Rittel and Webber's (1973) tenth point – 'the planner has no right to be wrong', and if the planner is wrong, then he might make matters worse.

The basic policy implication of the fact that there are many different ways to understand biodiversity is that interventions to enhance some specific attribute or component of biodiversity may have quite unanticipated effects on other measures of biodiversity. It is not possible to make any blanket predictions about whether these unanticipated effects are desired by policy makers and analysts.

Without careful incorporation of the multiple measures that tap specific combinations of attributes and components of biodiversity, policy interventions to enhance biodiversity and their assessments are likely to lead to outcomes whose complexity may not even be recognized.

From the perspective of reductionist science, interventions that aim to conserve biological diversity and alleviate poverty are very clearly shooting in the dark. Despite the experience gained from conservation and development projects, such projects largely remain within the realm of complex systems where outcomes cannot be predicted with any reliability. As the title of Kaplan's (2002) book suggests, conservation and development project designers and practitioners need to become 'artists of the invisible'. This may be difficult for large donor organisations and NGOs because they work from the perspective of an ordered world (Fig. 4), which assumes that CBNRM can be modelled and predicted.

Is small really beautiful?

Blaikie (2006) finds that despite its failures CBNRM is still an important strategy for conservation and development and uses case material from Botswana and Malawi to suggest that this persistence is due to the self-serving interests of donors and recipients of donor funds, when it is unpopular with local communities:

CBNRM remains a touchstone for much of rural development and sustainable natural resource management and has been promoted by most major IFIs [International Finance Institutions] since the early 1990s. Yet ... it has largely failed to deliver the ... predicted benefits to local communities. CBNRM has become and remains so popular to IFIs, but often so unpopular with target communities themselves.

The sub-headings in Blaikie's paper (Blaikie 2006) illustrate that he recognises the complexity of CBNRM:

'Almost all roads lead to CBNRM'

'Yet arrival is elusive ...'

'... And as Many Roads Lead Back Again: Our Theories Are Elusive'

... and he finds it difficult to make sense of what is going on within CBNRM systems, causing him to wonder whether there is a rational link between practice and policy:

... there is a rational and instrumental model of policy making and implementation, in which 'science talks to policy' - that better theory will be able to predict more accurately the outcomes of CBNRM from initial characteristics of the communities identified, and the natural resource(s) involved.

Blaikie (2006) somewhat cynically suggests that CBNRM policy is based on appealing theory that serves the interests of donors and recipient governments rather than the results of practice:

> An important aspect of this engagement [policy process] is between different IFIs and senior policy advisors of the recipient governments, where theories may be judged less on the grounds of their predictive value than on their discursive power and appeal to their audiences... other IFIs and their own political and financial constituencies...

> ... 'success' is reproduced within a network of multi-lateral and bi-lateral agencies, international NGOs, in-country NGOs and a limited number of senior government officials ... the discursive power of the theoretical benefits to environment and community of CBNRM, the need to proclaim success ... and the diffuseness ... of the social and environmental objectives, all lie behind representations of this 'success'.

While there may be some justification for this cynicism, Blaikie (2006) is merely reporting more examples of the 'wicked' problems of social-ecological systems, which is not particularly useful from the perspective of a practitioner looking for solutions to complex problems. The question of size of management regime in relation to ecological scale (Murphree 2000) which might be inferred from the title of Blaikie's paper is not addressed at all, while the implication that local people don't matter may be clear to those scholars who understand the pun and oblique reference to title of Schumacher's (1973) book[4].

Evolution & resilience or another case of CBNRM in crisis?

The Mahenye case study reported by Rihoy et al. (2007) tells how in contrast to the expectation of conventional CBNRM wisdom, interactions between local and district levels promote devolution:

> ... we would conclude that CBNRM is a process of applied and incremental experiments of democracy and most valuable in this because it involves not a single 'holy grail' of full devolution or 'ideal democracy' but the interaction of tiers of governance over time in adaptive processes.

> While in Zimbabwe RDCs are notoriously associated with 'capturing' Campfire benefits... the evidence from Mahenye indicates that in the current context of Zimbabwe, RDCs could provide a system of 'checks and balances' at the local level which can prevent capture of the process by local elites.

> ... the longstanding 'devolutionary' discourse which has dominated CBNRM debate within Southern Africa does not accommodate the realities of the highly politicized context in which CBNRM occurs.

This study illustrates how unintended consequences emerge as a result of the political processes that unfold once a particular plan has been put into operation. Even though implementation of the Campfire programme fell well short of the ideal of devolution to local level, villagers acquired sufficient power over time to form an alliance with their erstwhile opponent, the Rural District Council, that enables them to overcome a particularly rapacious local elite in the form of the chief and his cronies. The Mahenye community is learning and adapting:

> Contrary to perspectives of Mahenye as another example of CBNRM in crisis, our interpretation of Mahenye narratives is an optimistic one of evolution and resilience. [Mahenye] provides evidence that CBNRM is evolving and has empowered local communities with the means and incentive to engage and negotiate with their local government representatives.

From whence & to where?

As a social scientist and scholar-practitioner who has been intimately involved in CBNRM since its inception in Zimbabwe, Murphree's backward- and forward-looking paper (Murphree 2004) fully reflects the social complexities of communal approaches to conservation and development. In the backward-looking part of his paper, he gives an example of how state resistance to devolution can arise as an unintended consequence of economic arguments in favour of conservation as means to development:

> Paradoxically Campfire's emphasis on realizing true market values has had the unintended effect of inhibiting devolution. If these values are realized, the hegemonic interests of the state to retain their benefits are reinforced, and it is less disposed to surrender them.

Murphree (2004) then goes on to warn of the dangers of over-simplification of project design:

> One assumption in communal approaches has been that ... collectives of land and resources users ... can create viable regimes of common property use. Recent scholarship has pointed out major deficiencies in any simplistic programmatic application of this assumption.

... and echoing the words of Ruitenbeek and Cartier (2001) and Kaplan (1999) emphasises the importance of creating conscious awareness as a fundamental precursor to institutional development:

> Development is about increasing ... choice' ... '... about enabling people to understand themselves and their context such that they are better able to take control of their own future.

Murphree (2004) also brings the resilience perspective to CBNRM:

> ... [conservation] is better perceived as resilience in a complex, evolving biophysical-cum-social system comprised of structures which interact across

4   Schumacher (1973) 'Small is beautiful: Economics as if people mattered' is referenced by Murphree (2000) in his discussion of the problem of assigning jurisdictions for natural resource management.

scales of time and place and which move through adaptive cycles of growth, accumulation, restructuring and renewal.

... and argues strongly from a resilience perspective that institutional development is the foundation for biodiversity conservation and poverty alleviation:

> If however conservation is taken to mean systemic resilience in longer cycles of change then there is a strong case for making adaptive institutional capacity the central objective of communal approaches, providing the foundation on which ecological and economic concerns can effectively be addressed.

The forward-looking part of Murphree's paper can be summarised in five points which collectively focus on the importance of the need to develop new institutions for resource management and poverty alleviation that are responsive to local contexts:

- Communal approaches should be infused with the appreciation that institutional resilience is the pivotal variable determining their success or failure.

- Selective application of communal approaches by matching management regimes to the commonage to be managed, i.e. matching social and ecological scales.

- Integration of communal approaches with state or private regimes based on the principle of reciprocity so that resource management institutions may scale out and scale up.

- Disaggregatation of communal approaches by fitting the primary goal (conservation poverty alleviation or institutional development) and their attendant activities to the context of the environment within which the community resides.

- Replace the 'scientific-cum-bureaucratic paradigm which is deterministic, reductionist and inhospitable' with interdependent reciprocity between communal actors, scholars, practitioners, donors and policy-makers.

Conclusion

> [As development practitioners]... we are trying to hold infinity. Under such circumstances we must indeed beware the tendency to reduce. The challenge is rather to become discerning practitioners (Kaplan 2002).

This chapter is written by a CBNRM practitioner with some 18 years of accumulated biases who happens to think that the complex systems view of CBNRM will yield more understanding of CBNRM and ideas on how to improve practice, than a reductionist approach. The conclusions should be judged accordingly. Hopefully, there is now little doubt in the reader's mind that CBNRM mostly belongs in the realm of complex systems where interactions between people and nature at different levels of scale can lead to unpredictable and uncontrollable outcomes.[5] Cause and effect are only apparent in retrospect and decisions are best made on the basis of past experience, pattern recognition and forward projection (Kurtz and Snowden 2003), rather than the very incomplete predictions that might be possible based on reductionist approaches. Evidence suggests that resource managers who use traditional techniques and knowledge tend to manage complex systems better than scientific managers, particularly in the way they deliberately create disturbance to foster renewal (Berkes and Folke 2002). Traditional management will tend to be more adaptable and sustainable than scientific management which focuses on the fore loop of the adaptive cycle, optimisation and maximum sustainable yield which tend to create brittle systems that are prone to collapse (Walker and Salt 2006).

Two patterns emerge from the papers that were reviewed in this analysis: variation occurred with discipline, and familiarity with CBNRM in the field. Authors who work extensively in the field (e.g. Murphree 2004; Rihoy et al. 2007) seem to have a more perceptive grasp of the complexity of CBNRM than those who work out of academic institutions in Europe (e. g. Blaikie 2006). Indeed Murphree (2000) introduced complex systems perspectives in his paper on the issues of matching institutional and ecological scale, suggesting that in this regard he may be well ahead of his peers. Views of CBNRM also vary according to the biases of the authors, such as the political perspective from Blaikie (2006), compared to the rigorous reductionist perspective from Agrawal and Redford (2006).

A potential consequence of these different perspectives, which is consistent with Rittel and Webber's (1973) 'wicked' problems, is that academic discourse will tend to reflect different values and beliefs rather than real differences in what is good or bad CBNRM practice. As 'wicked' problems tend to be self-perpetuating, it is possible that there will be much sterile, even acrimonious, debate unless scholars recognise that CBNRM is part of complex systems space where solutions to problems are based on judgement that is informed by experience, beliefs and values.

Proceeding on the basis that a complex systems perspective of CBNRM is correct, the analysis of reviewed papers shows quite clearly that there is no major crisis in the sense of impending failure of CBNRM. Small crises have undoubtedly occurred (Hutton et al. 2006; Rihoy et al. 2007); donor agencies and recipient governments may be making lots of money out of CBNRM, as Blaikie (2006) implies; and it may be impossible to objectively measure biodiversity and poverty (Agrawal and Redford 2006) but there is no major crisis. What has occurred in CBNRM is consistent with the panarchy model

---

5   Although the outcome of events in complex systems cannot be predicted and complex systems cannot be controlled, they can be influenced (Ruitenbeek and Cartier 2001) hence the importance of leadership and developing social capital in the human component of social-ecological systems.

of social-ecological systems and is contributing to the development of more resilient approaches to the use of natural resources than old protectionist paradigms of conservation that seek to separate people from nature. Having dealt with the question of crisis, it is now more pertinent to ask how the practice of CBNRM can be improved.

Despite the findings of Rihoy et al. (2007) in Zimbabwe and some complementary findings from Botswana (Rihoy and Maguranyanga 2007), which suggest that devolution to the landholder is not necessarily a fundamental requirement for success, devolution remains an ideal for which CBNRM practice must continue to strive. No matter what the state and its laws might have to say, the landholder is the ultimate de facto arbiter of the fate of natural resources that occur on his land. Unless there are rights that give landholders the authority and responsibility to manage and benefit from the resources upon which their livelihoods depend (Murphree 2000), they are unlikely to develop the institutions necessary for effective management that yields a continuous supply of environmental goods and services required to support local economies. Furthermore, consideration of the complexity of CBNRM (Figure 2) suggests that the only pragmatic way to pre-empt many of the 'wicked' problems that can arise in hierarchical command and control organisations is to devolve authority and responsibility to the local level. This will reduce the number of problems; create the conditions necessary for the emergence of new institutions that match social and ecological scale; and create a resource management environment in which resilience is enhanced by encouraging local innovation as opposed to the decentralised[6] government model that puts all the institutional eggs in one basket. Devolution is necessary to enable the emergence of resilient institutions for natural resource management. Devolution can also be viewed as an emergent property of complex systems where access to benefit is a significant issue (Ruitenbeek and Cartier 2001) and a primary cause of the lack of devolution in CBNRM.

Murphree's (2004) focus on institutional development at the local level as the necessary precursor for poverty alleviation and biodiversity conservation is consistent with the panarchy. A 'discerning practitioner' (or discerning planner or policy designer) might therefore consider the conditions necessary for the emergence of new institutions for sustainable natural resource management. Ruitenbeek and Cartier (2001) suggest that in some situations the best policy might be no intervention, but where intervention might have a positive influence, the conditions of emergence can be protected by developing and maintaining social capital, and facilitating copying and variation. Timing of the intervention can be critical and some cunning may be needed to shift the balance of power.

---

6   Decentralised in the sense of Ribot (2005) where decentralisation is defined as the transfer of powers from central government to lower levels within government's political-administrative hierarchy.

References

Agrawal, A. and K. Redford. 2006. 'Poverty, Development, And Biodiversity Conservation: Shooting in the Dark?', WCS Working Paper No. 26. http://www. wcs. org/science.

Berkes, F. and K. Folke. 2002. 'Back to the future: ecosystem dynamics and local knowledge', in L.H. Gunderson and C.S. Holling (eds) *Panarchy: Understanding Transformations in Human and Natural Systems*. London: Island Press, pp. 121-46.

Blaikie, P. (2006) 'Is Small Really Beautiful? Community-Based Natural Resource Management in Malawi and Botswana', *World Development* 34 (11), pp. 1942-57.

Colding, J., T. Elmqvist, and P. Olsson. (2003) 'Living with disturbance: building resilience in social-ecological systems', in Berkes, F., J. Colding and C. Folke (ed)s. 2003. *Navigating social-ecological systems: building resilience for complexity and change*. Cambridge: Cambridge University Press.

Gunderson L.H. and C.S. Holling. (2002) 'Resilience and Adaptive Cycles'. in L.H. Gunderson and C.S. Holling (eds) *Panarchy: Understanding Transformations in Human and Natural Systems*. London: Island Press, pp. 25-62.

Hardin, G. 1969. 'The tragedy of the commons', *Science* 162, pp. 1243-8.

— 1985. *Filters Against Folly*. New York: Viking Penguin

Holling, C.S., 1978. *Adaptive Environmental Assessment and Management*. New York: John Wiley and Sons.

— 2001. 'Understanding the complexity of economic, ecological, and social systems', *Ecosystems* 4, pp. 390-405.

Holling, C.S. and L.H. Gunderson 2002. 'Resilience and Adaptive Cycles', in L.H. Gunderson and C.S. Holling (eds) *Panarchy: Understanding Transformations in Human and Natural Systems*. London: Island Press, pp. 25-62.

Holling, C.S., L.H. Gunderson, and D. Ludwig. (2002) 'In Quest of a Theory of Adaptive Change', in L.H. Gunderson and C.S. Holling (eds) *Panarchy: Understanding Transformations in Human and Natural Systems*. London: Island Press, pp. 3-22.

Hutton, J., B. Adams and J. Murombedzi (2006) 'Back to the Barriers: Changing Narratives in Biodiversity Conservation', *Forum for Development Studies* 2.

Jones, M.A. (in preparation) *The 'wicked' problems of CBNRM and their consequences for performance monitoring*.

Kaplan, A. 1999. *The Developing of Capacity*. Cape Town: Community Development Resource Association. http://www.cdra.org.za/.

— 2002. *Development Practitioners and Social Process: Artists of the Invisible*. London: Pluto Press.

Klein, G. 1998. *Sources of Power: How People Make Decisions*. Cambridge, MA: MIT Press.

Kurtz, C.F. and D.J. Snowden. 2003. 'The new dynamics of strategy: Sense-making in a complex and complicated world', *IBM Systems Journal*, 42 (3), pp. 462-83.

Murphree, M.W. 2000. 'Boundaries and borders; the question of scale in the theory and practice of common property management'. Paper resented at the Eighth Biennial Conference of the International Association of Common Property (IASCP). Bloomington, IN, 31 May.

— 2004. 'Communal approaches to natural resource management in Africa: from whence and to where?', *Journal of International Wildlife Law and Policy* 7: 203-216.

North, D.C. 1990. *Institutions, institutional change and economic performance*. Cambridge: Cambridge University Press.

Ostrom, E. 1990. *Governing the Commons. The Evolution of Institutions for Collective Action*. Cambridge: Cambridge University Press.

Ribot, J.C. 2005. 'Institutional Choice and Recognition: Effects on the Formation and Consoliation of Local Democracy', a natural resource and democracy concept paper, WRI, Washington, DC.

Rihoy, E., C. Chirozva, and S. Anstey. 2007. '"People are Not Happy" - Speaking Up for Adaptive Natural Resource Governance in Mahenye'. Occasional Paper No.31, Programme for Land and Agrarian Studies, Cape Town

Rihoy, E. and B. Maguranyanga. 2007. *Devolution and Democratization of Natural Resource Management in Southern Africa: A comparative analysis of CBNRM policy processes in Botswana and Zimbabwe*. Commons Southern Africa Series, Programme for Land and Agrarian Studies, Cape Town

Rittel, H., and M. Webber. 1973. 'Dilemmas in a General Theory of Planning', *Policy Sciences*, Vol. 4, pp. 155-69.

Ruitenbeek, J. and C. Cartier. 2001. *The Invisible Wand: Adaptive Co-management as an Emergent Strategy in Complex Bio-economic Systems*. Occasional Paper No. 34, Centre for International Forestry Research.

Snowden, D. 2002. 'Complex Acts of Knowing: Paradox and Descriptive Self-awareness', *Journal of Knowledge Management* 6 (2), pp. 100-11.

Snowden, D. and P. Stanbridge. 2004. 'The landscape of management: Creating the context for understanding social complexity', *Emergence: Complexity and Organisation* 6 (1-2), pp. 140-48. http://www.emergence.org/.

Walker, B. and D. Salt. 2006. *Resilience Thinking: Sustaining Ecosystems and People in a Changing World*. London: Island Press.

Walters, C.J. and C.S. Holling. 1990. 'Large-scale management experiments and learning by doing', *Ecology* 71, pp. 2060-68.

13

Taking Murphree's Principles into the Future:
The Research & Development Issues for CBNRM Initiatives in Southern Africa

Billy Mukamuri, Jeanette Manjengwa & Simon Anstey

Introduction

This concluding section is a synopsis informed partly by the contributions included in this book. Moreover, it is informed by discussions and deliberations that occurred during the conference held to honour Professor Murphree's contribution to scholarship and natural resources governance in southern Africa. The discussions held at the conference, and also implied in the chapters forming this volume, clearly highlight the fact that research and development are political processes, as is policy making. The authors of this concluding chapter have elected to discuss an issue often ignored by researchers and all those concerned with empowering marginalised communities across southern Africa, namely that both research and development are political processes.

Research & development as politics

Researchers are often not critical about issues such as who drives their research agendas. Generally speaking, research is a political process because it is done within a framework of interests, whether individually or collectively. Applied research is more political still because it seeks to change social structures so that they become more beneficial to a larger segment of society, particularly the marginalised and powerless. When talking about CBNRM initiatives, applied social scientists are more concerned with creating partnerships and capacity building in beneficiary communities.

Connectedness of policy and research is illustrated by Marshall Murphree's engagements with both academia and policy-makers in the wildlife arena. For example, his engagement as a Parks and Wildlife Board member and as the chairman of the Centre for Applied Social Sciences at the University of Zimbabwe, is illustrative of the continuum involving research and policy making. We should also not lose sight of his successful participation in the CITES Conference of Parties discussions at the international level.

Another lesson drawn from Professor Murphree's long academic and development career is that researchers need always to reflect on their work – past, present and ongoing – and to persevere, even if the working environment is hostile, with the aim of 'turning the tide' through lobbying. Applied research is all about changing lives for the better, for improving humanity's well-being. In addition, we are reminded that applied research is a lifelong engagement with a 'moral nature' and this reminds us of the need for commitment to the people we are engaged with, particularly the powerless, and marginalised communities.

Language is a central component of applied research. The general tendency by most researchers is to use complicated language, hardly comprehended by various stakeholders and end-users. Heavy-handed language mystifies research and development, and yet the purpose of research is to demystify issues. Researchers ought to write and speak in comprehensible languages.

Development, like research, is a political process involving multiple stakeholders and interests. Researchers need to be resolute and optimistic all the time. We are reminded that researchers and development practitioners need to view issues more as 'challenges' than as 'problems': 'problems disillusion', while 'challenges inspire'. Development will occur if the increasing tendency towards 'elite capture' of CBNRM initiatives is curtailed. More and more effort is needed to give priority to local communities so that they take charge of their own development. Further devolution of CBNRM initiatives to levels lower than RDCs continues to be called for. RDCs, though lower than governmental line ministries, are still strongly linked to the state and therefore constrained as key partners in a devolved or decentralised natural resources governance regime. In terms of wildlife management at the local level, there is a wide recognition of the need for more constituent-based institutions.

Towards a pro-poor research agenda

Deliberations at the conference and contributions to this book indicate the importance of understanding political dynamics at the local level. More research needs to be conducted to understand and hence improve 'democracy from below' and reverse the elite capture of CBNRM initiatives. An investigation into policy making processes remains an imperative for CBNRM researchers. Another key aspect of CBNRM research is understanding representation, and issues linking culture and politics such as natural resources management, property and democracy.

Legal aspects of CBNRM initiatives require full comprehension. There is a need to investigate and characterise property rights surrounding different CBNRM contexts, which may include public, private and common property regimes.

More research needs to be done into the nature of institutional resilience, and towards understanding adaptive management and 'scenario-building'. Researchers could focus on cultural framing, founding assumptions, the nature and levels of 'participation', taking local participation to the second generation, as well as evaluating institutional successes and failures.

Social science themes requiring further investigation relate to gender and how it informs access, governance and benefit sharing. Family dynamics and kinship ties require special attention because these inform how communities are internally configured and structured. Finally, consideration must be given to the impact of HIV and AIDS on CBNRM initiatives in southern Africa.

Notes on Contributors

Billy Mukamuri is a full-time lecturer and researcher at CASS. His research interests are on understanding local level institutional dynamics, particularly in communal areas. He has published extensively on social forestry issues, largely from south central Zimbabwe. He also published articles on the impacts of macro-economic changes and their impacts on natural resources management and rural people's livelihoods.

Jeannette Manjengwa is a lecturer and researcher at the Centre for Applied Social Sciences (CASS), University of Zimbabwe. She is the Team Leader of the IDRC-funded Local Level Scenario Planning, Iterative Assessment and Adaptive Management project, a regional research and development initiative being implemented with communities in the Great Limpopo Trans-Frontier Conservation Area.

Simon Anstey is a researcher and a PhD student at CASS. His thesis is based on local environmental and political processes in Mozambique. He has worked for the World Conservation Union (IUCN) in Jordan and is currently a consultant on natural resources projects in southern Africa.

Frank Chinembiri is a PhD student at the Institute for Environmental Studies (IES), University of Zimbabwe. He was a livestock specialist for the Department of Agricultural Extension and Technical Services for many years and is currently a consultant for the FAO sub-regional Office in Zimbabwe.

Chaka Chirozva holds a Masters in Social Ecology degree from the University of Zimbabwe, and is a former post-graduate student at CASS. He is a facilitator for the Local Level Scenario Planning, Iterative Assessment and Adaptive Management project.

Ben Cousins is a Senior Professor at the University of the Western Cape and Director of the Institute for Poverty, Land and Agrarian Studies (PLAAS).

His main research interests are common property management, land tenure reform, livestock production and communal rangeland dynamics, rural social differentiation and poverty, and the politics of land and agrarian reform.

Rosaleen Duffy is Professor of International Politics at the Centre for International Politics Manchester University, UK. She researches global environmental governance, transfrontier conservation areas, the environmental impact of illicit trading networks, the international politics of wildlife conservation and the politics of tourism.

Mike Jones has led a Community Based Conservation Network programme in Africa for the Sand County Foundation since 2001. He was part of a team that developed the Campfire programme in Matabeleland from 1989 and since then has worked on various community based conservation initiatives in different parts of southern and eastern Africa.

Tim Lynam holds a PhD degree and is an independent consultant currently working in Mozambique's Manica Province. He has carried out household baseline surveys in most of Campfire areas and was instrumental in generating socio-economic data for the Campfire Project in the late 1980s.

Rowan B. Martin is an ecologist and wildlife management specialist in Zimbabwe. He worked in the Department of National Parks and Wildlife in the 1980s and was instrumental in the conceptualisation and implementation of Campfire.

Bright Mombeshora holds an MSc from the University of Ile Ife (now Obafemi Awolowo) in Nigeria. He has worked as a senior research scientist under the Department Agricultural Research and Extension for more than 25 years.

Chipo Plaxedes Mubaya is a PhD student at the Centre for Development Support at the University of the Free State in South Africa, and formerly a Research Associate at CASS. She is involved in a collaborative project between Zimbabwe and Zambia on 'Building Adaptive Capacity to Deal with Vulnerability due to Climate Change'.

Shylock Muyengwa is a graduate student at the University of Florida School of Natural Resources and Environment and Managing Editor of the *African Studies Quarterly: The Online Journal for Africa Studies*. He has worked with CASS since 2003, and has conducted research on CBNRM in Botswana, Namibia and Zimbabwe.

www.ingramcontent.com/pod-product-compliance
Lightning Source LLC
Chambersburg PA
CBHW021816270326
41932CB00007B/208